Drug Use and Ethnicity in Early Adolescence

LONGITUDINAL RESEARCH IN THE SOCIAL AND BEHAVIORAL SCIENCES
An Interdisciplinary Series

Series Editors:

Howard B. Kaplan, *Texas A&M University, College Station, Texas*
Adele Eskeles Gottfried, *California State University, Northridge, California*
Allen W. Gottfried, *California State University, Fullerton, California*

DRUGS, CRIME, AND OTHER DEVIANT ADAPTATIONS:
Longitudinal Studies
Edited by Howard B. Kaplan

DRUG USE AND ETHNICITY IN EARLY ADOLESCENCE
William A. Vega, Andres G. Gil, and Associates

A Continuation Order Plan is available for this series. A continuation order will bring delivery of each new volume immediately upon publication. Volumes are billed only upon actual shipment. For further information please contact the publisher.

Drug Use and Ethnicity in Early Adolescence

William A. Vega
University of California, Berkeley
Berkeley, California

Andres G. Gil
Florida International University
Miami, Florida

and Associates

Plenum Press • New York and London

Library of Congress Cataloging-in-Publication Data

On file

ISBN 0-306-45737-7

© 1998 Plenum Press, New York
A Division of Plenum Publishing Corporation
233 Spring Street, New York, N.Y. 10013

http://www.plenum.com

10 9 8 7 6 5 4 3 2 1

To our wives
Roena and Margarita
whose support made the completion of this work possible

and appreciation to Roena Ravelo-Vega
for her editorial assistance and insights

Associates

Frank Biafora, Department of Sociology, St. Johns University, Jamaica, New York 11439

Elizabeth L. Khoury, Department of Sociology, University of Miami, Coral Gables, Florida 33146

Bohdan Kolody, Department of Sociology, San Diego State University, San Diego, California 91941

Eric Wagner, Nova Southeastern University, Fort Lauderdale, Florida 33314

George J. Warheit, Department of Sociology and Department of Psychiatry, University of Miami, Coral Gables, Florida 33146

Rick S. Zimmerman, College of Medicine, University of Kentucky, Lexington, Kentucky 40503

Preface

This book presents new and important information about adolescent drug use. The book is intended for human service professionals, teachers, researchers, and students interested in the issue of early adolescent drug use and its causes and pervasiveness in a multiethnic population. Today, the field of adolescent drug use research relies on integrative models that permit competing explanations of drug use. This approach promotes flexibility in testing hypotheses pertinent to adolescents of very different social and cultural backgrounds or personal characteristics. Longitudinal studies, including the one presented in these pages, have identified many risk and protective factors or processes that are linked to adolescent drug use. We review these throughout this book and present new information from our own research. Our point of departure is to extend and elaborate descriptive research and models of adolescent drug research to cover the unique and diverse experiences of adolescents who are Hispanic, African American, and White non-Hispanic.

The ultimate goal of this book is to stimulate new thinking about the pathways to drug use. American society is changing; assumptions about family, school, peers, and other social context variables that influence adolescent drug use need to be revisited and updated. We believe it is possible to achieve improved general explanations of adolescent drug use only if we can account for the uniqueness of ethnic group socialization and organizational patterns in the context of their environments. Due to the demographic changes in American society and changing patterns of drug distribution and consumption, our venerable models that explain adolescent drug use may also need reshaping. Adolescent drug use does not exist apart from the many other social features and partitions that characterize American society. Socioeconomic status differences, skin color, ethnic group identification, and language use are key factors operating to create and sustain social differences in the United States. The way these factors are transforming adolescent socializa-

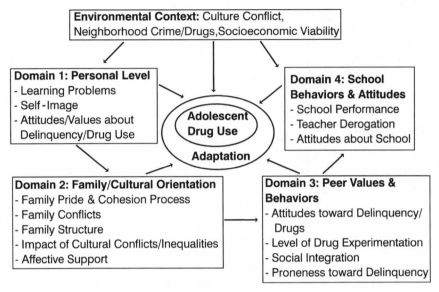

Figure P.1. Drug use vulnerability.

tion into drug use, especially for ethnic minorities, is only beginning to be appreciated or investigated. This volume is an initial step in that direction.

Figure P.1 presents a model of drug use vulnerability that structures the theoretical and empirical approaches taken in this book. The various components of the model are interactive. Therefore, the model serves as a basis for generating hypotheses and general research questions that are set in the context of ethnic adolescent experiences in group and social environments. The logic of our model is to integrate its components using three core explanatory theories, which are summarized below. A comprehensive review of supporting theories is presented throughout this volume. Many of the factors contained in the drug use vulnerability model were measured in repeated field questionnaire administrations, and are part of the data base presented in this book. Additional contextual information is drawn from documentation found in other special studies, institutional reports, and news media presentations.

Theoretical Models Used in the Research

Self-Derogation/Self-Esteem

The research model for this book was guided by three theoretical models. The first was the derogation-self-esteem model, often referred to as the esteem enhancement model, derived from the work of Kaplan and his colleagues (Kaplan, Martin, & Robbins, 1985; Kaplan, Johnson, & Bailey, 1986; Kaplan, Johnson, & Bailey, 1987). Very briefly, this model hypothesizes that adolescents characteristically behave so as to minimize the experience of self-rejection and, at the same time, to maximize experiences that enhance their self-esteem. The model hypothesizes that when adolescents perceive self-rejection they are motivated to alter the interpersonal circumstances responsible for these feelings. Negative assessments by valued others such as parents and teachers are hypothesized to produce subjective distress that, in turn, produces changes in behavior intended to reduce or eliminate negative self-evaluations. If these efforts are unsuccessful, there may be a subsequent willingness to seek alternative normative standards, for example, a disposition to deviance as well as a tendency to form ties with deviant peers. It is in this context that delinquent behavior, including drug use, is hypothesized to emerge. Our research addressed these issues in detail, and the findings are outlined in several of the chapters that follow.

Acculturation Stresses, Conflicts, and Gaps

The second class of theories tested in the research focused on acculturation-related issues. In the case of Hispanics, several hypotheses derived from earlier research were utilized as guidelines. For example, a number of investigators have reported that acculturation adjustment factors are related to personal problems including social deviance and substance use (Amaro, Whitaker, Coffman, & Heeren, 1990; Burnam, Hough, Karno, Escobar, & Telles, 1987; Rogler, Cortes, & Malgady, 1991). These findings prompted the testing of three major acculturation-related hypotheses. The first postulates that there will be positive relationships between increased acculturation into the social values and normative standards of dominant American social groups, thereby increasing drug use. The rationale for this position is the belief that American attitudes and norms regarding substance use are more permissive than those of the more traditionally oriented norms of immigrant families.

The second hypothesis postulates that there will be positive relationships between high levels of acculturation stress and conflict and drug use. The rationale for this postulate is derived from the literature that indicates that unmitigated acculturation strains and stresses are related to social disorganization and personal dysfunctionality and, further, that these processes are conducive to a wide variety of social deviance including increased substance use. The third hypothesis postulates that there will be a curvilinear effect between acculturation levels and drug use because those who are bicultural—rather than monocultural Anglo—or Hispanic will have optimal cultural adjustment and, therefore, less personal distress and lower drug use than their counterparts. An important variation of these formulations is embodied in the work of Szapocznik and his colleagues (Szapocznik, Daruna, Scopetta, & Arnalde, 1977; Szapocznik, Scopetta, Kurtines, & Arnalde, 1978; Sczapocznik, Scopetta, & Tillman, 1979). Utilizing clinical data, these researchers found that Cuban heritage adolescent boys tended to acculturate much more rapidly than other family members, especially their parents. This intergenerational acculturation "gap" was observed to produce a tendency on the part of parents to feel threatened. Parents were also found to be threatened by feelings of loss of control when their children's peer groups did not reflect their own value orientations. The researchers also observed that parents characteristically attempted to reestablish control over their children. However, many of these control activities had negative outcomes and deepened rather than diminished parent–child conflicts.

Perceptions of Racial and Cultural Prejudice and Discrimination

In addition to the derogation and acculturation stress theories, an additional theoretical approach was used to explore the effects of minority status factors on drug use. The role that the perceptions of prejudice and discrimination had on substance use was explored for Hispanic and African American adolescents, and the relationships between cultural protective factors that mitigate racial and ethnic stresses and substance use were also examined. The factors used in exploring the relationships between cultural, racial, and ethnic factors and nonnormative behaviors are incorporated in the drug vulnerability model in Figure P.1.

The findings reported in this book are derived from a carefully designed and successfully completed study of a disparate cohort of young adolescents residing in a rapidly changing major metropolitan area. Intercultural, interracial, and social structural conflicts, high crime rates, and a large, rapidly growing, and overcrowded public school system constituted some of the major contextual environments within which the research was conducted. The longitudinal nature of the research has provided an excellent foundation for the analyses of changes that occurred in substance use, social deviance, and mental health characteristics of those in the sample. In the chapters that follow, the analyses related to many of our aims and objectives are presented directly and fully, whereas space limitations dictate less attention to some of the others. However, all of them have been addressed and the results have been published in professional journals. These publications are identified in the reference list at the end of the book.

Overview of Chapters

The chapters are arranged to guide the reader from seminal constructs and an orientation to the environmental characteristics of the study site, through a concise understanding of the technical design and study procedures, before proceeding into the presentation of research findings and models of explanation. Chapter 1 provides a historical and contemporary overview of the dominant issues treated in the book, including the legacy of sociological thinking about social difference, social organization or disorganization, social control, and deviance. Chapter 2 details the social and ethnic history of the greater Miami area, a dynamic and culturally complex environment that in many ways is an archetype for the issues of social incorporation, intergroup conflict, and race relations in American cities. This chapter also provides complete documentation and design information on the longitudinal study presented in this book. Chapter 3 presents an overview of adolescent deviance theory and a summary of basic epidemiological findings about adolescent drug use in Miami. Chapter 4 provides an overview of issues and an operationalization of risk factor assessment among diverse ethnic group adolescents, information on protective factors, and an analysis of stages and sequences of drug use. Chapter 5 focuses on issues of gender differences in early adolescent development as these relate to drug use patterns in different ethnic groups. Chapter 6 addresses theoretical and empirical issues in acculturation and acculturative stress theory and drug use among Hispanic adolescents. This chapter also contains an elaboration of the self-esteem enhancement model using acculturative stress. Chapter 7 addresses some major unresolved issues pertinent to the epidemiology of African American drug use and presents new information about the reliability of their self-reported drug use. Chapter 8 discusses the implications of our study for preventive interventions and summarizes the recent history, dominant issues, and new directions in the field of drug abuse policy and prevention.

Recognizing that studies such as ours produce an enormous amount of information, and that it is only practical to present selected portions of that information, we have concentrated on a balanced presentation. Frankly, we believe the field of adolescent drug research could benefit from including much more information about culture, neighborhoods, and social differences as a basis for understanding life course drug use and behavior. Our efforts in this direction are modest and preliminary, motivated by the realization that this nation has an exceptional drug use problem; it is widespread and enduring. Thus, we need to expand our vision beyond the individual-level explanations of drug use and to accept the possibility that there are systematic factors operating in our society that create a special disposition toward using and abusing drugs by the American population.

We can assure readers that this study was very carefully conducted and great effort was given to produce data that would enable the researchers to address cross-ethnic comparisons and cross-cultural issues. It is our sincere hope that this book will serve the central purpose of stimulating others to conduct foundation research sensitive to processes of sociocultural adjustment, adolescent development and identity formation, and variations in family and environmental socialization. Improving our understanding of their influence in commencing and sustaining drug use careers is key to controlling adolescent drug abuse.

Acknowledgments

The research for this book was supported by a grant from the National Institute on Drug Abuse, R01 DA 05192, William A. Vega, Principal Investigator.

The authors wish to express their appreciation to Superintendent Octavio Visiedo, Dr. James Mennes, Dr. Sylvia Rothfarb, and the principals, assistant principals, teachers, and students of the Dade Country, Florida, Public School whose cooperation made the conduct of this research possilbe.

Contents

5. Are Girls Different? A Developmental Perspective on Gender Differences in Risk Factors for Substance Use among Adolescents

Elizabeth L. Khoury

6. Cultural Adjustment and Hispanic Adolescent Drug Use

William A. Vega and Andres G. Gil with Eric Wagner

1

Different Worlds
Drug Use and Ethnicity in Early Adolescence

This book is about drug use among youth of different ethnic and racial backgrounds in early adolescence. Only recently has the literature about adolescent drug use begun to reflect the social and cultural influences that are ubiquitous in American society. Consequently, knowledge gaps leave many issues unresolved about causal processes, social contexts, and the epidemiology of drug use among ethnic minorities over their life course. This volume addresses these influential issues in early adolescence for Hispanics, African Americans, and Whites who are not Hispanic. We begin by summarizing the poignant insights of theorists and researchers about ethnicity, cultural conflict, and social adaptation, understanding that these are critical factors that have influenced some adolescents toward deviant behaviors. These insights act as a foundation for this volume, using general explanatory models to examine early adolescent drug use across ethnic groups and to elaborate specific models based on culturally and racially salient factors.

Early Adolescent Experience and Social Context

The volatility of the contemporary American city reflects an array of formidable challenges: too much poverty, cultural diversity, immigration, homelessness and crime, too little new employment for the semiskilled, a declining tax base, and wide disinterest in supporting educational and social programs of the inner city. The decline in quality of urban life is obvious, as is the resistance by the affluent for any further income transfers to the vastly expanding ranks of the poor. As Bellah, Sullivan, Swindler, and Tipton (1985) note in their important book *Habits of the Heart*, radical individualism dominates and isolates the American middle class in

1

lifestyle enclaves, thereby absolving their sense of any broader civic responsibility. This dangerous combination of societal disassociation and personal detachment from the commonweal, in addition to financial exhaustion, renders the future of the American city a treacherous one and a challenging environment for the rearing of drug-free children.

More public money is spent on American children, per capita, than ever before in the nation's history; however, the end result of the investment has been increasingly disappointing. Teen violence and suicide rates have increased and academic performance scores have declined, accompanied by a major increase in sexually transmitted diseases (Fuchs & Reklis, 1992). These problems have been pervasive, however, unevenly affecting all ranks of society. Ultimately, answers to the American urban paradox must be sought in cultural terms. Decades ago Burgess (1954) noted that urban adolescents were emancipated from family control and strict community surveillance, opening their lives to freer choices that often included impulsive, irrational, or experimental activities experienced in the company of adolescent peer groups. The partitioned mosaic infusion of new immigrant Americans and the rapidly increasing disparities of income constitute social conditions that must be confronted by adolescents who usually have minimal preparation for the task. The study presented in this book took place in Miami; in this city, cultural ties that sustain civic interconnectedness and social integration are illusory, and residential segregation by income and ethnicity provides the environmental framework for the socialization of adolescents.

Postindustrial American society has evolved into a prefigurative culture (Mead, 1949/1970) in which adolescents are more likely to learn and be influenced by their peer group than by their elders. The experience of parents vis-à-vis their children resemble that of immigrant parents who find themselves in unfamiliar territory. These circumstances are directly related to structural and cultural shifts in our society. One of the most fundamental changes in U.S. society in the past 30 years has been the view about the nature of childhood and adolescence. There has been a transition on perspectives about children from innocence in the modern world of the nuclear family to competence in postmodern society (Elkind, 1995). Similarly, adolescents are increasingly seen as sophisticated and more capable to process information and interact in their environment as adults.

These transformations are fully congruent with the radical individualism of American society. The belief that children and adolescents are competent and able to fend for themselves facilitates, and perhaps justifies, parental and societal neglect or indifference. Personal and career goals have seemed to take precedence over the well-being of the family. Inasmuch as these changes have altered perceptions about childhood and adolescence, they also represent somewhat of a departure from developmental perspectives that tended to explain child development in terms of cognitive and psychological stages (Erikson, 1963; Freud, 1969; Piaget, 1971). In postmodern society, children are required to utilize "adult" thinking in dealing with the dangers of drugs and violence, and the lack of parental supervision in their environment.

This description of the effects of urban life on American youth is not unprecedented in our history. In the early twentieth century, similar conditions, including juvenile delinquency, were commonplace in large American urban centers (Burgess, 1926; Park, Burgess, & McKenzie, 1925; Wirth, 1928). There is, however, one distinctive aspect to contemporary adolescent behavior. Pervasive drug use now is endemic within American youth culture, with drugs accessible to adolescents from all economic and ethnic backgrounds. The availability does not mean that adolescents believe drug use, especially illicit drug use, to be a rite of passage to adulthood; more accurately, drugs saturate the environment and are readily accessible. However, social and cultural influences interact with the personal dispositions of adolescents to facilitate or impede the use of drugs.

It is misleading to conceive of today's adolescent experimental drug users as the product of either a purely pathological or random process. Licit drugs such as alcohol and cigarettes are so widely used that experimentation with these drugs is common by midadolescence and often no damaging social stigma results from their use. Nonetheless, it is clear that early experimental use of licit drugs increases the probability of using marijuana and other illicit drugs in later adolescence (Kandel, 1985). In the case of alcohol and cigarette experimentation, users are more likely than nonusers to have been exposed to common predisposing factors and processes generally associated with adolescent deviance. In other words, early adolescent drug experimentation is patterned behavior.

Explanatory models do not currently provide a full account of the adolescent drug use epidemic in U.S. society, There is much value in understanding the reasons that lead most preadolescents to remain drug free or to never progress from experimentation to more serious drug use or abuse. Interpersonal and psychosocial factors lead some adolescents to remain drug free, whereas others exposed to similar environmental circumstances become drug users. More importantly, the family and school experiences become a critical determinant in the progression and consequences of drug experimentation during early adolescence. It is less clear whether patterns of drug use, or their developmental sequelae, are experienced in precisely the same way by adolescents of different cultural backgrounds. Given the social inequalities, residential segregation patterns, and cultural diversity present in American society, it is premature to conclude that adolescent drug use unfolds with identical temporal stages and determinants. This could only occur if cultural background and social experiences were irrelevant and drug experimentation was primarily biologically determined. The evidence seems to support a different view. For example, the age of onset of drug experimentation and preferences for certain substances appear to be influenced by culture. African American adolescents have later onset of experimentation with licit and illicit drugs when contrasted with other ethnic groups (Warheit, Vega, Khouri, Gil, & Eifenbein, 1996); Hispanics are more likely to experiment with inhalants (Vega, Zimmerman, Warheit, Apospori, & Gil, 1993), and immigrants are less likely to experiment with drugs than are native-born Hispanic adolescents (Vega, Gil, & Zimmerman, 1993). These differences are reported consistently throughout the nation (Bachman et al., 1991). The cultural mechanisms guiding these choices and social patterns of drug use are not firmly established at this time.

These contextual differences pose special problems for improving our understanding of pathways to drug use. Greater sensitivity to these differences is important for refining both explanatory models and preventive interventions. Adolescent drug use has an uneven level of acceptance or toleration in different communities and among different ethnic groups. We find little crack consumed in the suburbs, and Asian adolescents consume very few illicit drugs in this country. We expect that adolescent drug use may be more tolerated by some parents and supported by adolescent peers in some neighborhoods more than in others, depending on the social and cultural circumstances. Furthermore, experimental drug use connotes a different level of risk from habituation that could dominate the lifestyle of an adolescent or become an impediment to conventional behavior. In part, this is why many researchers have turned to the use of broad explanatory models that assess a variety of factors or competing hypotheses to explain drug use and stages of use (De La Rosa, & Recio-Adrados, 1993; Petraitis, Flay, & Miller, 1995). We believe this trend is important and should be expanded because it permits testing a variety of explanations that are more plausible for one ethnic group than for another.

A central premise of this book is that only a comparative approach that truly allows consideration of the uniqueness of each ethnic group can provide a more accurate understanding of adolescent drug use. General explanatory theories have predictive value but lack cultural context and content, thereby providing insufficient insight for either a good description of the processes leading to experimental drug use in differing cultural contexts or a pragmatic model for intervention. Therefore, this book is cross-cultural not only in the usual sense of comparing rates of drug use and their risk factors, but also in attempting to understand the underlying uniqueness indicated by observed differences among ethnic groups.

Adolescence, Ethnicity, and Development

Adolescence is a period of biological growth and maturation, self-discovery, and social adaptation. Adolescents are challenged to experiment in order to understand and fit into the social world that surrounds them. Personal growth unfolds in tandem with opportunities for development of interests and strengths. Real or imagined weaknesses and deficits of self and environment provoke adolescents to redefine themselves. Many questions arise: What kind of people are they? What kind of people should they be? Early adolescence is particularly intriguing because in a few short years the child makes a transition into the role of adult-in-preparation and launches into a cycle of rapid learning that occurs in different settings such as the streets and in the schools where the rules of survival are learned and innovation is encouraged.

Freud made the link between the biological changes of puberty and what he considered one of the two major developmental concerns of adolescence: establishment of firm individuality, a sense of self and ego identity (Metcalf, 1995). In American society, developing a sense of affirming personal identity may be particularly problematic for adolescents who are members of ethnic minority groups. Awareness of differences in treatment and internalization of social distinctions based on affluence, physical features, and culture are part of adolescent social learning that becomes a foundation for identity formation, self-esteem, and peer association (Cross & Fhagen-Smith, 1996; Erikson, 1959, 1963). There is growing evidence that self-awareness of ethnic identity and inferior social status is related to the social behavior and attitudes of adolescents (Phinney, 1989, 1992). For example, Rumbaut (1994a, 1994b) reported from a multiethnic survey that self-selection of a "Chicano" ethnic identification among adolescents of Mexican origin, especially among U.S.-born males, was associated with lower grades, attenuated educational and occupational aspirations, and perceptions of discrimination.

However, the process and likelihood of selecting an ethnic identification or interpreting and internalizing one that is imposed from the outside world is conditioned by experiences in both the adolescent's external (secondary group contacts) and internal environment (primary group contacts). Being of Puerto Rican ethnic origin has different implications for ethnic identity formulation in New York that it has in Tampa, Florida. The degree of isolation, social distance from other ethnic groups, and hostility ethnic adolescents will experience is not consistent across environments, but is very consequential for social adjustment (Fabrega, 1969; Favazza, 1980). Whether in inner-city enclaves or middle-class suburbs, all adolescents face social testing in new situations that require immediate adaptation, self-control, aggressiveness, and other facets of adequate role performance.

The purpose of this book is to provide insight about the processes and determinants linked to early adolescent drug use in a multicultural American society. Current national surveys indicate increases in adolescent drug use despite extensive prevention efforts in both school-based and nonacademic programs. Another epidemic of drug experimentation and addiction appears to be on its way. Clearly, we continue to lack the necessary skills and resources to control the American drug problem.

Several assumptions have been made to guide our analysis about adolescent drug use. One is that adolescents are growing up in complex urban environments.

Cultural, racial, socioeconomic, and lifestyle variations are the paramount feature of social life in urban settings such as Miami, Florida, the location for the research we report here. As a result, our perspective is to contrast racially and culturally influenced characteristics of adolescents that we believe influence their development. A second assumption is that urban environments are rife with social conflicts, racial prejudice and income inequities, crime, and drug use that adolescents respond to in some way. A final assumption is that early adolescence is extremely dynamic, exemplified by escalating transactions with family and peers that often lead to conflicts around expectation of greater personal freedoms, especially when parents are antagonistic to new, and often experimental, language, behaviors, clothing, pastimes, or adolescent peer associations (Bowlby, 1982; Metcalf, 1995). Using a clinical standard, only about one-fifth of youth in early adolescence seem to experience acute adjustment problems. However, a much higher percentage will have transitory periods of significant stress, rebelliousness, and emotional problems (Offer & Schonert-Reichi, 1992).

Adolescent Development, Deviance, and Cultural Variation

The nineteenth-century social scientists studying the European transformation from traditional to modern society reflected on a central theme in their writings (Nisbet, 1966). They believed the primary challenge of modernity was to assure social cohesiveness and social order. Urbanization was eroding the last vestiges of feudal society, weakening a system based on tradition, reciprocity, and simple modes of production that were maintained by extended kinship networks and in-kind rural economies. The growth of European cities, such as London and Paris, during the industrial revolution provoked concern that class conflicts, social heterogeneity, and the weakening of traditional institutions would leave only a societal vacuum, as was evidenced by the degree of social disorganization routinely observed in these cities at that time. What force would hold these societies together in the face of a growing indifference to tradition, the absence of strong alternative institutions, and the vulnerabilities occasioned by the wanton criminality and vice that seemed organically related to the process of urbanization? Cities provided opportunities for a host of social affiliations and lifestyle opportunities that were unknown in rural society. The meaning of behavior, and how to control it, became more relative than absolute. Even divorce rates began climbing during the industrial revolution, a fact often overlooked with present-day concerns about the high rate of divorce (Demos, 1975).

In the early decades of the twentieth century these concerns were revived by an important group of sociologists at the University of Chicago. The Chicago School brought together a number of key thinkers of the period who formed the first school of urban sociology. They observed the social disjunctures of a city that was experiencing large-scale resettlement of migrants and immigrants. Distinctive ethnic groups coexisted and interacted in areas that tolerated or even supported both conventional and deviant behavior.

Park (1950) commented extensively on the social partitioning and obvious asymmetries of social position occasioned by ethnicity and race. His description of urban residential transitions, written over 60 years ago, echoes contemporary accounts of urban resettlement:

> It is significant also, that the migration of the Negroes to the northern cities took place at a time when urban residents were abandoning their homes in the center of the city for the more spacious suburbs. As these suburbs multiplied, the abandoned and the so-called "blighted" area surrounding the central business core steadily expanded. These areas are now largely occupied by immigrants and Negroes. (p. 173)

Park was convinced that urban social integration would not occur without extensive interracial conflict because, as he explained, non-Whites wore a racial "uniform" that provoked racial consciousness and segregation by the dominant society. Under these conditions, individuals of different racial backgrounds ceased to be persons and became "another example of the species merely" (p. 160). The result was conflict with its nexus in economic competition and maintenance of existing power relationships. However, Park was not a pessimist but more of a social evolutionist who believed interracial integration would occur through a historical process of face-to-face interaction between "races" leading to competition, conflict, and accommodation, but he set no time parameters on the completion of the process.

It is not our purpose to belabor the analysis or solutions to this dilemma invented by classical social philosophers or American sociologists. We highlight these issues because they are a primary thread in thinking about deviance and adolescent development that continues to be salient at the present time in both popular and academic circles. The concerns about social cohesiveness may turn out to be more relevant in the transition to postmodern and postindustrial society. The social environment is fractured, and its institutions, particularly churches and the family, have become less relevant for modeling behavior in the worlds of children and adolescents. As a result, the postindustrial family has been described as being more permeable, only minimally serving the basic needs of sustenance for its members, and less relevant to the lives of children. The institution of the family has evolved from a central source of material and emotional support, a source of identity and meaning, to a transitory "station" of minimal interaction between its members.

The essential nature of contemporary society constitutes the extreme outcomes of social disorganization and anomie that may surpass the most pessimistic evaluation of early industrialization philosophers. A society in which institutions are in flux and social cohesion is weak presents a challenging context for the socialization of the young and acculturation of newcomers. One of the major assumptions about the processes of acculturation and assimilation is that there is an existent set of values and beliefs to adopt or reject. The new challenge for immigrants, and particularly for parents vis-à-vis their children, is that norms and values are in a state of flux in U.S. society.

In this volume we speak more of ethnic or cultural differences than of racial ones because our current state of knowledge supports the reality of cultural differences, and the biological basis for racial genotypes has been discredited. Race is important today primarily because it is a social construction with far-reaching implications for intergroup relations and for understanding one's place in the social system and the prospects of changing that position. Our inclusion of ethnic groups in the study means that not race per se but rather the social constructions of culture, skin color, and poverty are the important foci.

In his classic book *The Gang*, Thrasher (1927) described 1,313 gang members he studied in inner-city Chicago in the 1920s as occupying "gangland," a socially "interstitial" area in the city exemplified by "fissures and breaks in the structure of social organization" (p. 20). The gang was an interstitial element that filled the void created in areas of the city where traditional institutions were weak. The gang provided alternatives for development, many being situational and opportunistic. Thrasher described Chicago's multiethnic gangland as consisting of various levels of organization and permanency that, in their aggregate, provided a spectrum of learning opportunities, and, for a few, even a ladder for social mobility. Delinquent behavior, some pernicious and some merely of recreational value, appeared as a normal adaptive response to the adolescent's need for positive evaluation and social support from peers.

The reasons why social disorganization led to criminal behavior were numerous. Sutherland (1934) cited discontinuities in the normative order, intensive communication and interaction, and economic inequalities as merging in American society with an individualism rooted in "mobility, competition, and conflict." This combination of factors was interpreted as a natural environment of deviance. Delinquent and criminal subcultures developed, providing a systematic basis for social learning, normative approval, and emotional support for non-law-abiding behavior. In addition, a gradient of opportunity existed ranging from minor delinquency to serious, organized, criminal activity. Sutherland believed that deviant behavior was learned in a process similar to learning conforming behavior. Both involved behavior modeling in a context of social approval, and both conventional and deviant subcultures had methods for teaching and enforcing their respective rules. It was inevitable that residents of impoverished slums would become crime prone because "the American culture which they see is a culture of competition, grasping greed, deceit, graft, and immorality" (p. 27). He noted that some ethnic groups in Chicago, such as Mexicans and Greeks, did not allow their children to play with children of other ethnic groups so they tended to have lower delinquency levels, but with the passage of time (5 to 10 years) delinquency increased in these groups as well.

Acceptance of deviant values and behavior by adolescents was predicated on the degree of attachment to conventional values and, conversely, the meaning assigned to deviant role models and behavior; this, in turn, was affected by exposure levels in neighborhoods and by cultural factors. Sutherland in his early criminological studies found that second-generation immigrants were more likely to become juvenile delinquents, specifically because of weakened traditional values (Sutherland, 1934). Wirth (1981) reported that cultural conflicts occurred in immigrant families when unassimilated parents were present, and this became an important contributory factor in delinquency and in other personal problems of their children.

Shaw (1929) determined that urban crime rates varied greatly by geographic area. He reported a 19.4% delinquency rate among Negroes in the blighted South Side of Chicago as contrasted with a rate of 3.5% in the same ethnic group five miles away from the inner city. High-crime areas had high residential mobility levels and low social control. Social contagion of mores supporting deviant behavior was held to be responsible for higher crime rates. Therefore, it was social characteristics of the areas rather than innate characteristics of ethnic groups that elevated crime rates—notwithstanding, the possibility that certain types of individuals were more likely to be drawn to these areas either because they could more easily practice deviant or criminal lifestyles or because they were chronically mentally ill (Faris & Dunham, 1939). This is a theme that is being reclaimed by contemporary researchers.

Robert Merton (1938), an important sociologist of this period, advanced the idea that the opportunity structure and values of American society created systematic psychological strain and a propensity toward deviance, which occurred because goals of material attainment were universally propagated and held forth as attainable for all citizens, in essence, the Horatio Alger myth. However, the means for attaining these material goals were not equally available to all, despite the fact that material goals were emphasized disproportionately as the basis for conferring status. This contradiction resulted in a "structured strain" within American society that in turn produced systematic "modes of adaption." Some of these modes involved potentially criminal, violent, and drug-using behaviors. The "structured strain" approach was very influential during the revival of delinquency and deviance theory during the 1960s. Structured strain is complementary to the Chicago School explanations of deviance and is also an important intellectual antecedent for explanations used in this book about the impact of racial discrimination on delinquency and drug use.

Ethnic Group Conflicts, Socialization, and Adolescent Deviance

The Chicago School tradition paid significant attention to the fact that immigrants and migrants, such as African Americans, moving to Chicago would face a difficult adjustment period. Racial tensions and race riots had already occurred in Chicago and in other major urban centers. Inner-city environments exposed adolescents to ethnic group segregation, inconsistent socialization, and widespread criminal behavior. New residents, such as "Negro" adolescents and others who were children of first-generation migrants or immigrants who settled in high-crime areas of the inner city, began to show increases in criminal behavior over time. From these observations it was apparent that social adjustment to new environments and cultures was disruptive to families and to the socialization of their children, particularly in communities that were replete with delinquent and criminal activities. The burden of maintaining traditional values and behaviors, establishing an economic foothold, and avoiding cultural and social network disintegration fell squarely on the internal resources of the new arrivals. Other Chicago researchers documented the struggle to establish new lives and the psychological pain endured by other groups, such as Polish immigrants cut off from their families and customs (Thomas & Znaniecki, 1918–1920).

Stonequist (1937) studied the process of intergroup, interethnic contact and psychological adjustment in the United States and internationally and elaborated the concept of "marginality." In contrast to the common understanding of marginality as group powerlessness, he created a nascent social psychological construct to explain personal adaptation to social interaction in complex cultural environments. Stonequist viewed culture contact and acculturation as inherently problematic, "an inner strain." In extreme situations there could be severe impact on identity development and functioning: "Inability to diagnose the source of the conflict, the conviction of an unscalable wall, and personal failures, overwhelm the individual. Mental conflict leads to discouragement and perhaps despair" (p. 201). Stonequist reasoned that individuals of diverse ethnic background would be faced with diverse, and at times conflicting, expectations, demands, and choices in the context of everyday life interaction. Expectations differing too radically from one culture group to another, Stonequist believed, could create problems in the successful adjustment of adolescents through loss of primary group support and deculturation. However, marginality also had positive aspects for those who could function well in this type of environment because they would have broader access to cultural groups and were perhaps more flexible, creative, and skillful at interpersonal relations as a result. Stonequist believed strong leaders could emerge from this process because the marginal man was a "key personality" in the contact between cultures, and the "crucible of cultural fusion."

The outcome of marginality experiences was dependent on (1) social conditions, such as the degree of competition between dominant and minority groups and the extent to which social distance and intolerance for cultural diversity was prevalent; (2) individual characteristics; and (3) cultural traits. In terms of importance, Stonequist believed the social, economic, and political environments were most critical. To the extent that an uncertain social status in two or more cultural groups prevailed it would have disorganizing effects on the individual. The psychological burden for the "marginal man" would be to construct an integrated, acceptable, and positively evaluated sense of self.

Large numbers of new immigrants continue to flow into the United States, especially Hispanics and Asians. Many settle in the same deteriorating neighborhoods that were once residential quarters of other impoverished ethnic and minority groups (Rumbaut, 1994b). This new phase of American immigration poses a fundamental question. Will incorporation of new immigrants who are increasingly nonwhite occur in a manner that approximates (1) intergenerational incorporation into American society that occurred with European groups, or (2) long-term segregation and creation of castelike minority status as has occurred for many African Americans and Hispanics? This is an important distinction because the ramifications for adolescent identity formation and development, and eventual social incorporation into American society, can be expected to differ if culture conflict is extensive and minority status becomes hardened. Furthermore, incorporation into a multiethnic, diverse, and dynamic society presents new and unique challenges. Whether or not one agrees with the vision and philosophy of the melting pot (Glazer & Moynihan, 1968), the reality is that the fundamental prerequisite of that assimilationist vision is the existence of a stable society in which the "melting" process can occur. Absent a stable and open society, the fundamental process of ethnic group and immigrant incorporation becomes replete with problems for all participants, newcomers as well as the receiving society.

Recent theories about acculturation and assimilation have focused on factors associated with cultural adaptation. The traditional straight-line, or linear, view of assimilation wherein ethnic groups are culturally transformed in a consistent and unimpeded way may continue to hold for some groups. Milton Gordon (1964) described American social class stratification as a basis for resocialization and social integration of disparate ethnic groups. However, other writers have described alternative models that extend these assimilation models. Bumpy-line, or segmented, assimilation (Abramson, 1981; Gans, 1992; Portes & Zhou, 1993) allows for new types of social incorporation. Segmented assimilation is dependent on social environment conditions and the degree of internal organization among ethnic groups, such as enclave formation, and availability of social and material resources (Portes & Rumbaut, 1990). The receiving environments or contexts of reception influence the adaptation of ethnic and minority groups, either favoring assimilationist approaches or creating reactive behaviors in response to perceived discrimination, boundary maintenance by dominant groups, and social conflicts

(Fabrega, 1969). These environmental conditions form what Rumbaut (1994a) calls the "crucible" without, which in turn conditions the "crucible" within: social experiences, information, and societal imagery that ultimately translate into messages that will shape adolescent self-concept.

What remains less well understood is how cultural differences and minority statuses are similar or different in terms of their consequences for healthy adolescent development and identity formation. Gibson and Ogbu (1991) highlight this question by distinguishing immigrant status from "involuntary" minority status. The crux of the matter lies in power relationships and "different historical experiences which lead to different adaptive responses" (p. 92). Nonoppositional experiences by immigrants and other ethnic groups who feel personally benefited by cultural change are not as likely to foster a minority group frame of reference; positive evaluation of the present compared to past circumstances in their nation of origin is crucial for this determination. In contrast, individuals who feel that their group (African Americans, Chicanos, Puerto Ricans) is exploited and discriminated against overtly and covertly are more likely to perceive themselves as oppositional and occupying minority statuses in American society. This is a question of central tendency in a subpopulation rather than a categorical endorsement on the part of any ethnic group. There are members of any ethnic group that will report they are discriminated against, just as there are members of minority groups who feel they are not being discriminated against.

Conceptually, there is unity between theoretical constructs such as cultural conflicts and minority perceptions of discrimination, but only when they are understood to exist in the same social and historical frame. It is within this context of cultural conflict and perceptions of minority adolescents that we explore drug use, particularly as it operates to facilitate or impede the successful personal adjustment and eventual social incorporation of adolescents of diverse cultural backgrounds. We propose that in many instances reasons for developing deviant behavior and drug use among adolescents include responses to externally imposed conditions and historical experiences of culture conflict and discrimination. These experiences are in turn perceived as derogatory by the adolescent, and can render that individual an involuntary minority group member. This process sets up contingencies as well. Personal distress results from the development of oppositional attitudes when cultural expectations of important social reference groups are competing and conflicting. This process is an entry point into many delinquency theories. Our supposition is that there can be a social and cultural basis for negative self-evaluations produced by social experiences that reinforce or precipitate other risk factors to increase vulnerability to delinquent and drug-using behavior among ethnic minority adolescents (Vega, Gil, Warheit, Zimmerman, & Apospori, 1993).

2

Context and Design of the Study

George J. Warheit

Introduction

The findings reported in this book were obtained as part of a major epidemiological study that focused primarily on the substance use attitudes, beliefs, and behaviors of a multiethnic cohort of young adolescents residing in Dade County, Florida. The research was conducted between 1989 and 1995. The aims and objectives of the research resemble those of studies conducted by other researchers and scholars interested in adolescent substance use (Rachal et al., 1975; Guinn & Hurley, 1976; Wilsnack & Wilsnack, 1978; Jackson, Greenaway, & Zalesnick, 1981; Ensminger, Brown, & Kellam, 1982; Barnes & Welte, 1986; Maddahian, Newcomb, & Bentler, 1986; Mata, 1986; Newcomb & Bentler, 1986; Gilbert & Alcocer, 1988; Oetting & Beauvais, 1990; Bentler, 1992; Chavez & Swaim, 1992; Kandel, Yamaguchi, & Chen, 1992; Brook, Whiteman, & Cohen, 1995; Kaplan, 1995; Warheit, Biafora, Vega, & Zimmerman, 1995; Johnston, O'Malley, & Bachman, 1996). However, our findings extend present knowledge in several areas. Perhaps most importantly, they contribute new and unique information on a large and disparate group of Hispanic adolescents, and, inasmuch as many of those in the study cohort were foreign born, it was possible to determine the relationships between acculturation processes and related conflicts and substance use patterns. The findings on Hispanic adolescents are enriched by comparative analyses with large subsamples of African American and White non-Hispanic adolescents who were members of the same school cohort.

A second contribution accrues from the unusual contextual elements of the research environments. The authors believe strongly that the attitudes, beliefs, and behaviors associated with adolescent substance use and other forms of social deviance cannot be explained entirely by the idiosyncratic characteristics of individuals. To the contrary, they believe that systems of explanation are incom-

13

plete if they fail to take into account the social and cultural milieu present in the families, schools, communities, and neighborhoods in which individuals live. In keeping with these beliefs, the first part of this chapter describes the social and cultural environments extant in Dade County at the time the study took place, and it includes a brief summary of the impact that Hurricane Andrew had on the community and on our research, which was underway at the time. It also outlines some of the defining features of the Dade County Public School System (DCPS) in whose schools the student data were gathered. A full discussion of these contextual factors and how they affected the outcomes of our research is beyond the scope of this chapter. However, even an abbreviated description of them illustrates the aspects of the environments in which the data were gathered, and it facilitates the interpretation of many of the findings presented in the chapters that follow.

In the second part, the objectives and design of the research are listed, the sample characteristics are described, and there is a discussion of the theoretical models that guided many of our major analyses.

The Two Faces of Miami

Miami is the principal city in Dade County, Florida, and because the city and county are so highly interrelated the two designations are often used interchangeably throughout this chapter. Dade County and Miami can be viewed as a community with two faces—one very positive, the other equally negative. Although each is a gross oversimplification, stated most succinctly, Dade County and the city of Miami is perceived by many as a beautiful and vibrant place, a tropical paradise, an exciting place to visit, and a pleasant place to live. Many others view the county and city as a crime-ridden, drug-dominated, lawless, and corrupt place, overrun by immigrants and filled with racial and ethnic conflicts. Undoubtedly, the true character of the community includes dimensions of both views.

The positive image of Miami and its environs is supported by the area's tropical climate, exotic vegetation, beautiful beaches, fashionable residential neighborhoods, and the city's gleaming new skyline. Its positive image is further enhanced by its many elegant hotels, excellent restaurants, nightclubs, recreational facilities, and a wide variety of tourist attractions. Further evidence of Miami's mystique is its ability to attract millions of visitors every year and the fact that it is home to thousands of winter residents from all over the world. Many of the rich, famous, and politically powerful have residences scattered among the small islands just off the shoreline or in one of the county's many upscale residential enclaves. Since its early origins, the tropical climate and the social and cultural ambiance of the city have played important roles in Miami's establishment and growth, and these factors continue to define and shape it today.

A second set of factors associated with the area's positive image is its increasing importance as part of the world's expanding market economy. Situated at the southern tip of the United States, it is ideally situated for international business, commerce, and tourism. International banks are found on its downtown streets; there is a large and growing number of multinational businesses located in the city and county; and hundreds of flights leave the airport daily for destinations throughout the Caribbean basin, Central and South America, Mexico, and other cities all over the world. In addition, the Port of Miami is one of the busiest on the East Coast, home base for more ocean cruise liners than any other port in the world. Dade County's location has also made it increasingly important in a political sense. As a port of entry and home to approximately one and a half million persons from the Caribbean basin and South America, Dade County has become a focal point for political activity associated with United States foreign affairs. This is especially true for policies regarding Cuba, Haiti, Nicaragua, El Salvador, Panama, and the other countries in the region. As the gateway to Central and South America, nearly all of the nations from the hemisphere have major consulates in the county, and in 1994 the city hosted a major summit meeting of hemispheric political leaders. Dade County's role as the primary liaison between the United States and the countries of Latin America is well established, and as the economic ties between the two regions expand, the county's international importance will probably increase as well. The area's tropical climate, social ambiance, cultural diversity, and its emergence as a focal point for U.S. political and economic activities related to other countries in the hemisphere make Dade County one of the most attractive metropolitan areas in the United States.

Another use of images is far less attractive. Television shows, movies, and the mass media have offered a different, far more negative view. And although much of what has been presented is stereotypically media image construction and nonfactual, much is not. Over the past three decades, the massive flood of Hispanics, Haitians, and other immigrants arriving in South Florida has generated a wide array of problems for public officials in every agency of government, including the DCPS, and it has been accompanied by pervasive anti-immigrant beliefs and feelings on the part of many of the area's residents. Moreover, this huge immigrant presence has coincided with a strong and growing anti-immigrant sentiment throughout the United States; because of its visibility, Dade County and Miami have often been a lightning rod for those attacking immigrants and U.S. immigration policies (Beck, 1996). Miami's image has also suffered as a result of its periodic civil unrest and riots, its high crime rates, and its political corruption, which brought it to the verge of bankruptcy ("Florida Officials," 1996). The reputation of the county is further tarnished by its role as a major port of entry and distribution center for illicit drugs. Singly and together, these and other factors have created a counterimage to that conjured up by the phrase "tropical paradise." In sum, its most severe critiques fear that Dade County and Miami represents a microcosm of what U.S. urban areas could be like in the twenty-first century:

places filled with immigrants who are not very interested in speaking English or becoming assimilated into the mainstream of American life; places of cultural parallelism; places filled with dysfunctional racial and ethnic tensions; places of political unrest and malfeasance; places where property and life are not safe; places without any defining social cohesiveness; places of widespread personal alienation and social anomie.

A discussion of the absolute merits of these two perspectives is open for discussion, but a large body of data makes it very apparent that Miami does have two faces and the vignettes outlined above accurately reflect elements of each. It is a city of contradictions, and perhaps this duality of sunshine and conflict are what attracts the attention of so many and why those who focus on the city do so in such a polarized fashion. In any event, civic and business leaders along with the general populace are very conscious of Miami's image, and this consciousness is very much a part of the city's collective psyche.

Dade County at the Time of the Research

As noted above, we believe that background contextual information provides an important framework for understanding the attitudes and behavior of individuals, and for this reason we have explored in greater detail certain aspects of the county's sociocultural milieu. Stated most succinctly, as we gathered our data, the county and city were undergoing vast demographic, social, economic, and political changes; racial, ethnic, and cultural tensions were manifested daily; drug use was widespread; crime rates were high. A major hurricane occurred between the second and third waves of data collection, and its impact intensified many existing ethnic conflicts and adversely affected both the physical structures and psychological well-being of many residents of the county. Throughout the course of our research, the basic institutional structures, including those related to the public school system, were being challenged to meet the demands of a community in transition. Because of their importance, a more detailed discussion of these contextual factors is presented next.

Conflicts between Immigrants and the Native Population

Strained relations between immigrants and their hosts are not unusual; they have been commonplace throughout U.S. history. However, the in-migration of individuals from Cuba and other countries of the region to South Florida has been qualitatively and quantitatively different in many ways from earlier waves of immigration to the United States, and some of these differences underlie immigrant–host animosities. First, unlike many immigrant groups before them, a large number of the early immigrants from Cuba were from the upper-socioeconomic groups, and they brought with them both personal and economic resources that facilitated their adjustments to a new homeland. Second, the immigrants from Cuba came as political refugees and, as a consequence, were the beneficiaries of preferential treatment not afforded other groups. Third, the immigration to Dade County has been very large vis-à-vis the host population, and these large numbers provided the critical mass of persons and institutions required to transfer large segments of the Cuban culture to South Florida. Fourth, as a result of the transplantation of intact components of their native culture, and the subsequent business and cultural enclave development, many immigrants were not compelled to learn to speak English, which allowed them to resist successfully the pressures to conform to host expectations regarding acculturation and assimilation. (Nevertheless, their children do succumb to the relentless pressures of acculturation.) And fifth, Cuban immigrants, as well as Latin Americans from other nations, have attained dominant economic and political influence over many aspects of the community. However, even within the Latin American community of Miami there is extensive social and economic stratification, and most of the immigrants that have arrived in the last 20 years remain low income. These internal variations in national origin and socioeconomic status among Latin Americans further intensify the social fragmentation of Dade County (Gil & Vega, 1996). In more recent years Dade County's Hispanic population has become more diversified, with increases in the population from Central and South American groups.

Demographic Changes Underlying Immigrant–Host Conflicts

Portes and Stepick (1993), in their excellent book, *City on the Edge*, have appropriately defined Miami as a community that has undergone a dramatic transformation from a relatively small, sunbelt tourist city to a vast and rapidly expanding metropolitan area. They also correctly attribute many of the changes taking place to the arrival of over one million immigrants over the past 25 years. The data presented in Table 2.1 illustrate the extensiveness of the demographic changes that have taken place in Dade County in recent decades. As shown, the increase in absolute numbers and percentages of Hispanics is remarkable. Estimates indicate that in 1950 only 4.0% of the population of Dade County was Hispanic (Special Populations Reports, 1996). In the four decades that followed, the percentage of Hispanic heritage individuals residing in the county increased to 49.0% (U.S. Bureau of the Census, 1990) and the trend continues.

Researchers at the University of Florida have placed the 1995 Hispanic population in the county at 1,126,929; this represents 56.0% of the county's estimated total population of 1,990,445 (Special Populations Reports, 1996). During the same four decades, a White flight resulted in a decrease in both the

Table 2.1.   Population Characteristics: Dade County, Florida, 1950–1990,
White Non-Hispanic (WNH), Hispanic, Black

Year	Total population	WNH	%	Hispanic	%	Black[a]	%
1950[b]	495,100	410,200	82.9	20,000	4.0	64,900	13.1
1960[b]	935,047	747,748	80.0	50,000	5.3	137,299	14.7
1970[b]	1,267,792	778,909	61.4	299,217	23.6	189,666	15.0
1980[c]	1,625,781	775,117	47.7	580,994	35.7	269,670	16.6
1990[c]	1,937,094	585,607	30.2	953,407	49.2	397,993	20.6

[a]The Black category includes persons from Haiti, the West Indies, the Bahamas, and other Caribbean island areas. Approximately one-thrid of Blacks enumerated in 1990 were foreign born. The 1990 figures for the Hispanic category includes 28,372 persons identified as Black.
[b]From *Dade County, Florida Characteristics: U.S. Decennial Census*, Metro Dade County Department of Human Resources, Miami, Florida, 1983. The 1950 and 1960 data for Hispanics are estimates derived from archival data, not from actual census counts.
[c]From *Hispanic Popluation Estimates by Age and Sex for Florida and Its Counties, No. 4*, Bureau of Business and Economic Research, University of Florida, Gainesville, Florida, August 1996.

number and percentage of White non-Hispanics, or so called Anglos, in the county. The percentage of White non-Hispanic residents decreased from 82.9% in 1950 to 30% in 1990, and their out-migration continues. It has been estimated that there was an overall net loss of 6,290 White non-Hispanic persons through out-migration between 1990 and 1994 (*Florida Statistical Abstract*, 1995; Special Populations Reports, 1996). Some of this loss can be attributed to Hurricane Andrew which devastated the area in 1992, but some undoubtedly reflects the ongoing flight of the White non-Hispanic population.

Although the number and percentage of Blacks in the population has increased over the past 40 years, growing from 64,900 (13.1%) in 1950 to 397,993 (20.6%) in 1990, their growth does not parallel that exhibited by the Hispanic groups. Moreover, the 1995 estimates indicate that the percentage of Blacks in the county was approximately the same as it was in 1990 (*Florida Census Handbook*, 1995).

Conflicts over Language and Citizenship

The 1990 census reported that Spanish had become the dominant language in the community. In 1990, 562,948 of the county's population over 5 years of age indicated that they spoke English less than well, and 1,031,921 persons in the county spoke some language other than English in their homes. Of this number, 901,270 spoke Spanish or Spanish Creole, 69,032 spoke French or French Creole, and approximately 62,000 spoke other languages (U.S. Bureau of Census, 1990). The pervasiveness and continued use of other languages, especially Spanish, has been a persistent source of irritation between immigrants and native-born White non-Hispanic and African Americans.

The divisions over language use that were often unstated became manifest in 1980 when a local White non-Hispanic group, Citizens of Dade County, was able to pass an ordinance that prohibited the use of county funds for the purpose of utilizing any language other than English or any culture other than that of the United States. This ordinance was reinforced in 1988 when the voters of Florida overwhelmingly passed an English-only amendment to the state's constitution. The passage of these measures, which galvanized the ethnic groups in the community, has had little practical significance. Spanish was and is omnipresent in almost all public sectors of the city and county's private and corporate life, including the DCPS, and its usage continues to be a source of conflict between groups in the community. Nevertheless, our study demonstrates that adolescent children of Hispanic immigrants do assimilate and learn English.

The seeking of citizenship is another factor related to interethnic tensions in Miami. The U.S. census reported that there were 1,937,094 persons residing in Dade County in 1990 and that 874,569 (45%) of them were foreign born. Census data also revealed that only 315,777 (36%) of the foreign born had become naturalized citizens (U.S. Bureau of the Census, 1990). This low percentage gaining citizenship may be attributed in part to the recent arrival of numerous immigrants. However, the large number of longtime residents who have not sought citizenship suggests that other factors are also involved. For example, some people in the Cuban community regard themselves as temporary residents in the United States, as exiles who will return to their native land once Castro and communism disappear. Regardless of the underlying factors, the preoccupation with Cuba has been interpreted by many in the host population as resistance to assimilation by immigrant groups. Recent legislation severely limiting access by immigrants to social security and welfare benefits appears to be dramatically increasing the percentage of naturalizations among the immigrants.

Political Changes and Conflicts

By the time of our last data collection period in the spring of 1994, Hispanics had not only become the dominant ethnic group in the county and city, but they were well on their way to being the most powerful political group as well. They were in control of both county and city governments, and they occupied the top posts in most county and city departments, including the offices of city manager and county manager. The voices and images of Hispanic leaders were heard and seen over numerous radio and television stations that broadcast exclusively in Spanish, and events of consequence for Hispanics were covered extensively in the Spanish edition of the *Miami Herald, El Nuevo Herald.* The growing Hispanic political control of Dade County and Miami, which was very much in evidence as our study began, culminated in the fall of 1996 when the county and city elected its first "strong mayor," that is, an elected executive officer with far-reaching authority over and above that enjoyed by the county and city managers and commissions. The race for the position of county mayor involved two members of the county commission. One was a 34-year-old male whose parents were born in Cuba; the other was a 50-year-old African American male with a long history in both local and national politics. The Cuban American won the election with 60% of the vote.

More money was spent on this election than any of its kind in South Florida, with most of it being expended by the winning candidate, who had a 2.4 million dollar campaign budget. During the last month of the campaign, he received 1.1 million dollars in campaign contributions; his African American opponent was able to raise only $225,000 during the same period ("Peak of Power," 1996). Racial and ethnic tensions that were near the surface for a long time became manifestly obvious in the closing days of the campaign, in spite of the candidates' disclaimers to the contrary. The day after the election, the *Miami Herald* reported that the election

> ... was sparked by last minute incendiary ethnic appeals ... Miami's black and Cuban radio stations kept up nonstop appeals for their listeners to vote to beat out the other group. Spanish radio called on Cubans to come out to deal with "a problem of race" and a black station warned of Spanish becoming the official language of Dade county and of a "master plan by Cubans" to take over. ("Peak of Power," 1996).

The sharp ethnic divisions were also reflected in the voting patterns. The Hispanic candidate received 92% of the Spanish vote; the African American candidate received 96% of the Black vote. The day after the election the mayor-elect indicated that one of his first tasks was to heal the wounds occasioned by the ethnic conflicts, with clear racial overtones, which pervaded the election.

In recent decades, as the dominance of the Hispanic community grew in size and power, the political influence of the White non-Hispanic group was being significantly diminished. At the local level, even though individual Anglos had for the most part become minor players in the politics of the county and city, they sometimes had the swing votes in the county and city commissions and could not be totally discounted. Moreover, there were strong vestigial remnants of the social, cultural, economic, and political power once enjoyed by the White non-Hispanic elites, and these remnants were frequently at odds with the newly dominant Hispanic groups. As discussed by Portes and Stepick (1993), for many Hispanics the most bothersome of these was the area's most influential newspaper, the *Miami Herald*, whose editorial policies tended to represent older, more traditional U.S. perspectives on a wide range of social, cultural, and political issues. The *Miami Herald* was routinely castigated (often in its own pages) by members of the most powerful Cuban political action group in the United States, the Cuban American

National Foundation. The leadership of the foundation regarded the paper as biased against Hispanics, nonsupportive in areas of great interest to Cubans (e.g., U.S. foreign policy as it relates to Castro), and hypercritical of Hispanics in South Florida for their real or perceived resistance to "Americanization" and assimilation into U.S. society.

The majority of persons in the multiethnic Black communities of Miami, unlike many in the Anglo one, are more or less trapped in Miami. Although there has been evidence of a Black brain drain from the area, for most Blacks in the county it has not been economically feasible to relocate. As a consequence, they have been engaged in a struggle to maintain a modicum of social, economic, and political power. As described by Portes and Stepick (1993), African American leaders have often referred to their status as "double subordination," a term reflecting both racial and ethnic disadvantage. Pervasive poverty, the decline of the African American business community, competition for jobs with Blacks from the Caribbean as well as with other immigrants, and the deterioration of older, more stable Black neighborhoods occasioned, in part, by the movement of African American professionals to suburban areas have combined to pose significant problems for African Americans in Dade County and Miami.

In the realm of politics, Blacks in Dade county have been compelled to establish alliances with both White non-Hispanic and Hispanic brokers, but these are situational and subject to ongoing negotiation. In addition, there have been signs of distrust and disagreement between African Americans and immigrant Blacks from other regions of the hemisphere, particularly those from Haiti. Differences in language, culture, religion, competition for jobs, disagreements over wages, and conflicting attitudes toward the dominant society have separated Black ethnic groups in the county, and these divisions have been a factor in keeping Blacks relatively impotent in the face of the strong, large, well-organized, economically and politically powerful Cuban ethnic enclave. To a lesser extent, a similar situation exists for Hispanics who are not Cuban, such as Central Americans from Nicaragua and El Salvador, many of whom are poor refugees. Although they can speak Spanish, many of these people are undocumented, poorly educated, and have no legal right to employment or health and human services. This situation limits their earning and mobility potential even within the Miami Latin American enclave. This will be an important factor in the future as Miami's Hispanic population continues to become increasingly diverse with the end of the "open arms" U.S. policy toward Cuban immigration.

Historical Perspectives on Change and Conflict in Dade County

The tensions and conflicts in South Florida around the issues of language, citizenship, and assimilation are redundant in twentieth-century American history.

The expectations of American popular and political culture have been that immigrants would become citizens and assimilate into "American" life. However, in practice, this rarely happened. In their classic work, *Beyond the Melting Pot*, Glazer and Moynihan (1968) observed that, in spite of a widespread belief to the contrary, the United States was never a single melting pot filled with indistinguishable elements, each added from a plethora of immigrant cultures. Historically, although the ethos of U.S. society granted immigrants some freedom to maintain portions of their native culture, it was a freedom bound by the expectations that they would ultimately embrace the language, social values, belief systems, institutions, history, and traditions of their hosts. And an overriding expectation was that immigrants, especially the young and those in the second and third generations, would relinquish all but minimal vestiges of their cultural heritage. This limited diversity within the broader context of eventual assimilation was the expected pattern in the United States. Departures from these expectations have traditionally led to social resistance of immigrants, and on many occasions to prejudice, discrimination, and conflict. Given this historical context, it is not surprising that Dade county was rife with interethnic and interracial tensions at the time of our research.

Those wishing a more extensive discussion of historical views on the assimilation of immigrants in the United States are referred to Thomas and Znaniecki (1927), Child (1943), Wittke (1952), Handlin (1959), and Gordon (1964). More recent sources that include discussions of assimilation include Acuña (1981), Portes and Bach (1985), and Portes and Rumbaut (1990). Those interested in a discussion of the ecological processes associated with the transformation of social areas resulting from cultural, ethnic and racial in-migrations and their concomitant conflicts are referred to the classic work of Park and his colleagues (Burgess, 1927; McKenzie, 1933; Park, 1952; Park et al., 1925).

Racial Tensions and Violence

The city of Miami has had a history of racial unrest and on occasion it has erupted in instances of both major and minor violence. In 1968 there was a major civil disorder in Miami. Although prompted in part to attract the attention of the Democratic party, which was holding its national (presidential) convention in the city at the time, the rioting reflected local racial unrest that had been smoldering as a consequence of long-term unresolved problems between members of the Black community and the existing White political leadership. A second source of tension was the perception that the preferential treatment being afforded by federal statutes to immigrant Cubans was diminishing the resources and opportunities available to the Black community. The 1968 civil disorder was followed in 1980 by a major riot that erupted when four White policemen charged with the beating death of a young African American male were acquitted by an all-White jury.

Several smaller disturbances have occurred since 1968, including one that took place just as our research was getting underway. Specifically, two nights of rioting followed an incident in 1989 when a policeman of Hispanic origin (Colombia) shot and killed an African American as he rode through the streets of Liberty City, one of the large, historic Black ghettos in Miami. A rider on the motorcycle being driven by the victim was also killed when the vehicle crashed following the shooting. Subsequent trials and appeals further heightened already tense relationships. Although convicted of manslaughter and sentenced to 7 years in prison, the policeman, with massive moral and financial support from the Hispanic community, secured the services of a nationally famous trial lawyer who was successful in getting a new trial, a change of venue, and a reversal of the conviction and sentence. The support given by the Hispanic community intensified conflicts between Blacks and Hispanics, as did its reaction to a visit by Nelson Mandela in the summer of 1990. Just prior to his arrival, the Hispanic mayors of five incorporated municipalities in Dade County unanimously "uninvited" Mandela, after a national news service carried a story in which the South African leader expressed some friendship with Castro. Mandela came, as scheduled, but without any recognition from the political leadership of the county or city, and a planned ceremony at which he was to receive the key to the city was canceled. This action was viewed as an affront to Mandela and to the Black community, and it resulted in Black leaders calling for a boycott of Miami on the part of conventioneers.

The boycott, while never fully realized, lasted for several months and resulted in the cancellation of a number of large conventions, and it produced ongoing tensions as local Black leaders urged the boycotting of businesses that did not support their position. It is worth noting that the boycott extended to other segments of the community and, in fact, during the fall of 1990 as we were preparing to gather the first wave of data, our efforts were canceled in several schools as large numbers of bus drivers and teachers stayed away from work. Although not as dramatic as the cases just cited, as our research was being conducted, there was a stream of public displays of interracial and intraracial tensions and conflicts between all of the major ethnic groups living in the area, and these tensions had a chilling effect on intergroup interactions including those occurring in the classrooms of the DCPS.

Crime

One of the most powerful factors associated with the negative images of Miami is its reputation for being lawless and violent. Official crime statistics verify this image. Law enforcement data indicate that in 1991 Miami had the second highest overall reported crime rate in the United States. There were 18,256 crimes per 100,000 persons. Only Atlanta, Georgia, with 18,953 crimes per 100,000 had a slightly higher rate. By way of comparison, Los Angeles reported 9,730 crimes for

100,000, and New York City reported 9,236. Miami also led the nation in violent crimes (i.e., murder, rape, robbery, and aggravated assault). It reported 4,191 such crimes per 100,000; again by way of contrast, New York reported a rate of 2,318 per 100,000, Los Angeles reported a rate of 2,526 per 100,000, and Washington, D.C., reported 1,422 violent crimes per 100,000. The data on property crimes indicated that Miami ranked third in the country with a rate of 14,065 per 100,000. It was exceeded only by Ft. Worth, Texas (15,023), and by Atlanta (14,912 per 100,000; *American Almanac*, 1995).

The high levels of crime in the community are reflected by illegal acts committed in the schools. The *Miami Herald* reported that in the 1991–1992 school year there were 415 robberies; 2,125 assaults; 558 cases of weapons possession; 110 instances of illegal drug possession, sale, or use; and 3,240 other miscellaneous crimes committed in the DCPS ("School Crimes," 1996). It is important to note that the highest crime rates were found in the county's middle schools. On average, there were 20 physical assaults per 1,000 students in the middle schools as contrasted to 11 per 1,000 in the county's high schools ("New Crime Wave," 1996). In addition to assaults, the prevalence of gangs, guns, knives, and other weapons in the schools led to the installation of metal detectors in many of them and to an increased police presence in and around some schools as well.

Hurricane Andrew

Hurricane Andrew, which struck South Florida during the early hours of August 24, 1992, posed a vast array of problems for Dade County and the city of Miami, and, inasmuch as it occurred between the second and third waves of data collection, it created a large number of unanticipated problems for the research group as well. The hurricane was one of the most devastating and costly disasters in U.S. history. Direct economic losses have been estimated at between 20 and 25 billion dollars; more than 130,000 homes were damaged or destroyed; approximately 160,000 persons were forced into temporary housing; and an estimated 86,000 persons were left unemployed ("Aftermath of Hurricane," 1992). The stresses associated with the loss of homes and jobs were compounded by the perception that widespread looting was taking place immediately after the storm. Gun purchases increased at unprecedented rates as citizens armed themselves to protect their families and possessions ("Aftermath of Hurricane," 1992).

At a personal level, a sharp increase in family conflicts reflected the stresses associated with the storm and its aftermath. As reported in the *Miami Herald*, family violence, including spousal and child abuse, rose so dramatically that local officials had to appoint additional judges to process the complaints ("Violence Follows Hurricane," 1992). Heavy rains, high temperatures and humidity, the lack of electricity and potable water, and overcrowded housing conditions added to the hassles confronting Florida residents as they attempted to deal with the consequences of the storm. Thousands of students and teachers were dislocated, school openings were postponed, and many of the schools were severely damaged. The dispersion of students throughout Florida and the rest of the country posed a challenge to the research group, who made vigorous and largely successful efforts to locate respondents and to secure Time 3 data from them.

The impacts of the hurricane were not only extensive, they were also persistent. Eight months after the storm, a survey of 14,937 households conducted by community officials revealed that only about 5% of the most badly damaged homes had been fully repaired ("Hurricane Recovery Slow," 1993), and an article published in *Newsweek* magazine in April of 1993 reported that children and adolescents were still suffering psychological traumas and that 12 had attempted suicide ("Trauma after the Storm," 1993). On March 7, 1994, nearly 19 months after the hurricane, a front-page article entitled "Unrecovered: Many Lives Still Shattered in South Dade" appeared in the *Miami Herald*. The article chronicled the continuing, unresolved stresses still confronting many of those who resided in the area most affected by the storm ("Unrecovered," 1994).

The hurricane was extremely disruptive, pervasive, and persistent, and as we have reported elsewhere, it had significant deleterious mental health and social consequences on adolescents (Khoury et al., 1997; Warheit, Zimmerman, Khoury, Vega, & Gil, 1996). Anecdotal data obtained from classroom teachers reinforce these findings and support our conclusion that the hurricane was a major disruptive force in the lives of many in our sample.

The Dade County Public School System

School and Staff Characteristics

All school systems in the state of Florida are county based and a county board of education controls all public schools in each county. Therefore, the 48 middle schools that served as our sources for the first wave of data were all part of the Dade County Public School System (DCPS). At the time of the first data collection period in the fall of 1990, the DCPS was the fourth largest in the United States with a total of 289,687 students, and it was growing rapidly. At the beginning of the 1995–96 school year, enrollment had reached 326,296 students, and 94% of the regular schools in the county were significantly overcrowded ("New Housing Overloading Dade's Schools," 1995). The system included 185 elementary schools, 48 regular middle schools, 27 senior high schools, and 40 alternative, specialized, or adult education schools and centers. The instructional staff included 13,580 classroom teachers, 75% of whom were female. Slightly less than one-half of the teachers (49%) were White non-Hispanic; 27% were Black, and 23% were of Hispanic origin. Almost one-half (49%) of the principals were White non-Hispanic, 35% were Black, and 15% were Hispanic (Dade County District and School Profiles, 1990–1991).

The superintendent of the DCPS at the time of the study's initiation was Hispanic. He left to become superintendent of the New York City School System shortly after the research got underway and was replaced with an interim superintendent who was African American. Vigorous efforts on the part of the African Americas community failed to have him named to the office, and an administrator of Cuban heritage became the superintendent and remained in that position during the time these data were being gathered and analyzed. In every instance, these administrators and their assistants were extremely cooperative with the research group during all phases of the research. Their assistance was crucial, particularly in our gaining access to students. The DCPS has a school-based management system that empowers individual principals to control much of what takes place in their schools. Their consent and the cooperation of key staff members had to be secured before access to schools was allowed. The superintendent and his assistants were instrumental in gaining that access. In addition to the superintendent and his assistants, the principals, assistant principals, trust counselors, and teachers in all schools were extremely cooperative throughout the study. All 48 middle and 40 alternative schools in the DCPS participated in the research during all three data collection periods, and further, all of the county's high schools cooperated as students moved into them.

The overwhelming number of tasks being placed on the staff of the middle and junior high school principals, teachers, and trust counselors in the individual schools could have led them to deny our request for research privileges. Among other factors, a large volume of research was already being conducted in the schools as ours was being planned. Our request to access 48 middle and junior high schools, and later to add 25 high schools to our sample, involving thousands of individual classrooms, represented an additional set of extensive demands on an already burdened staff. In addition, we were asking a large number of teachers to provide ratings of approximately 3,000 students, and we were requesting access to the parents of these students. Thankfully, we received permission to conduct the research, and in addition, we are grateful for the tremendous assistance provided by the DCPS throughout the project.

Socioeconomic Status of the Students

At the time of our research, the overall socioeconomic status (SES) of students in the DCPS was relatively low, as indicated by the percentage of them on free or reduced-cost lunch programs. Among the sixth graders in our cohort, 57%

were on free or reduced-cost lunch programs, and for the seventh graders the percentage was 48% (Dade County District and School Profiles, 1990–1991). These data are consistent with the findings of researchers from the University of Florida and Florida State University who have reported that 62% of the children in the kindergarten classes of the DCPS were living below the poverty level, that is, they lived in households that had a family income of $13,400 or less for a family of four. The data on Black and Hispanic children are even more arresting. The same study concluded that approximately 80% of the Black children and 65% of the Hispanic children in kindergarten were living in families with household incomes below the poverty level. By comparison, White non-Hispanic rates of children in poverty were near the national average, 23% ("Dade Kids Face Hardships," 1993).

Racial and Ethnic Composition of the Students

The DCPS reported that in 1990–91 about one-half of all middle school students were of Hispanic origin, approximately one-third were Black, and about one-fifth were White non-Hispanic. Approximately one-fourth of all students in the DCPS in 1990 were foreign born, and an even larger percentage of the sixth and seventh graders in the research cohort (38.6%) were born outside the United States. This relatively large percentage of foreign-born students is reflected in the DCPS programs related to language. At the time of our first data collection, there were 40,520 students enrolled in classes for English for Speakers of Other Languages (ESOL), 29,394 enrolled in classes with bilingual curriculum content, and 83,175 students enrolled in classes for students of Spanish origin with limited use of English (Dade County District and School Profiles, 1990–1991).

In 1990, in spite of the fact that the DCPS was bussing nearly 68,000 students daily, many schools in the system were predominantly of one race or ethnic group. Hispanics and Blacks often constituted the majority of students in individual schools, and in many instances one of these two groups represented 80% to 90% of the total enrollment. White non-Hispanic students were a majority in six of the schools, with percentages ranging from 49% to 61% (Dade County District and School Profiles, 1990–1991). The DCPS is one of the most highly segregated school systems among major metropolitan areas in the United States.

Student Achievement

The nationally normed Stanford Achievement Tests (7th edition) are administered annually to all DCPS students in Kindergarten through eleventh grades. Given the large percentage of low-SES and foreign-born students in the system, it is not surprising to find that the scores on these tests were below national levels as determined by percentile scores. (Scores below the 50th percentile are regarded as being below the national norm or average.) The reading comprehension percentile score for sixth graders in our study cohort was 41; for the seventh graders it was 39. The mathematics comprehension percentile score for sixth graders was 60 and for the seventh graders it was 45 (Dade County District and School Profiles, 1990–1991). Parenthetically, it is important to note that in 1995, the DCPS was notified by educational officials in the Florida Department of Education that 52 of their schools had fallen so far below national and state norms on reading, mathematics, and/or writing skills that it was possible they would receive state-imposed sanctions including the complete revamping of school faculties. Four of the 50 middle schools in the county were reported on this list of schools with critical test performance scores ("Dade Schools on Notice," 1995).

As our research was being conducted, the DCPS, as were many other school systems in urban areas throughout the United States, was confronted with a large variety of problems that made great demands on their resources. These included overcrowding; the need for new schools; extensive bussing; high dropout rates among some groups; racial and ethnic conflicts; gangs, crime, violence, and drugs in and around schools; high rates of teacher turnover in troubled schools; student attrition resulting from the growing numbers of parents practicing home schooling or sending children to private schools; and a growing indifference on the part of many in the community.

It is clear from the above description that Dade County and the city of Miami were undergoing a great many demographic, social, and cultural changes in the early 1990s and, further, that these changes were transforming the institutional structures and social patterns of the community. The historical core values of the community were in a transitional state; there was pervasive behavioral ambiguity and normative confusion; crime rates were high; racial and ethnic tensions were often near the surface and frequently found expression in both public and private settings. In addition, there was a lack of consensus on how the social, cultural, and racial tensions and conflicts could be ameliorated. A large body of both anecdotal and empirical evidence suggests that these profound tensions and conflicts were producing personal alienation and social anomie (e.g., Durkheim 1951) and, further, that this alienation and anomie were related to feelings of social and cultural marginality among the diverse ethnic groups of Miami. We also believe that these conditions were related to substance use and other forms of social deviance on the part of the young adolescents in our study cohort. These factors, along with the impact of one of the most destructive hurricanes in recent history, were very much a part of the environment within which our research took place, and many of the findings presented in subsequent chapters are best understood when these contextual elements are taken into account.

Design of the Study

Introduction

The findings presented in the chapters that follow were secured from a major epidemiological project that had the following aims and objectives:

1. To identify the factors associated with the initiation, habituation, and cessation of substance use among a cohort of Hispanic, Black, and non-Hispanic White adolescents.
2. To identify the role that cultural orientation, cultural values, ethnic pride, perceptions of prejudice, racial mistrust, acculturation processes, and acculturative conflicts have on drug use among Hispanic origin and/or Black adolescents.
3. To identify whether the sequence and stages of drug use are similar among Hispanic, White non-Hispanic, and Black adolescents.
4. To test the esteem enhancement theory of delinquency as an explanatory model for understanding deviance and drug use among those in the cohort, and to determine if acculturative strain theory is consistent with this model.
5. To determine whether risk factors and related processes identified in a comprehensive theoretical framework predict substance use among Hispanic and non-Hispanic adolescents.
6. To identify access points and modifiable risk factors appropriate for designing future school-based interventions. An overview of the design is presented in Figure 2.1.

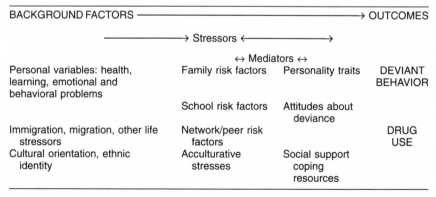

Figure 2.1. Overview of model: Relationships between cultural, and ethnic factors and nonnormative behaviors.

The selection of ethnic group identifiers in this book was done with the aim of assuring the broadest comprehension by readers. We are critically aware of the social contentiousness and scientific inadequacy of ethnic and racial labels (Zimmerman, Vega, Gil, Warheit, Apospori, & Biafora, 1994). This issue presents a particularly thorny problem in Miami, where people of diverse international, especially Latin American, nationalities coexist. Our first choice was to use actual national origin (e,g., Cuban) for specific subgroups, or Latino to designate all ethnic groups with a Latin American heritage, as we have in many of our published research articles. However, we later changed to Hispanic for two reasons. This is the standard U.S. census ethnic category for Latin Americans, and somewhat surprisingly, we found that adolescents in Miami now preferred Hispanic over Latino. We were equally unsatisfied with the use of White non-Hispanics as the reference category to compact a highly diverse subpopulation in Dade county. In order to maintain some clarity of ethnic identification for African Americans, we have tried to use this term consistently when referring specifically to this ethnic group, and we used Blacks when referring to the broad grouping of all people in Dade County of African ancestry, including people from nations of the Caribbean basin and African Americans. In years to come, given the extensive rates of interethnic unions in all U.S. ethnic groups, the problem of accurate ethnic labeling can only worsen, and ethnicity may become increasing pervaded by political meaning. Nevertheless, we made every effort to be consistent in ethnic terminology throughout the book to assist readers unfamiliar with the enigma of American ethnic identity.

Overview of the Study Design

The data required to address these goals were obtained from three sources: (1) a large sample of boys and a smaller sample of girls entering the sixth and seventh grades of the DCPS in the fall of 1990, (2) a sample of parents of students included in the samples and (3) a nonprobability sample of teachers who rated the same students on whom parent and family data were secured. Three waves of data were secured on the student sample; two were gathered from the parents; and, one was conducted with the teachers at Time 1. The teacher and parent samples were discontinued at waves two and three, respectively, as a consequence of a reduction in funds for these phases of the research.

Student Sample

As the research was being planned, the investigators decided to focus primarily on boys, inasmuch as data obtained as part of the Hispanic Health and Nutrition

Examination Survey (HANES; National Center for Health Statistics, 1985) and from independent researchers (National Institute on Drug Abuse, 1987; Page, McCoy, Sweeney, & Rio, 1985; Szapocznik, Ladner, & Scopetta 1979) indicated very low prevalence rates of illicit substance use among Hispanics in the county. Detailed power analyses predicated on these low rates suggested that, even with the inclusion of all middle school girls in the county, the power to find a significant difference, if it existed between Hispanic and non-Hispanic girls, was less than .6. However, data were obtained on a stratified probability sample of 626 girls enrolled in six of the county's middle schools. These six schools were selected so as to approximate the ethnic composition of all middle schools in the DCPS. When appropriate, data on girls are included in the analyses within individual chapters.

Prior to the first wave of data collection, informed consent forms, printed in both English and Spanish, were sent to the parents of prospective participants. Only students returning affirmative responses were included in the study. Informed consent was also secured from students at the time of the questionnaire administration. Altogether, consent forms were sent to the parents or guardians of 9,763 boys and 669 girls. Among boys, 8,234 (83.4%) of the forms were returned and of this number, 6,934 (84.0%) granted permission to have their sons included in the research. Of the 669 consent forms sent to the parents of girls, nearly 90% were returned and almost all of these granted permission to have their daughters involved in the study. At the time of the first data collection period (T-1), data were obtained on 6,760 boys and 626 girls. The T-2 sample included 6,089 boys and 549 girls. This represents 90% and 87% of the T-1 samples, respectively. The T-3 sample consisted of 5,370 boys and 554 girls. The increase in the sample of girls at T-3 was the result of an improvement in the tracking methods, which allowed the research group to identify some T-3 girls not identified at T-2. Approximately 80% of the participants were included in all three data collection periods. The ethnic composition of the sample of boys at T-1 is shown in Table 2.2; Table 2.3 reports data on the total sample for all three data collection periods.

The T-1 data were gathered in the fall of 1990 when students were entering the sixth or the seventh grade. The T-2 data were collected in the fall of 1991. Hurricane Andrew, which occurred on August 24, 1992, delayed the T-3 data collection to the spring of 1993.

As noted, all 48 of Dade County's public middle schools participated in the study, and as students progressed from middle school to high school, all 25 high schools also cooperated, as well as alternative schools.

Approximately one-half the Hispanic boys and girls in the study were foreign born. Among Hispanic subgroups, 33% of the Cubans were foreign born, 92% of the Nicaraguan heritage students were foreign born, and the percentages for Colombians and Puerto Ricans who were born outside the continental United States were 69% and 81%, respectively. Approximately three-fourths of the

Table 2.2.   Ethnic Characteristics
of the Sample at Time 1, Boys Only

	N	%
White non-Hispanic	899	13.3
Hispanics	4,296	63.5
Cubans	(1,745)	(25.8)
Nicaraguans	(576)	(8.5)
Others	(1,975)	(29.2)
Blacks	1,328	19.6
African Americans	(946)	(14.0)
Haitians	(196)	(2.9)
Other Caribbean Blacks	(186)	(2.8)
Other Ethnic/Racial Groups	190	2.8
Unknown	47	0.7

foreign-born Cubans had lived in the United States for more than 10 years; only 12.4% had lived in the country for less than 6 years. Nicaraguan students tended to have shorter lengths of stay in the United States than any of the other groups. About one-half of them had lived in the United States for less than 6 years, whereas one-third of the Colombian and Puerto Rican heritage students had lived in the country for the same time period. No single pattern was found for the other Hispanic subgroups included in the sample.

The mean age of the sample at T-1 was 11.6 years, and there was little difference in the ages by race and ethnic group. However, the living arrangements of those in the sample varied significantly. Close to three-fourths (74.0%) of the White non-Hispanic students, 71.8% of the foreign-born Hispanic, and 66.3% of the U.S.-born Hispanic students lived in households with two parents. By contrast,

Table 2.3.   Sample Selection/
Retention, Boys and Girls

		Participants	
Consent requested	T-1	T-2	T-3
Students			
10,432	7,386	6,646	5,924
Parents			
3,592	2,992	2,676	0
Teacher ratings			
2,992	2,853	300*	0

*This was an additional group for which teacher ratings
were obtained.

only 42.1% of the African Americans lived in two-parent households. Only 11.7% of the White non-Hispanic students lived in single-mother households, and the percentage was only slightly higher for foreign-born Hispanic students (12.0%) and higher for Hispanics born in the United States (16.15%). Close to one-third, 29.9%, of the African Americans in the sample lived in single-mother households. At T-3 the proportion of adolescents in single-mother households increased for all groups: 32.2% for African Americans, 19.6% for U.S.-born Hispanics, 14.4% for foreign-born Hispanics, and 13.7% for White non-Hispanics. As noted above, approximately one-half the total cohort was living at or near the poverty level as determined by their inclusion in free or reduced-cost lunch programs.

Representativeness/Attrition of the Student Sample

Data from six variables provided by the school system were analyzed to determine if there were significant differences between eligible students in and not in the total sample and in each of the ethnic groups. The variables were race or ethnicity, age, reading level, year in school, native or foreign born, and the number of parents in the household. Overall, the results showed that those in the sample were significantly different from the nonparticipants in only 1 of 216 cells as defined by the other five comparison variables. African American students with reading levels in the fourth through seventh stanines had small but significantly lower rates of representation in the sample than their counterparts in the lowest and highest stanine groups. Inasmuch as there were no other significant differences between those in and not in the sample for any of the other within-race or within–ethnic group comparisons, for most of the analyses the data were not weighted to control for nonresponse rates. The convention in this volume is to use the term *ethnicity* rather than *race*, except in instances where race is more appropriate as a social designation.

The tests for representativeness were followed by analyses designed to determine whether there were significant differences between those remaining in the study over all three data-gathering periods and those dropping out. Four separate procedures were utilized. First, chi-square and *t* tests were calculated to determine if there were social and demographic differences between participants and dropouts. No significant differences were found. The second method involved logistic regression analyses to determine the contribution of key variables in the prediction of attrition. A third test was composed of different weighting techniques to determine if corrections were required as a consequence of attrition. The fourth method compared the dropouts to those in the study on a number of the key independent and dependent variables. The differences in the correlation matrices were assessed using LISREL covariance structure analysis. The outcomes of these analyses indicated that there were no systematic or significant differences between those in the study over the three waves and those lost through attrition, As a consequence of these findings, it was determined that it was not necessary to assign weights to correct for possible attrition biases as analyses were conducted.

Collateral Data

Parent Sample

In addition to data from the students, the study design called for the securing of three waves of collateral information from a stratified probability sample of parents with quotas for each of the three major ethnic groups. Stratification insured adequate numbers for the planned analyses. Once selected, parents were contacted by telephone and told of the study, and its objectives and potential risks and benefits were described. Once informed, consent was requested. The refusal rate was very low—less than 10%. After consent was given, the questionnaire was administered over the telephone. Parents were given the choice of responding in English or Spanish. On average, it took approximately one-half hour to complete the protocol. All interviews were conducted by a professional survey research group with offices in Coral Gables, Florida. The principal investigators and other staff members of the project were able to monitor the interviewing of parents by patching into the phones being used by the survey group. When it was deemed necessary, the principal investigators or staff would meet with interviewers and their supervisors to discuss problems and to offer guidance.

The parent interview schedule included the Parent Report Form (PRF), which is used in association with the Child Behavior Checklist (CBCL) developed and tested by Achenbach and Edelbrock (1983, 1986a). It also contained questions regarding family life; alcohol and drug use by family members; measures of family cohesion, pride, and support; questions regarding income and education; and, for Hispanics and Blacks, measures of perceived prejudice and discrimination and acculturation processes and conflicts. A total of 2,992 parent interviews were secured.

Teacher Ratings

At T-1, information was secured from teachers on the same students whose parents and guardians were included in the parent substudy. As discussed above, budgetary restraints restricted the obtaining of teacher information on the student sample at T-2 and T-3. A total of 2,853 students were assessed by their teachers at T-1. The teacher data were obtained by means of the Teacher Report Form (TRF) version of the CBCL (Achenbach & Edelbrock, 1986b). As with the parent interviews, the primary purpose of the teacher substudy was to provide collateral information on students from the teacher's perspective. These data were of value in themselves and, in addition, they were used to compare teacher assessments with those made by students and their parents.

Questionnaire Construction and Administration

The construction and testing of the student questionnaire, which took approximately 18 months to complete, involved the use of four focus groups and two pilot studies. The normal difficulties associated with questionnaire construction were compounded by the fact that the school population included many foreign-born students with poor reading skills and limited knowledge of English. These language and reading difficulties were addressed through concerted efforts to develop items that could be understood by the students and to word the items in language consistent with their grade levels. After the English version of the questionnaire was developed, it was translated, back-translated, and retranslated into the Spanish forms most likely to be understood by the heterogeneous Hispanic groups included in the sample. A number of different administration procedures were developed to facilitate the gathering of information from those with special language or reading difficulties. At T-1, and to a lesser degree at T-2, several different methods of administration were used. These included the gathering of data during one class period for those who had no difficulty in reading or responding to the items in the protocol. Some students were given the questionnaire over two class periods, and, in a few instances, students who had difficulty reading any language had the instrument administered to them orally. By T-3, all but a very small number of students were able to complete the instrument in one class period. All questionnaires were administered in school settings by trained members of the project staff. Privacy was enhanced by seating arrangements and students were encouraged to use the large envelope that contained their questionnaires to cover their answers.

Human Subjects, Confidentiality, and Tracking of Students

As noted earlier, all participants in the study were requested to sign informed consent forms prior to their inclusion in the research. In addition, a Certificate of Confidentiality was secured from the National Institutes of Health to safeguard the anonymity and confidentiality of the data. Although students and parents were given assurances of confidentiality, inasmuch as the longitudinal design involved tracking them over time, anonymity was not possible. However, the confidentiality of participants was provided at two levels: (1) no visible identifiers of any kind were included on the protocols and (2) project identifiers of students and parents were kept secure by the principal investigators. Students were identified and tracked between waves by using data secured from them at the time of the initial data collection period and from information supplied by the DCPS. Parents were followed using procedures that included DCPS records and a payment to parents when they notified research staff of changes in address or telephone numbers. At T-3, some modifications were made that simplified the tracking process for students. Once again, relying on the DCPS management information system, individual students were located in specific schools and classrooms. However, at T-3 the DCPS student number was written on the protocol using invisible ink. Project staff went to schools and classrooms, assembled participants in the study, and distributed envelopes containing the protocols. Once completed, the envelopes were returned to the project office, and a special scanning instrument was used to determine the ID number. The T-3 procedures were much more efficient than those used in the earlier data collection waves. Positive identification was obtained and, as a consequence, some of those who could not be matched at T-2 because of inconsistencies in information given at T-1 or T-2 were matched. After the data were checked, coded, and transferred to computer files, all student questionnaires and parent interview schedules were destroyed.

3

Substance Use and Other Social Deviance

George J. Warheit and Andres G. Gil

Introduction

This chapter presents data on the prevalence of substance use and its relationships to other social deviance among two cohorts of young adolescents residing in Dade County, Florida. Four racial or ethnic subgroups are included in the analyses: (1) those of Hispanic heritage born in the United States, (2) those of Hispanic heritage born outside the United States, (3) African Americans, and (4) White non-Hispanics (WNH). The chapter begins with a general discussion of social deviance and substance use followed by a brief outline of the most salient components of a number of theories postulated to explain the origins, development, and cessation of deviant behaviors. The analyses include basic descriptive longitudinal findings for both substance use and social deviance among those in the sample, and they center on how these two sets of behaviors are related over the three time periods in which the data were collected. The chapter concludes with a summary and discussion of the findings.

Social Deviance

Ancient codes of conduct that include bodies of prescribed and proscribed behaviors, as well as guidelines regarding punishments for those violating those codes, offer strong historical evidence that deviance has always been present in social groups and societies. Moreover, ethnographic studies reveal that throughout much of human history, deviance was attributed largely to devils, witches, evil spirits, demon possession, and other supernatural sources. Given these presumed causes, it is not surprising that deviants were most often subjected to exorcism rituals and rights of purification designed to placate angry deities, as well as physical punishment, death, and excommunication. Modern societies, as with those of antiquity, are confronted with individuals who violate the norms that define the boundaries of behavior. However, for the most part, social deviance is no longer attributed to supernatural forces; modern social and biological sciences have largely supplanted these earlier explanatory systems. Modern sciences, notwithstanding, the etiologic factors underlying deviant behavior have not been definitively identified, in spite of massive and prolonged efforts, and the search goes on.

Definitions of Deviance

The literature is replete with varying definitions of social deviance with most of the differences being attributable to the theoretical, philosophical, and heuristic orientations of those offering them. In spite of these differences, there is a consensus regarding the key elements found in most definitions. At the broadest level, deviance can be said to occur when the attitudes, beliefs, characteristics, and behaviors exhibited by individuals or classes of individuals violate the normative standards of groups that have the power to impose negative sanctions on those judged to be in violation of those standards. It is important to note that those being judged as deviant may or may not be members of the group imposing the standards and sanctions. Deviants may hold membership in the judging group, they may be nonmembers seeking admission to the judging group, or they may be nonmembers not desiring membership in the judging group.

Explicit in the definition offered above is the supposition that *attitudes* and *beliefs*, as well as behaviors, that do not coincide with the normative values of the larger society are sometimes regarded as deviant and can lead to negative sanctions. And in many societies, violations of traditional attitudes and beliefs are still taboo. However, it is obvious that in contemporary America the mere possession of attitudes and beliefs that are incompatible with those of society at large does not necessarily produce social conflicts or negative legal sanctions. For example, individuals whose attitudes and beliefs lead them to conclude that there is nothing morally or ethically wrong with the use of marijuana or cocaine are not likely to come to the attention of the criminal justice system unless they act on those attitudes and beliefs; neither are they likely to incur extralegal negative sanctions. This does not mean that those wishing to understand social deviance should discount the role that attitudes and beliefs play in producing deviant behavior. Kaplan and his colleagues have shown conclusively that attitudes and beliefs that predispose individuals to deviance are excellent predictors of subsequent deviant behaviors (Kaplan, Martin, & Johnson, 1986; Kaplan, Johnson, & Bailey, 1987).

In Kaplan's discussion of deviance he distinguishes between motivated and unmotivated deviance (Kaplan, 1995). Motivated deviance, on the one hand, is perceived as involving rational (willful) behaviors that are intended to achieve a wide range of instrumental goals including the enhancement of one's self-esteem. The origins of unmotivated deviance, on the other hand, are seen as occurring as a consequence of one's ascribed or achieved statuses, for example, race, ethnicity, religion, or sociocultural characteristics. Blacks, ethnic minorities, immigrants, gypsies, and other groups have often been defined as deviants even though they may not have engaged in overt deviant behaviors. Their deviance is regarded as being unmotivated because those labeled as deviant have no control over the factors that precipitate their being defined as deviant.

Deviance and U.S. Belief Systems

In the United States, deviance has two distinguishing characteristics: It involves a behavioral act and it is presumed to be motivated. Deviance is perceived as a volitional act. The social and cultural origins of this perception have many roots, but none is more influential than that derived from the notion of free will—a belief system that is deeply embedded in the religious and philosophical foundations of U.S. society. The centrality of belief in free will is manifested in many of our institutional structures, and it is one of the cornerstones on which our criminal justice system has been built. Moreover, it is clearly reflected in our admonition to adolescents to "just say no to drugs." In short, there is a pervasive belief that drug use and nonuse are largely a function of one's will, a matter of free choice, and all that one has to do to avoid drug use is to exercise that choice. Inasmuch as the notion of free will is part of an extremely powerful and pervasive belief system, those identified as deviants who wish to be spared negative sanctions must demonstrate to those in authority that their behaviors were not willful but, rather, the result of factors beyond their control (e.g., ignorance, poverty, racism, prejudice, substance use, sexual/physical abuse as a child, dysfunctional family life, and/or mental incompetence).

Substance Use as Deviance in the United States

Throughout much of our national history, our society has emphasized sobriety and abstinence as highly prized virtues. They are prized because they are regarded as prerequisites to other valued behaviors including personal rationality, self-control, reliability, predictability, self-reliance, and a sense of personal and social responsibility, including taking care to safeguard one's physical and mental well-being. As a consequence of the high value assigned these behaviors, the use of any substance that interferes with their fulfillment has been regarded as very undesirable, illegal, sinful, and a vast array of institutionalized moral and legal prohibitions regarding their use has been woven into the social and legal fabric of the society.

As noted, throughout most of our national history, abstinence from drug use has been preferred. However, this long-held value has undergone substantial changes in recent decades and at present the norm regarding legal substance use among adults in the United States is that it is acceptable as long as it is in moderation and it takes place in appropriate environments. In addition, although there are both laws and other normative prohibitions regarding the use of marijuana, cocaine, and other illicit drugs, their use among adults is more or less tolerated as long as it does not involve any of these three dimensions: (1) they refrain from the sale or distribution of substances; (2) users do not run afoul of the law for offenses that bring their substance use to official disclosure; and (3) their illicit substance use does not result in social dysfunctionality, that is, the inability to perform adult-related social roles. Somewhat curiously, as attitudes toward alcohol, and to a lesser degree the use of illicit drugs, has softened for adults, the use of tobacco has in recent decades been singled out as being especially harmful, and there is a growing negative national consensus and an increase in the number of legal prohibitions regarding its use (e.g., in theaters, restaurants, public shopping malls, places of employment, and on buses and airplanes).

On the one hand, current normative standards of substance use for adults are largely predicated on the assumption that they possess the maturity and judgment required to avoid becoming addicted and/or from engaging in substance use behaviors that are dysfunctional at personal and social levels. On the other hand, the use of cigarettes, alcohol, and illicit drugs on the part of adolescents is viewed with considerable angst among those in the general population, and legislative and massive educational efforts have been put forth to prevent such use. The reasons underlying these legal and attitudinal differences regarding adult vis-à-vis adolescent drug use are extremely complex, but they include deep-seated religious, cultural, and social values. Although it is not often stated formally, it appears that substance use among children and adolescents is proscribed because it is assumed that they lack the judgment required to use these substances in moderation; that is, they are viewed as being more susceptible to abuse and addiction than their adult counterparts. In addition, it is believed that substance use has more deleterious physical and mental health consequences for children than for adults, and it is assumed that early substance use among adolescents leads to a diminution of their chances for future educational, occupational, and social successes. In short, tobacco, alcohol, and illicit drugs are regarded as dangerous for adolescents, and our society has attempted to erect social and legal barriers that isolate adolescents from their use.

Approaches to the Study of Deviance and Substance Use among Adolescents

Studies of adult crime and juvenile delinquency have been of interest to researchers and scholars from both the social and biological sciences for a very long time, and they have developed a number of theoretical postulates and paradigms to guide their thinking and research. An exhaustive listing of contributors is beyond the scope of this chapter; however, those wishing contemporary summaries of deviance theories are referred to Akers (1994), Hirschi (1969), Hirschi and Gottfredson (1983), Kaplan (1984a), Messner, Krohn, and Liska (1989), Shoemaker (1990).

The dramatic increase of illicit substance use among both adults and adolescents, which began in the late 1960s and has continued to the present, prompted great interest on the part of scientists, governmental legislative bodies and agencies, criminal justice officials, health and human service providers, and the general public. This interest has resulted in massive efforts to understand the factors producing this "epidemic," and research funded by a variety of government agencies and private foundations has resulted in the publication of hundreds, if not thousands, of books and articles dealing with the subject.

Illicit substance use, by definition, is a deviant act, and it is not surprising that as social scientists have attempted to explain these behaviors they turned to previously developed theories to guide their efforts. Moreover, inasmuch as researchers from a wide variety of academic disciplines have become involved in investigating the causes of substance use, it is understandable that divergent and sometimes competing theoretical models have been explored.

A review of the literature indicates that although there has been a tremendous volume of research conducted on substance use and deviance, relatively few researchers have utilized fully specified theoretical models in their designs and as explanatory frameworks for interpreting their results. To the contrary, most research designs have utilized implicit theoretical frameworks, and a very large number of them have been descriptive or atheoretical in nature. It should also be noted that none of the theoretical models utilized are unique; all share common elements and overlapping boundaries and, as such, any review will reveal a cross-borrowing of concepts. With these contextual observations in mind, the following brief summary of the most prominent theories and research approaches is offered.

Social Control

Historically, one of the most commonly cited theories of social deviance has been social control (Eliot, Huizinga, & Ageton, 1985; Hirschi, 1969; Jessor & Jessor, 1977; Jessor, Graves, Hanson, & Jessor, 1968). Most succinctly stated, social control theory postulates that deviance occurs as a consequence of faulty or inadequate socialization experiences, which result in the failure of individuals to internalize the social norms of their membership groups and those of the community and society. As a consequence, the normative restraints required for social conformity are lacking and deviant behaviors ensue. The factors underlying this faulty or inadequate socialization have been attributed to dysfunctional family structures and social environments, exposure to nonnormative influences including those of peers, lack of native intelligence, and psychological or psychiatric disorders. Social control theory conjectures that each of these factors, singly or in combination with others, inhibits individuals from establishing bonds to either primary or secondary social groups and to the conventional institutions of the society. This lack of bonding is seen as a prelude to subsequent social deviance.

Social Learning

In addition to social control, theories of social learning have been utilized by a large number of researchers and scholars. This theoretical position shares many of the assumptions found in social control theory in that it includes the notion of faulty or inadequate socialization. However, learning theory differs from control theory in that it emphasizes the role that deviant groups have in producing value systems that are in conflict with those of the dominant society. Leading proponents of this position (Akers, Krohn, Lanza-Kaduce, & Radosevich, 1979; Bandura, 1977) have drawn heavily on Sutherland's (1939) early and highly influential work on differential association. The basic assumption of differential association is that individuals acquire deviant behavioral patterns the same way they do normative ones; that is, they learn them. Specifically, individuals are hypothesized to learn deviant behaviors through interactions with those whose attitudes, beliefs, and behaviors are at variance with those of the social groups and/or society of which they are a part. Persons are said to become deviant

> when they possess an excess of definitions favorable to the violation of the law over definitions unfavorable to violations of law, ... and when persons become criminal, they do so because of contacts with criminal behavior patterns and also because of isolation from anti-criminal patterns. (Sutherland and Cressey, 1960, p. 74)

Thus, the ratio of contacts with those inclined to obey the law vis-à-vis those inclined not to do so is postulated to produce either conventional or deviant behaviors.

Social learning theories have been an unstated, but guiding, framework for a very large body of research that has explored the relationships between family factors and deviant behavior among adolescents (Barnes, 1990; Brook, Whiteman,

Gordon, & Brook, 1983; Eliot et al., 1985; Glueck & Glueck, 1962; Kandel, Kessler, & Margulies, 1978; Krohn, Skinner, Massey, & Lauer, 1983; Krohn, Skinner, Massey, & Akers, 1985; Laub & Sampson, 1988; Loeber & Stouthamer-Loeber, 1986; Maccoby & Martin, 1983; McCord, 1991; Robins, West, & Herjanic, 1975; Wu & Kandel, 1995). Its concepts are also widely found in research on the relationships between peer influences and deviance (Brook, Whiteman, & Gordon, 1983; Farrell, Danish, & Howard, 1992; Forney, Forney, & Ripley, 1991; Huba & Bentler, 1984; Jessor & Jessor, 1977; Kaplan et al., 1987; Newcomb & Bentler, 1986a; Warheit et al., 1995).

Although not always specified, a majority of the studies just cited have assumed that deviance on the part of adolescents is at least partially related to their interaction with parents, siblings, close relatives, or peers. However, it is often difficult to determine whether the theoretical orientation underlying these studies is derived from theories of social control or from learning theory. In most instances, they probably rely on elements of both.

Structural Strain Theory

A third theoretical approach postulated to explain social deviance is structural strain (Cloward, 1959; Merton, 1957). The most fundamental assumption of this position is that deviance occurs when the behaviors of individuals are in conflict with the goals of the society and when the means used to achieve those goals violate societal norms. The sources of this deviation are not always made explicit but three are implicit: Individuals have not been adequately socialized regarding societal goals or means of goal achievement; through differential association and other processes, goals and means of goal attainment are learned that are in conflict with those promulgated by the society; deviance is seen as a response on the part of individuals who perceive that the goals or means of goal attainment are blocked by racism, prejudice, and other social structural factors.

Merton's goals–means schema (Merton, 1957) is one of the most widely cited descriptive models of social deviance found in the sociological literature, and there has been a number of studies that have elements of strain theory in their design. For example, much of the research on social deviance among African Americans often includes the assumption that racism, prejudice, and discrimination are underlying causes for their disproportionately high rates. In addition, research on acculturation processes and conflicts assumes that the cultural heritage of immigrants, including their language, often results in prejudice, minority status, discrimination, and denial of access to the opportunity structures of the host society. It is postulated that when this occurs, individuals respond in a variety of nonnormative ways including criminal activity and substance use. For a detailed discussion of acculturation stresses and their relationships to substance use, see Chapter 6 in this volume.

Social Psychological Theories

In addition to theories of social control, social learning, and structural strain, which were often grounded in sociological principles, there is a large and growing body of researchers who have relied on concepts drawn from social psychology to guide their efforts (Kandel & Logan, 1984; Kaplan, 1980, 1984a,b; Kaplan et al., 1987; Kaplan, Johnson, & Bailey, 1988a,b; Reckless, Dinitz, & Murray, 1956; Rosenberg, 1989; Smith & Fogg, 1978; Stacy & Newcomb, 1995). These and many other researchers have explored a variety of presumed causal factors including the psychosocial stresses associated with conflicts between first- and second-generation immigrant adolescents and their peers, siblings, and parents (Szapocznik, Scopetta, & Tillman, 1979a). However, the largest single body of research utilizing social psychological principles has focused on the relationships between self-esteem, self-rejection/derogation and social deviance. The most systematic and fully specified model of self-rejection and deviance has been developed and tested by Kaplan and his colleagues (Kaplan, 1980; Kaplan, 1984a,b, 1986; Kaplan, et al., 1987, 1988a,b). Kaplan's theory contains three basic assumptions. First, individuals come to a conscious and rational conclusion that they are being rejected by their membership and reference groups. Second, rejected individuals experience psychic distress, which they recognize and dislike. Third, those experiencing painful psychic distress seek membership in alternative groups where they feel accepted and comfortable. The key concept in the model is psychic stress, for it is hypothesized that consciously recognized stress arising from rejection *causes* individuals to seek membership in alternative groups, some of which may have core values that violate those of society. Stated differently, the avoidance of ongoing membership in groups where individuals are emotionally uncomfortable, and the seeking of membership in groups where they feel accepted, can be viewed as an attempt to resolve the dissonance between what they feel about themselves and the perceptions that they believe others have of them.

Kaplan's carefully crafted research and that of others whose central notions include concepts drawn from social psychology have antecedents in the works of early symbolic interactionists who emphasized the role that society and socialization play in identity formation. They also share elements of other theories, including social control, social learning, and structural strain, as well as components of theories found in developmental and behavioral psychology.

Research Based on Psychological and Psychiatric Postulates

There is an extensive literature on findings from research that utilize all or elements of the theories just enumerated, and in addition, there has been a rapid increase in the number of studies that have relied on assumptions drawn from psychology and psychiatry. These can be placed in one of three broad and sometimes overlapping categories: those that draw on developmental psychology, those based on theories of personality, and those that derive theoretical direction from abnormal psychology and psychiatry.

Psychological Studies

In recent decades there has been a growing interest in theories of *developmental psychology* to help explain substance use and other forms of social deviance, and the number of studies using principles from this academic discipline has increased rapidly (Baumrind & Moselle, 1985; Bowlby, 1988; Brook & Cohen, 1992; Brook, Whiteman, Cohen, Shapiro, & Balka, 1995; Kandel, 1975, 1988; Urban, Carlson, Egeland, & Stroufe, 1991; Windle, 1993). These research efforts have emphasized parental attachment and bonding, family interaction patterns, stresses associated with maturational conflicts, identity formation, and related factors.

Closely related to research based on developmental issues are studies of deviance that focus on specific psychological factors, including *personality characteristics and personality problems* (Bates, Labouvie, & McGee, 1986; Brook & Newcomb, 1995; Brook, Whiteman, Finch, & Cohen, 1995; Guy, Smith, & Bentler, 1994a; Hirschi & Gottfredson, 1983; Martin & Robbins, 1995; Milgram, 1993; Reebye, Moretti, & Lessard, 1995; Shedler & Block, 1990; Sutker, Archer, & Allain, 1978; Swaim, Oetting, Edwards, & Beauvais, 1989). Variables of interest have included aggression, violence, and other behaviors associated with antisocial personality, sensation seeking, risk taking, and impulsivity. Deviance is hypothesized to be a manifestation of deeply seated characteristics of one's personality, and, as stated by Martin and Robbins (1995), personality-centered theories serve as a corrective for sociological theories that fail to take into account biological and personality factors that may predispose individuals to antisocial behaviors including substance use.

Psychological/Psychiatric Problems and Disorders

In addition to the growing number of studies utilizing concepts from developmental psychology and personality theory, there has been increased interest in examining the relationships between psychological and psychiatric disorders and deviance (Blau, Gillespie, Felner, & Evans, 1988; Brook, Whiteman, Finch, & Cohen, 1995; Friedman, 1987; Hansell & White, 1991; Lavik & Onstad, 1986; Lynskey & Ferguson, 1995; Shedler & Block, 1990; Smith & Fogg, 1978). Overall, research based on this orientation represents a small percentage of the total found in the literature, and findings in this area are often blurred by the use of clinically based rather than population-based samples. Nonetheless, current trends in the biological sciences that are emphasizing the importance of biogenetic factors as determinants of behavior, including deviance, are likely to increase in the decades ahead.

Problem Behavior Syndrome

A relatively recent development in the field that focuses on the global and multifactorial character of deviance is generally referred to as problem behavior syndrome (Donovan & Jessor, 1985; Eliot, Huizinga, & Menard, 1989; Gottfredson & Hirschi, 1990; Jessor & Jessor, 1977). The basic assumption of this approach is that deviance is not caused by individual factors such as faulty socialization, peer associations, poor self-esteem, or the lack of adequate coping resources but, rather, is best understood within the context of a multifactorial framework that includes a broad spectrum of interrelated attitudes, beliefs, and behaviors. Gottfredson and Hirschi (1990) represent the basic tenets of this position when they write:

> Thieves are likely to smoke, drink and skip school at considerably higher rates than non-thieves. Offenders are considerably more likely than non-offenders to be involved in most types of accidents, including household fires, auto crashes, and unwanted pregnancies. They are also considerably more likely to die at an early age. (p. 93)

Numerous research efforts have been designed to test elements of problem behavior syndrome (Brook, Whiteman, Cohen, Shapiro, & Balka, 1995; Cohen & Brook, 1987; Eliot et al., 1989; Farrell et al., 1992b; Newcomb & Bentler, 1988; Penning & Barnes, 1982). As with other approaches, many of these studies have had equivocal outcomes. Nonetheless, the approach holds considerable promise for future research on deviance. It prompts more specificity in the aspects of deviance being tested, and it has the potential to produce greater theoretical integration than now exists.

Approaches That Explore the Relationships between Substance Use and Other Forms of Social Deviance

In addition to the problem syndrome approach, the literature contains a substantial corpus of findings on the relationships between substance use and other forms of social deviance that are not driven by any specific theoretical model (Apospori, Vega, Zimmerman, Warheit, & Gil, 1995; Bentler, 1992; Brook, Whiteman, & Finch, 1992; Dembo et al., 1990; Gillmore, 1991; Guy, Smith, & Bentler,

1994b; Huizinga, Loeber, & Thornberry, 1993; Kleinman, Wish, Deren, & Rainone, 1988; McBride, Joe, & Simpson, 1991; O'Donnell, Hawkins, & Abbott, 1995; Watts & Wright, 1990; Windle, 1993). Many of these studies could be placed within the problem syndrome category, but because they tend to emphasize the relationships between substance use and other manifestations of deviant behaviors, they are separated for purposes of discussion only.

The findings from these and similar studies indicate that there are significant relationships between substance use—especially behaviors that involve frequent and heavy use—and a wide variety of other deviant behaviors. Apospori et al. (1995) have identified three major sets of hypotheses offered to explain these relationships. The first postulates that drug use causes crime (Watters, Reinarman, & Fagan, 1985); the second hypothesizes that delinquent behaviors precede substance use (Eliot & Huizinga, 1984; Eliot et al., 1985; Inciardi, 1981); the third proposes that substance use and other forms of deviance have common etiologic agents (Akers, 1984; Fagan & Hartstone, 1984; Jessor & Jessor, 1977). The third, or common-cause, position appears to be attracting the greatest interest at present, but in spite of a large and expanding body of empirical literature supporting this view, a substantial number of issues remain. These include the empirical identification of which factors influence which behaviors, how different factors function within and between different demographic groups, the type of delinquency involved, and the relationships between the volume and type of substance use and the characteristics of the deviant behaviors.

Risk Factor Approaches

Risk factor research has a long tradition in the field of epidemiology and related disciplines that have emphasized prevention and early intervention more than they have theory development or the establishment of specific etiologic linkages. The basic tools of risk determination include probability theory and other statistical techniques that allow for the quantification of various types of risks, for example, attributable risks, relative risks, and risk ratios (for a history and discussion of risk factor research see Covello & Mumpower, 1985; Skolbekken, 1995.) As commonly utilized in substance use studies, risk factor approaches are predicated on the assumption that there are no single definitive cause of use or nonuse but, rather, multiple pathways through which individuals are led to initiate, habituate, or cease involvement with drugs. As such, this approach borrows concepts from a variety of theoretical approaches, and it most often assumes that substance use is related more to the total number of risk factors experienced by individuals rather than to their exposure to specific factors (Bry, McKeon, & Pandina, 1982; Labouvie, Pandina, White, & Johnson, 1990; Newcomb, Maddahian, & Bentler, 1986; Scheier, Newcomb, & Skager, 1994; Vega, Zimmerman, et al., 1993).

The growth of risk factor research over the past decade may reflect the inadequacies of individual theoretical models to explain substantial portions of the variance between a wide range of putative causes and substance use. It may also be reflecting a more pragmatic, public health orientation on the part of researchers; that is, there is a strong current interest in identifying groups at risk and in planning programs of prevention and early intervention. Chapters 4 and 5 in this volume explore in detail the risk factors for substance use among adolescents included in our samples.

Summary

Research on social deviance has a long history in the social and behavioral sciences, and over the years a large number of theoretical paradigms have been developed and tested to explain its origins. Early sociological theories that once dominated research in the field have been complemented by those from several other disciplines, including psychology and psychiatry. Many of these various approaches have distinctive characteristics, but at the same time, most share some overlapping boundaries. Regrettably, to date, very few efforts have been made to integrate different but complimentary aspects of these theories, and, at present, attempts to elaborate particular theoretical models have frequently given way to more pragmatic approaches, including risk factor–based studies.

In Chapter 2, the overall research design was explained. The study was guided in part, by two primary theoretical positions, self-rejection–derogation as outlined by Kaplan and his colleagues (Kaplan, 1980; Kaplan, Johnson, & Bailey, 1986) and acculturation conflict perspectives (stress theories), including those of Szapocznik, Scopetta, and Tillman (1979a) and Vega, Gil et al. (1993). Chapters 6 and 7 of this volume report findings related to these two perspectives. The research design also obtained data that focused on research questions related to structural strain theories. Chapter 7 reports findings on the relationships between race, culture, and substance use, and part of the interpretation of the data on these associations relies on theories of structural strain.

The data presented in the remainder of this chapter were gathered from items that were guided by several different theoretical perspectives. Although the analyses are mostly descriptive in nature, they can best be interpreted within the context of problem behavior syndrome theory and structural strain theory as it relates to issues of acculturation, assimilation, and racial differences and, most often, from the position that asserts that substance use is but one aspect of a fundamental predisposition to deviance and to deviant behaviors as well. In subsequent chapters these theoretical postulates guide multivariate analyses.

Design of the Study

As stated in the introduction, one of the objectives of this chapter is to present information on the prevalence of substance use behaviors among four ethnic groups of young adolescents. Another objective is to report findings on the relationships between early substance use and other forms of social deviance among these same groups. Implicit in the second objective is an effort to determine if early use of alcohol and illicit drugs is associated with subsequent deviant behaviors. It is recognized that causal links between these two sets of factors cannot be definitively established by the analytic methods utilized; nonetheless, the findings can provide strong clues as to these relationships, and they can offer information on the similarities and differences between the subgroups included in the sample.

The data reported in this section were obtained as part of the South Florida Youth Development Project, and inasmuch as the design of the study was outlined in detail in Chapter 2, only a brief summary is offered here. Three waves of data were collected (T-1, T-2, and T-3) on a large sample drawn from all sixth- and seventh-grade boys who entered the Dade County, Florida, Public Schools in the fall of 1990. The mean age of the sample for boys at T-1 was 11.6 years. The T-3 data collection scheduled for the fall of 1992 was delayed by Hurricane Andrew, which occurred in August of that year. The T-3 data were obtained in the spring of 1993, at which time the mean age of the sample was 14.3. Data were also secured on approximately 600 girls from the same student cohorts, but because their illicit drug use and deviance rates were low, especially at T-1, they have not been included in the analyses presented in this chapter. However, data on their substance use behaviors are presented in Chapter 5. The T-1 to T-3 retention rate for boys in the sample was approximately 80%; it was slightly higher for girls.

For purposes of this chapter, the following procedures were followed. All 4,184 male students on whom data were obtained at all three time periods were selected as the sample. It included 632 White non-Hispanics, 618 African Americans, 1,466 foreign-born students of Hispanic origin, and 1,468 students of Hispanic heritage born in the United States. The data on race and ethnicity were obtained from students and, where feasible, from their parents. Information on race and ethnicity was supplemented by information secured from the Management Information System of the Dade County Public School System (DCPS).

The data on substance use were derived from questions that determined ever in lifetime use, grade at time of first use, and frequency and amount of use. Those who indicated only small tastes or who said they had used alcohol for religious purposes only were considered nondrinkers. Lifetime illicit drug use behaviors were determined from individual questions that asked, "Have you ever smoked marijuana or hashish; coke, crack cocaine, angel dust (PCP); uppers, downers, and tranquilizers (without a doctor telling you to take them)?" The data on inhalant use were obtained from items formatted in similar fashion to those regarding other drug use.

In an effort to determine the magnitude of substance use behaviors among the four groups, two scales and two indexes were constructed. The cigarette scale consisted of one item with multiple responses. These were no use, used once or twice, used occasionally, regular use of less than one pack a day, and regular use of one or more packs a day. Former users were not included in the analyses. The scores on the scale ranged from 0 to 4. The alcohol scale was developed from the responses to items that determined the number of times alcohol was used in lifetime, the number of drinks consumed on last drinking occasion, how often the subject drank enough to get drunk, the grade of first use, and whether the use of alcohol had caused problems. The scores ranged from 0 to 62. The marijuana use index was composed of one item, which determined the number of times marijuana was used in lifetime. The range of scores was 0 to 6, with 6 indicating 40 or more times. The other drug use index was developed from responses to a series of questions that asked students about their use of cocaine, crack cocaine, barbiturates, amphetamines, and tranquilizers not prescribed for them. The response choices were yes and no. The scores ranged from 0 to 5.

In order to determine the relationships between alcohol and illicit drug use and other deviant attitudes and behaviors, three deviance measures were utilized. These were disposition to deviance, minor deviance, and major deviance. The deviance measures were adapted from the work of Kaplan and his colleagues (Kaplan, Johnson, and Bailey, 1986; Kaplan et al., 1987). The disposition to deviance measure consisted of four items that tapped attitudes toward a variety of deviant behaviors; the minor deviance scale was composed of seven items that parallel those found in Kaplan's most and moderate deviance scales; and the major deviance measure included six items from Kaplan's least common deviance scale. It is important to emphasize that the questions utilized to elicit information about minor and major deviant behaviors were asked for the last month.

The items used to obtain substance use information and a description of the various substance use scales, indexes, and deviance measures are outlined in the appendix. All scales were tested for internal consistency using procedures developed by Cronbach (1951a) for each of the subgroups in the sample. Very small variations were found, and in every instance the scales had acceptable levels of internal consistency.

Findings

Lifetime Prevalence of Substance Use

The findings on lifetime prevalence of cigarette, alcohol, marijuana, and other illicit drug use for all three time periods are presented in Table 3.1. The data are analyzed for both within-group and between-group differences.

Table 3.1. Lifetime Substance Use at Three Time Periods

Ethnic groups	Cigarettes			Alcohol			Marijuana			Other drugs		
	T1	T2	T3	T1	T2	T3	T1	T2	T3	T1	T2	T3
Total sample (N = 4,184)	19.2	31.1	49.7	40.6	53.8	74.7	2.0	6.4	18.7	2.7	7.4	12.5
White non-Hispanics (WNH)	26.9	37.5	55.2	51.0	61.7	81.5	1.9	7.4	21.6	2.7	7.8	15.2
(N = 632)	(1.8)	(1.9)	(2.0)	(2.0)	(2.0)	(1.5)	(.60)	(.90)	(1.7)	(.60)	(1.1)	(1.4)
African Americans	10.5	20.7	39.8	31.5	46.3	65.6	2.1	5.3	16.1	1.8	4.0	5.3
(N = 618)	(1.3)	(1.7)	(2.0)	(2.0)	(2.0)	(1.9)	(.60)	(.90)	(1.5)	(.50)	(.80)	(.90)
Foreign-born Hispanics	18.3	30.1	47.8	35.0	49.4	70.6	1.8	5.5	15.6	3.3	8.1	12.8
(N = 1,466)	(1.0)	(1.2)	(1.3)	(1.3)	(1.3)	(1.2)	(.40)	(1.0)	(1.0)	(.50)	(.70)	(.90)
U.S.-born Hispanic	20.3	33.7	53.4	45.4	58.0	79.5	2.1	7.4	21.6	2.6	7.8	14.0
(N = 1,468)	(1.1)	(1.2)	(1.3)	(1.3)	(1.3)	(1.1)	(.40)	(.70)	(1.1)	(.40)	(.70)	(.90)

Note. All figures are percentages. Figures in parentheses are standard errors for the adjacent percentages. T1, Time 1; T2, Time 2; T3, Time 3.
Chi = square comparisons:
WNH/African Americans: Cigarettes T1, T2, T3 (.001); Alcohol T1, T2, T3 (.001); Marijuana T3 (.001); Other Drugs T2, T3 (.001).
WNH/Foreign-born Hispanics: Cigarettes T1, T2, T3 (.01); Alcohol T1, T2, T3 (.001); Marijuana T3 (.001).
WNH/U.S.-born Hispanics: Cigarettes T1 (.001).
African Americans/Foreign-born Hispanics: Cigarettes T1, T2, T3 (.001); Alcohol T1, T2, T3 (.001); Other Drugs T1 (.05), T2, T3 (.001).
African Americans/U.S.-born Hispanics: Cigarettes T1, T2, T3 (.001); Alcohol T1, T2, T3 (.001); Marijuana T2 (.03), T3 (.001). Other Drugs T2, T3 (.001).
Foreign-born/U.S.-born Hispanics: Cigarettes T2 (.04), T3 (.001); Alcohol T1, T2, T3 (.001); Marijuana T2 (.04), T3 (.001).

Within-Group Differences

   Cigarettes.   As shown, all four groups reported highly significant increases in the lifetime use of cigarettes over the three time periods. The rates of cigarette use more than doubled for all groups. At T-3, they ranged from a low of 39.8% for African Americans to a high of 55.2% for White non-Hispanics. Foreign-born Hispanics had rates more similar to African Americans than to their native-born Hispanic counterparts, whose rates resembled those of White non-Hispanics. Overall, 49.7% of the total sample reported lifetime use of cigarettes at T-3.

   Alcohol.   The findings on lifetime alcohol consumption also showed highly significant increases between T-1 and T-3 for all four groups. The lifetime use of alcohol at T-3 was highest among White non-Hispanics, 81.5%; it was lowest for African Americans, 65.6%. As with cigarettes, the two Hispanic groups had contrasting rates. The alcohol use rate for the foreign born, 70.6%, closely resembled that of African Americans, 65.6%, and the rate for the native born 79.5%, was very similar to that of White non-Hispanics. Overall, 74.7% of the total sample reported alcohol use at some time in their lives.

   Marijuana.   The findings on lifetime use of marijuana revealed very dramatic increases for all ethnic groups between T-1 and T-3. White non-Hispanic adolescents and U.S.-born Hispanics had identical T-3 rates, 21.6%; their rates of increase were also the highest. They had an approximate tenfold increase between T-1 and T-3. The T-3 rates for African Americans, 16.1%, and for foreign-born Hispanics, 15.6%, were similar, and for each group they were approximately eight times higher than those reported at T-1. By T-3, 18.7% of the total sample reported ever in lifetime marijuana use.

   Other Illicit Drugs.   The use of other illicit drugs also showed highly significant increases over the three time periods for all groups. At T-3, the highest rate was found for White non-Hispanics, 15.2%. This rate was nearly equaled by those of U.S.-born Hispanics, 14.0%, and foreign-born Hispanics, 12.8%. The T-3 rate for African Americans was 5.3%. The T-3 rates for White non-Hispanics and U.S. Hispanics were approximately five times higher than those reported at T-1. The increase for foreign-born Hispanics was approximately fourfold, and the T-3 rate for African Americans was 2½ times greater than that reported at T-1. The lifetime rates of other drug use for White non-Hispanics and the two Hispanic groups at T-3 were 2½ to 3 times greater than those reported by African Americans. At T-3, 12.5% of the total sample reported ever in lifetime use of these other substances.

Between-Group Differences

   The between-group differences in use rates are also reported in Table 3.1. The chi-square analyses showed that White non-Hispanics had significantly higher lifetime rates of cigarette and alcohol use than African Americans at all three time periods; in addition, they had significantly higher scores on the marijuana and other drug measures at T-3. With one exception, there were no significant differences in use rates between White non-Hispanics and U.S.-born Hispanics: White non-Hispanics had significantly higher cigarette use at T-1. The differences between White non-Hispanics and foreign-born Hispanics were significant for cigarettes and for alcohol at all three time periods.

African Americans had significantly lower lifetime rates of cigarette and alcohol use than foreign-born and native-born Hispanics at all three time periods. The rates for marijuana use were not significantly different for African Americans and foreign-born Hispanics at any time period; however, African Americans had significantly lower rates of marijuana use than U.S.-born Hispanics at T-2 and T-3. African Americans also reported significantly lower rates of other drug use than foreign-born Hispanics at all three time periods; they also had significantly lower rates of other drug use than U.S.-born Hispanics at T-2 and T-3.

Significant differences between the two Hispanic groups were found for cigarettes at T-2 and T-3. The differences in alcohol rates were also significant at all three time periods, and for marijuana at T-2 and T-3. In every instance, the U.S.-born Hispanics had higher lifetime rates than their foreign-born counterparts. However, there were no significant differences in other drug use rates between the two Hispanic groups at any time period.

Inhalant Use.   The findings on inhalant use are reported in Table 3.2. Once again, they show highly significant within-group increases for all four groups

Table 3.2.   Lifetime Inhalant Use

	Time 1	Time 2	Time 3
Total sample	3.9	6.7	15.3
White non-Hispanics	4.5	8.9 a*** b*	17.7 a***
	(.80)	(1.1)	(1.5)
African Americans	3.1 d*	3.8 c* d***	7.9 c*** d***
	(.70)	(.80)	(1.1)
Foreign-born Hispanic	3.1 e**	5.9	14.5
	(.50)	(.60)	(.90)
U.S.-born Hispanics	4.8	7.6	18.1
	(.60)	(.70)	(1.0)

Note. All figures are percentages. Figures in parentheses are standard error for the adjacent percentages.
Group comparisons:
   a, White non-Hispanics differ from African Americans; b, White non-Hispanics differ from foreign-born Hispanics; c, African Americans differ from foreign-born Hispanics; d, African Americans differ from U.S.-born Hispanics; e, foreign-born Hispanics differ from U.S.-born Hispanics.
*$p < .05$; **$p < .01$; ***$p < .001$.

across the three time periods. The highest T-3 rate of inhalant use was found for U.S.-born Hispanics, 18.1%, closely followed by the rate for White non-Hispanics, 17.7%. The lowest rate was found for African Americans, 7.9%. The T-3 inhalant use rate for foreign-born Hispanics was 14.5%. The T-3 rates were approximately four times higher than the T-1 rates for White non-Hispanics and for both Hispanic groups. For African Americans, the rate was about 2½ times greater at T-3 than at T-1. The between-group differences in inhalant use were significant for White non-Hispanics and African Americans at T-2 and T-3; the differences were significant between White non-Hispanics and foreign-born Hispanics at T-2. None of the differences between White non-Hispanics and U.S.-born Hispanics were significant. African Americans had significantly lower rates than U.S.-born Hispanics at all three time periods, and they had significantly lower rates than the foreign-born Hispanics at T-2 and T-3. The differences in inhalant use rates between foreign- and U.S.-born Hispanics were significant in only one instance. At T-1, the foreign born had a significantly higher rate than the native born. The data on lifetime use of all substances present clearly discernible patterns. African Americans had consistently and, most often, significantly lower rates of substance use than the other three groups. The differences were especially noteworthy when African American rates were compared to those of White non-Hispanics and U.S.-born Latinos. The differences between White non-Hispanics and U.S.-born Hispanics were not significant in almost all between-group comparisons; foreign-born Hispanics tended to have significantly lower rates of substance use than their U.S.-born counterparts.

Regular/Past Month Substance Use

The findings on regular cigarette use and past month alcohol, marijuana, and inhalant use are presented in Table 3.3. Regular cigarette use was defined as smoking one pack or more of cigarettes per day. Past month use indicates one or more occasions in the past 30 days on which individuals drank alcohol, used illicit drugs, or sniffed inhalants to get high.

Within-Group Differences

Cigarettes. The findings on regular use of cigarettes resemble those reported for lifetime use. The prevalence of regular cigarette use increased dramatically over the three time periods and the increases were significant for all four groups. For example, at T-1, less than 1% of the U.S.-born Hispanic and White non-Hispanic adolescents reported regular cigarette use. However, by T-3, 6.3% of the U.S.-born Hispanics and 5.9% of the White non-Hispanic students reported regular use. African American students had the lowest levels of increase; the

Table 3.3. Regular Cigarette and Past Month Alcohol, Marijuana, and Inhalant Use

Ethnic groups	Regular cigarettes			Past month alcohol			Past month marijuana			Past month inhalant		
	T1	T2	T3	T1	T2	T3	T1	T2	T3	T1	T2	T3
Total sample	.50	2.1	4.9	10.4	18.0	23.7	.40	1.7	7.1	.90	1.9	3.0
White non-Hispanics	.70	3.2	5.9	13.8	20.9	30.1	.30	1.0	8.7	1.6	2.5	4.6
	(.30)	(.70)	(1.0)	(1.5)	(1.8)	(2.0)	(.20)	(.40)	(1.1)	(.50)	(.60)	(.80)
African Americans	.50	.20	.90	4.8	9.3	11.9	.50	.80	5.6	.50	1.3	1.0
	(.30)	(.02)	(.40)	(.90)	(1.3)	(1.4)	(.30)	(.40)	(1.0)	(.30)	(.50)	(.40)
Foreign-born Hispanics	.30	1.8	4.7	9.1	16.6	22.8	.40	2.1	5.5	.60	1.4	2.8
	(.10)	(.40)	(.60)	(.80)	(1.1)	(1.2)	(.20)	(.40)	(.60)	(.20)	(.30)	(.40)
U.S.-born Hispanics	.60	2.8	6.3	12.4	21.7	26.6	.40	2.1	8.6	1.1	2.4	3.3
	(.20)	(.40)	(.70)	(.90)	(1.2)	(1.2)	(.20)	(.40)	(.70)	(.30)	(.40)	(.50)

Note. All figures are percentages. Figures in parentheses are standard errors for the adjacent percentages. T1, Time1; T2, Time 2; T3, Time 3.

Chi = square comparisons:

WNH/African Americans: Cigarettes T2, T3 (.001); Alcohol T1, T2, T3 (.001); Marijuana T3 (.05).

WNH/Foreign-born Hispanics: Cigarettes T2, (.05); Alcohol T1, (.01), T2 (.05), T3 (.001); Marijuana T3 (.05).

WNH/U.S.-born Hispanics: All comparisons nonsignificant.

African Americans/Foreign-born Hispanics: Cigarettes T2, T3 (.001); Alcohol T1, T2, T3 (.001); Marijuana T2 (.05); Inhalant T3 (.001).

African Americans/U.S.-born Hispanics: Cigarettes T2, T3 (.001); Alcohol T1, T2, T3 (.001); Marijuana T2 (.01), T3 (.001); Inhalant T1 (.05), T3 (.001).

Foreign-born/U.S.-born Hispanics: Alcohol T1 (.01), T3 (.001); Marijuana T3 (.001); Inhalant T1, T2 (.05).

percentage of regular use among this group was .50% at T-1; at T-3 it was .90%. The rate of regular cigarette use among foreign-born Hispanics is especially noteworthy. At T-1, they reported a regular use rate of .30%; this was even lower than the rate found for African Americans. However, by T-3, 4.7% of this group reported smoking one pack or more of cigarettes per day.

Alcohol.   The rates of past month alcohol use showed the same patterns found for cigarettes. Overall, the highest T-3 rates were found for White non-Hispanics, 30.1%. African Americans had the lowest past month rates at all three time periods, and their T-3 rate of 11.9% was only slightly less than one-third that of the White non-Hispanic rate. Approximately one-fourth of both Hispanic groups reported past month alcohol use at T-3.

Marijuana.   At T-3, past month use of marijuana for all groups was significantly higher than those reported at T-1 and T-2. At T-1, .30% of the White non-Hispanic cohort reported past month use; by T-3, the percentage had increased to 8.7%. Similarly dramatic increases were reported for the other groups as well. The T-3 rate for U.S.-born Hispanics was very similar to that reported by White non-Hispanics, 8.6%. The T-3 rates for African Americans and foreign-born Hispanics closely resembled one another. They were 5.6% for African Americans and 5.5% for foreign-born Hispanics.

Inhalants.   The findings on the past month use of inhalants also showed significant increases between T-1 and T-3 for all four groups, but the changes were not as pronounced as those found for marijuana. White non-Hispanics had the highest T-3 rate of past month inhalant use, 4.6; African Americans had the lowest rate, 1.0. The T-3 rates for U.S.- and foreign-born Hispanics were 3.3 and 2.8, respectively. With a few very minor exceptions, African Americans reported lower rates of regular/past month use of all substances than their ethnic counterparts, and, in most instances, White non-Hispanics and U.S.-born Hispanics had rates more similar to one another than those found between the two Hispanic groups.

Between-Group Differences

The between-group differences in regular cigarette use and past month use of alcohol, marijuana, and inhalants, were significant in several instances. White non-Hispanics had significantly higher regular cigarette use rates than those of African Americans at T-2 and T-3, and for alcohol at all three time periods. A significant difference between these two groups was also found for past month marijuana use at T-3. White non-Hispanics also had higher rates of regular cigarette use than foreign-born Hispanics at T-1 and for marijuana at T-3. They also had significantly higher past month alcohol use at all three time periods. There were no significant differences in the rates of regular or past month use for any of the substances for White non-Hispanics and U.S.-born Hispanics.

Foreign-born Hispanics had significantly higher rates of regular cigarette use than African Americans at T-1 and T-2, and they had significantly higher rates of past month alcohol use at all three time periods. Foreign-born Hispanics also had a significantly higher past month marijuana use rate than African Americans at T-2, and past month inhalant use at T-3. U.S.-born Hispanics had consistently higher regular and past month use rates of all substances than those reported by African Americans, and their T-3 rates were significantly higher for all substances. The differences between U.S.- and foreign-born Hispanics were significant for alcohol at T-1 and T-3, for marijuana at T-3, and for inhalants at T-1 and T-2. In all instances where significant differences were found, they were attributable to the higher rates reported by Hispanics born in the United States.

Substance Use Scale/Index Scores

As noted above, one of the objectives of the research was to determine the magnitude of substance use among the four ethnic groups, for which two scales and two indexes were constructed to facilitate the analyses. The results and the significance levels derived from *t*-test analyses are presented in Table 3.4.

Within-Group Differences over Time

The analyses revealed significant increases in the scale scores for cigarette use between T-1 and T-3 for all groups. The increases were about threefold for all groups except White non-Hispanics; their scale score was about 2½ times greater at T-3 than at T-1. None of the T-1 to T-3 alcohol mean score changes were significant. However, the increases in marijuana scale scores between T-1 and T-3 were significant for all four groups, a finding that reflects the increased lifetime and past month use of this substance reported above. The data for the other drug scale revealed significant changes over the three time periods for all groups except African Americans.

Between-Group Differences

The findings on between-group differences on the substance use scales reveal that White non-Hispanics had significantly higher mean cigarette and alcohol scores than African Americans at all three time periods. They also had significantly higher mean scores for marijuana use at T-3 and for other drugs at T-2 and T-3. A very similar pattern was found when White non-Hispanic scores were compared with those of foreign-born Latinos, with one major exception. White non-

Table 3.4. Substance Use Scale Scores by Racial/Ethnic Group

	Cigarettes			Alcohol			Marijuana			Other drugs		
	T1	T2	T3	T1	T2	T3	T1	T2	T3	T1	T2	T3
White non-Hispanics	.30	.50	.74	1.1	1.6	1.7	.03	.29	2.1	.03	.09	.17
Significance of group comparisons	a*** b*** c***	a*** b***	a*** b***	a*** b***	a*** b***	a*** b***		c*	a*** b***		a*	a***
T1/T3 change:	**			***			***			**		
African Americans	.12	.21	.36	.71	1.1	1.0	.02	.16	1.0	.03	.05	.03
Significance of group comparisons	a*** d*** e***	a*** d*** e***	a*** d*** e***	a*** d*** e***	a*** d*** e***	a*** d*** e***		a***	a*** e***		a* d* e**	a*** d*** e***
T1/T3 change:	N.S.			N.S.			*			N.S.		
Foreign-born Hispanics	.19	.37	.59	.83	1.3	1.4	.02	.30	1.2	.05	.09	.14
Significance of group comparisons	b*** d*** f***	b*** d*** f***	b*** d***	b*** d*** f***	b*** d*** f***	b*** d*** f***		f***	b*** f***		d*	d***
T1/T3 change:	N.S.			N.S.			**			*		
U.S.-born Hispanics	.23	.44	.70	1.0	1.5	1.7	.03	.62	2.0	.03	.11	.19
Significance of group comparisons	c** e*** f***	e*** f***	e*** f***	e*** f***	e*** f***	e*** f***		c* e***	e*** f**		e**	e***
T1/T3 change:	N.S.			N.S.			***			***		

Note: Values given are mean scale scores; *t*-test analyses were conducted.
Group comparisons: a, White non-Hispanics/African Americans; b, White non-Hispanics/foreign-born Hispanics; c, White non-Hispanics/U.S.-born Hispanics; d, African Americans/foreign-born Hispanics; e, African Americans/U.S.-born Hispanics; f, foreign-born Hispanics/U.S.-born Hispanics.
*p < .05; **p < .01; ***p < .001; N.S., nonsignificant.

Hispanics had significantly higher scores on the cigarette and alcohol measures at all three time periods, and on the marijuana index at T-3. However, no significant differences in other drug use scores were found. The comparisons between White non-Hispanics and U.S.-born Hispanics revealed only one significant difference: White non-Hispanics had significantly higher cigarette scores at T-1.

Foreign-born Hispanics had significantly higher cigarette and alcohol scores than African Americans at all three time periods, and they had significantly higher other drug use scores at T-2 and T-3. No significant differences were found for the marijuana index scores. U.S.-born Hispanics also had significantly higher scores on the cigarette and alcohol measures than African Americans at all three times, and they had a significantly higher marijuana score at T-3 and higher other drug scores at T-2 and T-3. U.S.-born Hispanics had significantly higher cigarette scale scores than foreign-born Hispanics at T-2 and T-3, and they had significantly higher alcohol scores at all time periods. The U.S.-born Hispanics also had significantly higher marijuana scores at T-2 and T-3. However, the mean scores on the other drug use index were not significant for the two groups at any time period.

Substance Use and Other Deviance

One of the emerging areas of inquiry among researchers interested in adolescent deviance is that pertaining to the relationships between substance use and other deviant behaviors. In the sections that follow, these relationships are explored.

Alcohol and Illicit Drug Use and Disposition to Deviance

The data on alcohol and illicit drug use and disposition to deviance are presented in Table 3.5. Respondents whose alcohol scale scores at T-1 were one standard deviation or more above the mean for the entire sample were placed in the high-use category, and those who had used *any* illicit drug at T-1 were placed in the yes category for that substance. Those whose scores on the disposition to deviance scale were one or more standard deviations above the mean for the entire population were classified as being high on that dimension. The relationships between T-1 alcohol scores and illicit drug use and high disposition scores at all three time periods (continuous) were tested for significance using chi-square procedures.

Alcohol. As shown in the table, there were significant differences between those with high and low T-1 alcohol scale scores and continuous high disposition to deviance scores among all four ethnic groups. Approximately 20% of the adolescents with high T-1 alcohol scores had high disposition to deviance scores at all three time periods. By contrast, between 5% and 10% of those with low alcohol

**Table 3.5. Relationship between Early
(Time 1) Alcohol and Illicit Drug Use
and Disposition to Deviance**

Groups	Repeated high disposition to deviance[a]
White non-Hispanics	
Alcohol use scale	
High	20.8***
Low	4.8
Illcit drug use	
Yes	23.5***
No	8.8
African Americans	
Alcohol use scale	
High	16.3*
Low	10.4
Illcit drug use	
Yes	36.4***
No	10.5
Foreign-born Hispanics	
Alcohol use scale	
High	23.3***
Low	8.5
Illcit drug use	
Yes	26.5***
No	10.8
U.S.-born Hispanics	
Alcohol use scale	
High	20.3***
Low	8.6
Illcit drug use	
Yes	31.6***
No	10.6

Note. All figures are percentages.
[a]Repeated disposition to deviance indicates high scores (1
standard deviation above mean) on all three waves of data
collection.
$*p < .05; **p < .01; ***p < .001.$

scores had continuous disposition to deviance scores. Only 4.8% of the White non-Hispanics with low alcohol scores had high continuous disposition to deviance scores. Overall, the relationships between high T-1 alcohol scores and disposition to deviance scores were very similar for all ethnic groups. The relationships were greatest for foreign-born Hispanics; 23.3% of the adolescents in this group who had high T-1 alcohol scores had continuous disposition to deviance scores. The lowest level of relationships were found for African Americans; 16.3% of those with high scores on the alcohol scale had high disposition scores at all three time periods.

Illicit Drug Use.   The findings on any illicit drug use at T-1 indicated that between one-fourth and one-third of the users had high disposition to deviance scores at all three time periods. The highest relationships were found for African Americans; 36.4% of this group who had tried any illicit drug had continuous high disposition to deviance scores. This was closely followed by the rates for U.S.-born Hispanics, 31.6%. Overall, only about 10% of the nonusers at T-1 had continuous high scores on the disposition to deviance measure.

Alcohol and Illicit Drug Use and Minor and Major Deviance

The data on the relationships between high T-1 alcohol and illicit drug use and T-3 minor and major deviance are reported in Table 3.6. As noted above, the questions related to minor and major deviant behaviors were asked within the context of the past month. Chi-square tests were completed to test for significance. The categories for alcohol and illicit substance were the same as those used above, and high minor and major deviance designations were assigned those with scores one standard deviation or more above the mean on these measures.

Minor Deviance.   The findings indicated that T-1 high alcohol use scores were significantly associated with high T-3 minor deviance scores for all four ethnic groups. Nearly 90% of all adolescents in the sample who had high alcohol scale scores had high minor deviance scores. However, approximately three-fourths of the nonusers also had T-3 high deviance scores. Regardless of alcohol use, minor deviance was very prevalent among all adolescents in the sample at T-3.

The relationships between T-1 illicit substance use and minor deviance were significant in two of the four comparisons. The differences were significant for White non-Hispanics and foreign-born Hispanics. The lack of significant levels for African Americans and for U.S.-born Hispanics, as well as the low levels of significance for the other two groups, may be due to the very high rates of minor deviance reported for those in the sample. As with the alcohol analyses, approximately three-fourths of the nonusers in all four groups had high minor deviance scores. Moreover, the findings for African Americans indicate that the nonusers of illicit drugs had higher T-3 minor deviance scores than those found for the users. These findings are probably reflecting the relatively low rates of illicit substance use among African Americans, on the one hand, and their relatively high minor deviance rates, on the other. Nonetheless, in spite of these high minor deviance rates, the differences between users and nonusers remained significant for White non-Hispanics and foreign-born Hispanics.

Table 3.6.   Relationship between Early
(Time 1) Alcohol and Illicit Drug Use
and Time 3 Deviant Behavior

Groups	Minor deviance	Major deviance
White non-Hispanics		
Alcohol use scale[a]		
High	87.5***	53.6***
Low	69.6	26.7
Illicit drug use[b]		
Yes	94.1*	52.9*
No	73.6	33.2
African Americans		
Alcohol use scale		
High	88.3*	42.9**
Low	75.9	29.1
Illicit drug use		
Yes	66.7*	66.7*
No	78.0	31.3
Foreign-born Hispanics		
Alcohol use scale		
High	88.2***	43.4***
Low	71.7	25.2
Illicit drug use		
Yes	87.8*	44.9**
No	74.4	28.1
U.S.-born Hispanics		
Alcohol use scale		
High	88.1***	45.1***
Low	75.3	29.6
Illicit drug use		
Yes	89.2*	64.9***
No	77.9	32.1

Note. All figures are percentages.
[a]High scores on alcohol scale are 1 standard deviation above the mean.
[b]Illicit drug measure indicates the use of marijuana, cocaine, crack,
barbiturates, or pills.
$*p < .05; **p < .01; ***p < .001.$

Major Deviance.   The findings on the relationships between T-1 alcohol scale scores and T-3 major deviance scores revealed significant differences for all four groups. Approximately 45% of those with high alcohol scores at T-1 had high T-3 major deviance scores; this compares to about 30% for those with low T-1 scores. The percentages of those with both high alcohol and major deviance scores were much lower than those found for minor deviance. White non-Hispanics with high alcohol scores were twice as likely as those with low scores to have high T-3 major deviance scores.

The data on T-1 users of any illicit drug and T-3 major deviance indicated that users had higher deviance scores than nonusers and, further, that the differences were significant for all four groups. Approximately two-thirds of the African Americans and U.S.-born Hispanics who had used any drug at T-1 had high major deviance scores at T-3. In contrast, approximately one-third of the T-1 nonusers had high T-3 deviance scores. Foreign-born Hispanics had the lowest percentage of their T-1 illicit substance users with high T-3 deviance scores. Less than one-half, 43.4%, of those in this group who had used any illicit drug by T-1 had high major deviance scores. This percentage is about one-third lower than the ones reported by African Americans and U.S.-born Hispanics.

Alcohol and Illicit Drug Use and Continuous Deviance

In order to explore more fully the relationships between early substance use and minor and major deviance, additional analyses were completed that centered on repeated deviant behaviors, that is, those that occurred at all three time periods. The results of these analyses are presented in Table 3.7. As with previous analyses, adolescents were placed in high and low groups on the T-1 alcohol scale and into yes and no groups on the T-1 illicit substance measure.

Minor Deviance: Alcohol.   The data on T-1 high alcohol scores and continuous minor deviance show highly significant relationships for all four groups. About two-thirds of the White non-Hispanic adolescents with high T-1 alcohol scores had high minor deviance scores at all three time periods. The proportions for the other groups, while not as high, ranged between 50% and 60%. Approximately one-third of those with low T-1 alcohol scores had high minor deviance scores at all three data collection periods.

Minor Deviance: Illicit Drugs.   The findings on use of any illicit drug at T-1 and continuous minor deviance indicated there were significant associations for White non-Hispanics and both Hispanic groups. However, these relationships were not significant for African Americans. Almost 90% of the White non-Hispanics who had used any drug at T-1 had high continuous minor deviance scores. The rates for users for both Hispanic groups approximated 70%. It is of interest to note that only 41.5% of the African Americans who had used illicit drugs by T-1 had continuous high minor deviance scores, a rate that was about one-half that found for White non-Hispanics. Overall, the percentage of nonusers who had high continuous minor deviance scores ranged from 42.9% for White non-Hispanics to 27.3% for African Americans. The rates for nonusers among foreign-born and U.S.-born Hispanics were 34.3% and 41.7%, respectively.

Major Deviance: Alcohol.   The data on high T-1 alcohol use scores and continuous major deviance indicated that there were highly significant relation-

Table 3.7.   Relationship between Early (Time 1) Alcohol and Illicit Drug Use and Repeated Deviant Behavior[a]

Groups	Minor deviance	Major deviance
White non-Hispanics		
Alcohol use scale[b]		
High	65.5***	15.5***
Low	36.3	3.9
Illicit drug use[c]		
Yes	88.2***	35.3***
No	42.9	6.5
African Americans		
Alcohol use scale		
High	58.8***	16.3***
Low	38.0	5.4
Illicit drug use		
Yes	41.5	9.1
No	27.3	6.9
Foreign-born Hispanics		
Alcohol use scale		
High	55.0***	11.5***
Low	30.4	2.8
Illicit drug use		
Yes	67.3***	20.4***
No	34.3	4.2
U.S.-born Hispanics		
Alcohol use scale		
High	58.2***	13.5***
Low	37.8	5.3
Illicit drug use		
Yes	68.4**	34.2***
No	41.7	6.6

Note. All figures are percentages.
[a]Repeated deviant behavior indicates that the behavior was reported in the past month on all three waves of data collection.
[b]High scores on alcohol scale are 1 standard deviation above the mean.
[c]Illicit drug measure indicates the use of marijuana, cocaine, crack, barbiturates, or pills.
*$p < .05$; **$p < .01$; ***$p < .001$.

ships for all four groups and, further, that their rates were very similar. They ranged from 16.3% for African Americans to 11.5% for foreign-born Hispanics. Unlike the data on minor deviance, all four groups reported very low rates of continuous deviance among those with low T-1 alcohol scores. The range was from 2.8% for foreign-born Hispanics to 5.4% for African Americans.

Major Deviance: Illicit Drugs.   The findings on T-1 use of any illicit drug and continuous major deviance were highly significant for the White non-Hispanic and two Hispanic subsamples. The relationships were not significant for African American adolescents. Slightly more than one-third of the White non-Hispanics and U.S.-born Hispanics who reported T-1 use of any illicit substance had continuous high major deviance scores. About one-fifth of the foreign-born Hispanics who used illicit drugs at T-1 had continuous high major deviance scores. The findings on African Americans stand in sharp contrast to those of their counterparts. Only 9.1% of those in this group who reported illicit substance use at T-1 had continuous high major deviance scores. This compares to 6.9% for the nonusers.

Summary of Findings and Conclusions

Findings on Substance Use

The findings on lifetime substance use revealed that there were significant increases in the use of all substances between the T-1 and T-3 data collection periods. This was true for all four groups. The rate of cigarette use between T-1 and T-3 doubled for White non-Hispanics, it nearly quadrupled for African Americans, and among the two Hispanic groups, the use rates were approximately 1½ times higher at T-3 than they were at T-1. Similar patterns were found for alcohol. Alcohol use among White non-Hispanics and U.S.-born Hispanics increased more than 1½ times between T-1 and T-3, and the percentages of African Americans and foreign-born Hispanics using alcohol at T-3 were approximately twice as high as those reported at T-1.

Marijuana use also showed very dramatic increases over the three time periods. The percentage increases were approximately tenfold for White non-Hispanics and U.S.-born Hispanics; they were about eightfold for African Americans and foreign-born Hispanics. Other illicit drug use among White non-Hispanics and U.S.-born Hispanics was approximately five times higher at T-3 than at T-1; the increase was about fourfold for foreign-born Hispanics, and it was nearly threefold for African Americans. Inhalant use also showed large percentage increases for all groups between T-1 and T-3. They were approximately fourfold for White non-Hispanics and the two Hispanic groups, and they were about 2½ times higher for African Americans.

The data on frequency of use over the three time periods indicated highly significant increases in regular use of cigarettes and past month use of alcohol, marijuana, and inhalants for adolescents in all groups. Regular cigarette use rates among foreign-born Hispanics was 15 times higher at T-3 than at T-1; they were approximately 9 times higher for White non-Hispanics and U.S.-born Hispanics. While less dramatic, the regular use of cigarettes by African Americans was still almost twice as high at T-3 as at T-1. Past month alcohol use was about twice as high at T-3 as at T-1 for all groups, and there were very large increases in the past month use of marijuana. Among White non-Hispanics, the past month use rate for marijuana was 29 times higher at T-3 than at T-1; it was 21 times higher for U.S.-born Hispanics, 13 times higher for foreign-born Hispanics, and 11 times higher for African Americans. In most instances, the greatest increase in marijuana rates occurred between T-2 and T-3. While significant, the rates of past month use of inhalants were not as great as those found for the other substances.

The findings on the magnitude of use revealed that although the score changes were not always significant, there was increased use of all substances for all groups. The findings on lifetime, regular, past month, and magnitude of substance use reflect those of others who have found that alcohol is typically the first substance used by most adolescents and that it is followed by cigarettes, marijuana, and other illicit drugs (Barnes & Welte, 1986; Kandel, 1988; Kandel et al., 1992; Newcomb & Bentler, 1986b). The findings also confirm those reported by others that indicate that substance use of all kinds begins at a relatively young age (Jackson et al., 1981; Johnston et al., 1996; Maddahian, Newcomb, & Bentler, 1985; Robins, 1984) and that it increases sharply as adolescents mature chronologically (Barnes & Welte, 1986; Johnston et al., 1996; Newcomb & Bentler, 1986b). By age 12, between one-third and one-half the adolescents had used alcohol at some time in their lives; by age 14, the proportions ranged from two-thirds to four-fifths. The use of marijuana and other illicit drugs were especially associated with increased age. At T-1, when the mean age of the total sample was 11.7 years, only about 2 out of every 100 adolescents had ever used marijuana; by T-3, when the mean age was 14.3, between 15 and 22 out of every 100 had used it at some time in their lives. While not as pronounced, a similar age-related pattern was found with increases in other illicit drug use. The analyses on between-group differences showed that there were significant differences between the four groups for all substances, and although the patterns were not always the same, they generally revealed that White non-Hispanics and U.S.-born Hispanics had higher rates than African American and foreign-born Hispanic adolescents. African Americans, almost without exception, reported the lowest rates and magnitude of use at all three time periods.

The findings that African Americans had lower substance use rates than their ethnic counterparts replicates those of almost all other researchers (Barnes & Welte, 1986; Harford, 1986; Maddahian et al., 1985; Newcomb, Maddahian, & Bentler, 1987; Ringwalt & Palmer, 1990; Windle, 1991). However, a caveat is in order. Data collected in 1994 and 1995 as part of the Monitoring the Future Survey (MFS) indicated that White non-Hispanics and African Americans in the eighth grade had very similar lifetime, past year, past month, and daily use rates of alcohol and marijuana. White non-Hispanics still had higher rates of inhalant and other illicit drug use. The findings also indicated that racial differences in the use of all substances were much more pronounced for those in the twelfth grade than for those in the eighth grade. Among twelfth graders, White non-Hispanics had much higher use rates for all substances than African Americans (Johnston et al., 1996). It is not possible to determine from the MFS data whether the similarity in alcohol and marijuana use for African Americans and White non-Hispanics in the eighth grade in 1994 and 1995 was an aberration, or whether it marks a trend in earlier and greater lifetime use of these substances among African Americans. It is possible that the data on African Americans and White non-Hispanics in the twelfth grade were reflecting cohort effects that may not be present among younger African American adolescents.

Regrettably, the factors underlying the differences in substance use among Whites and African Americans have not been clearly identified. Ringwalt and Palmer (1990), who found that African Americans were less likely than White non-Hispanic adolescents to use alcohol, attributed these lower rates to the fact that African Americans had far more negative views regarding the health effects and addictive characteristics of alcohol use than their White counterparts. African Americans also reported greater concern for parental disapproval, whereas White non-Hispanics were more concerned with peer disapproval. To date, however, our knowledge regarding the factors producing the differences in substance use between African Americans and other ethnic groups is fragmentary, and it is an area that needs additional verifying hypothesis-testing research. It is also an area of inquiry that would benefit immensely from carefully crafted ethnographic studies involving young African American adolescents, their families, and the social environments within which they live. Chapter 7 will address African American drug use patterns more thoroughly.

As reported elsewhere by our research group (Warheit, Vega, Khoury, Gil, & Elfenbein, 1996), we found highly significant relationships between length of time in the United States and increased substance use rates among foreign-born Hispanics. The increases in their rates may be attributable to the greater availability and acceptability of substances in the United States than in the countries from which the foreign born originated. The differences may also be accounted for by the more tolerant norms regarding substance use in the United States vis-à-vis the foreign borns' countries of origin, and they may be reflecting the impact of acculturation factors, including a lessening of family influences and increased peer pressures. The relationships between acculturation processes and conflicts and substance use are analyzed in detail in Chapter 6.

The overall prevalence rates found for the subgroups in our sample are similar to those reported by others whose findings were based on regional and national samples (Johnston et al., 1996; Oetting & Beauvais, 1990). In addition, our findings—which showed large increases in substance use between 1990 and 1993—while related to the aging of the sample, may also be reflecting the overall increases in substance use among adolescents nationwide during the first 5 years of the current decade (Johnston et al., 1996).

As noted by Johnston and his fellow researchers, substance use among adolescents peaked in the late 1970s and declined in the 1980s. However, it has been increasing over the first half of the present decade in spite of numerous efforts to discourage it. The early and continued use of licit and illicit substances among a disparate ethnic sample of young adolescents residing in South Florida appears to have mirrored the substance use behaviors among adolescents generally throughout the United States.

Substance Use, Disposition to Deviance, and Minor and Major Deviance

The analyses indicated that those with high alcohol scores and those who had used drugs at T-1 had significantly higher predisposition to deviance scores at all three time periods than those with low scores or nonusers. This was found for all four groups. In addition, the findings on the relationships between T-1 alcohol and illicit drug use and T-3 minor deviance scores revealed significant differences for all four groups with one exception. African Americans who had not used illicit drugs at T-1 had higher minor deviance scores than those who had used them. This finding is regarded as an aberrant one and is considered to be the result of the high minor deviance scores found for all groups in the sample. Overall, nearly 90% of those in the entire sample who had high alcohol use scores or had used any illicit drug at T-1 had high minor deviance scores at T-3. Concurrently, about three-fourths of those with low scores or who had not used illicit drugs also had high scores on the minor deviance scale. Obviously, the endemic prevalence of minor deviance obfuscates some of the relationships between these behaviors and early substance use. Nonetheless, users had significantly higher minor deviance scores than nonusers, and this finding reinforces others that show powerful relationships between these two sets of behaviors among all adolescents in the sample.

The findings for both T-1 alcohol scores and illicit substance use revealed highly significant differences between users and nonusers and high major deviance scores for all four groups. However, the overall percentages of T-1 users, and nonusers with high deviance scores, were much lower than those found for minor deviance. Whereas nearly all of those who had high alcohol scores or had used illicit drugs at T-1 had high minor deviance scores, less than one-half those with comparable alcohol and drug behaviors had high major deviance scores.

The analyses also indicated there were significant relationships between early alcohol and illicit drug behaviors and continuous minor and major deviance. A disproportionately large percentage of the adolescents who used substances a T-1 were much more likely than non-users to have high minor and major deviance scores at all three data collection periods. The one major exception was found for

African Americans. There were no significant relationships between T-1 illicit drug use scores and continuous minor and major deviance scores for this group. This finding, along with several others, indicates that the relationships between illicit drug use and other forms of deviance were different for African Americans than they were for the other ethnic groups in the sample. Although some of the relationships between early use of substances and minor deviance were confounded by the very high prevalence rates of minor deviance reported by adolescents in all four groups in the sample, overall, the findings indicated highly significant relationships between early alcohol or substance use and subsequent deviant behaviors.

In sum, the analyses revealed significant relationships between high T-1 alcohol scores and illicit drug use and continuous disposition to deviance scores and to high T-3 minor and major deviance scores as well. With few variations, these relationships were found for all four ethnic groups. Once again, it is acknowledged that definitive statements regarding the relationships between early substance use and subsequent deviant attitudes and behaviors cannot be made from the analyses outlined in the chapter. Nonetheless, the weight of the evidence is very strong, and we believe additional, multivariate analyses will confirm the findings presented. Some of this information is presented in Chapters 6 and 7.

The overview of the theoretical models and other approaches utilized to study deviant behavior outlined earlier, along with the results of the analyses described in this chapter and from others throughout this volume, clearly and convincingly demonstrates the complex, multifaceted nature of social deviance among adolescents in our society. If this is the case, as we believe it is, those interested in developing a more complete understanding of these complex relationships must work toward the empirical development of theories that integrate the cultural, social, psychological, psychiatric, and biogenetic factors underlying social deviance. This task is an extremely challenging one, and its completion will undoubtedly depend on future advancements in each of the identified disciplines. Nonetheless, the establishment of more integrated theories must be one of the long-term goals of those whose research interests fall within the purview of social deviance. Without these integrated theories, the field will continue to be marked by fragments of findings that can be interpreted only within the context of the theoretical orientations, biases, and design limitations of those conducting the research.

Finally, it should be acknowledged that the present epidemic of substance use among both adults and adolescents in our society, as well as in other societies around the world, is a relatively new phenomenon. Given this fact, theories developed to identify the underlying causes of this epidemic are still in a nascent stage and, perhaps, tied too closely to older theoretical models designed originally to identify the etiologic factors associated with criminal deviance. While it is evident that many individuals engage in a broad spectrum of nonnormative activities, including concurrent illicit substance use and crimes against persons and property, it is also evident that there are many who are involved in one set of these behaviors but not the other. There are, after all, fundamental differences between using illicit substances and crimes involving physical violence and theft. It is apparent, therefore, that more comprehensive theoretical models must be created if we are to explain the causal factors associated with substance use, apart from other forms of deviance, including criminal behavior.

4

Pathways to Drug Use

William A. Vega and Andres G. Gil
with Bodhan Kolody

Introduction

As shown in the previous chapter, the profiles of early adolescent drug use differ greatly among ethnic groups. White adolescents begin drug experimentation early in their teenage years, whereas African Americans get a later start; U.S.-born Hispanics commence drug use before Hispanic immigrants do. These and other findings indicate that there are systematic differences in age of first use and cessation of use and, further, that there are differences in reasons for selecting and using specific drugs. Thus, progression from no use to experimental or serious drug abuse cannot be explained without taking some heed of the social, cultural, and economic factors that influence drug use at various stages over the life course. In short, the risks for use and the stages of use are dissimilar within and across racial and ethnic groups.

This chapter begins with a review of issues related to the evaluation of risks, then moves to a discussion about recent research that looks for differences in the patterning of risks and stages of adolescent drug use by taking into account ethnic group differences. Chapter 5 reviews risk patterns associated with gender differences. As noted by Homans (1967), science has two reciprocal functions: to *discover* and to *explain*. Although risk factor studies would appear to belong more to the former category than to the latter, these studies are often grounded on either implicit or explicit theoretical foundations. Pulkkinen (1988), citing Lerner (1986), states: "A theory is a set of propositions comprising defined and interrelated constructs that integrate laws concerning regular, predictable relationships among variables" (p. 187). If one accepts this definition of theory, it is clear that risk factor research, unlike theory-driven, verifying research, is concerned more with the identification of factors associated with increased or decreased vulnerability than with testing specific hypotheses. However, it is important to note that risk factor studies routinely include variables derived from a theoretically based research literature, including variables incorporated within specific theoretical formulations.

Many contemporary risk factor studies of adolescent drug use are based on "organismic-type" theories (Pulkkinen, 1988) that presume that the stages of development are universal, even as all adolescents routinely progress through physical and psychological stages of maturational experiences. As a result, increased or decreased vulnerability for drug use is often viewed as being nonrandom and patterned by exposures to specific conditions and social learning experiences. This position also presumes that vulnerability to substance use is more heightened at some maturational stages than at others, and that the effects, or meaning of these exposures, are modified by contextual circumstances (Pulkkinen, 1988). Thus, this approach views risk as being best understood within the framework of adolescent development. Given this perspective, known risk factors, such as family influences, that vary between different ethnic groups must be explored independently; in addition, gender differences in substance use, as discussed in Chapter 5, and peer associations are also logical sources of inquiry. Similarly, peer associations and family environmental factors, such as cohesion and attachment, vary within and between different racial and ethnic groups, and they, too, must be taken into account in developmental models of substance use and other forms of social deviance.

One of the guiding assumptions operative in this chapter is borrowed from Magnusson (1987), who states: "... the characteristic way in which individuals develop, in interaction with the environment, depends upon and influences the continuous reciprocal process of interaction, among the subsystems of psychological and biological factors in the individual" (p.6). Specifically, we assume that the reciprocal interactions between adolescents and their environment are heavily influenced by ethnicity, especially when adolescents are members of ethnic communities that are socially marginalized. In other words, although we can operationally assume universality of maturational stages, the person-level interaction with the social environment that produces or attenuates adolescent risk for drug use is linked to experiences occurring in ethnic communities, themselves embedded in a highly stratified and segregated society. Consequently, understanding the differential effects of risk factors among adolescents of diverse ethnic groups is an important step in the discovery process leading to refinement of theory.

From our perspective, ethnicity is a fundamental exogenous variable in risk factor research. Regrettably, it has, for the most part, been overlooked in much prior research, and as a consequence, there is a very limited fund of information regarding differences in adolescent drug use trajectories within and between ethnic groups in the United States. At present, however, the results from comparative research that focused on risk factors and stages of drug use progression are beginning to appear in the literature. A brief summary of these research efforts will be outlined as a prelude to a presentation of the results of our own longitudinal research, which centered on risk factors and stages of substance use.

Risk as a Concept and Method

Risk is a basic concept in epidemiology. Exposure, present or absent, is the basis for estimating the degree of likelihood that a given pathological outcome will occur. Ultimately, the abundance and configuration of putative risk factors form the foundation for theory about how vulnerability is produced. Rarely is a singular exposure to a risk so powerful that a one-to-one relationship with an outcome is established. Even exposure to powerful disease pathogens will not produce illness or death with perfect reliability. In identifying potential risk factors for potency and consistency as causal agents in drug use, we encounter four major categories of explanatory variables: culture and society, and interpersonal, psychosocial, and biogenetic factors (Hawkins, Catalano, & Miller, 1992). Moreover, each of these categories contains an array of variables, some of which are unique and some of which are shared with one or more of the other factors.

Adolescent drug use, as noted in Chapter 1, poses a particular challenge because certain types of drug use are often considered normative and situational, not pathological as assumed in deterministic models of causation. This possibility produces threats to the validity of our research paradigms but does not totally negate their value. Drug use may be normative in many sectors of American society, but certainly not in all. Indeed, frequent (past month) use of any illicit drug occurs only in a small fraction, or about 8%, of American adolescents (U.S. Department of Health and Human Services, 1995). Moreover, we can compensate for the "normalizing" effect by including a wide range of factors that could be expected to have differential distribution among ethnic and socioeconomic groups, such as variables representing personal, family, and peer factors. In this chapter, we present risk profiles that, within the limitations of our data base, reflect lifestyle variations and adaptations that foster vulnerability or resistance to drug use in early adolescence. To the extent that these risk factor profiles reflect the social contexts of race, ethnicity and class in America, they will, presumably, be more useful for elaborating and testing theories and for designing programs of prevention and treatment as well.

If risk factors had identical implications for behavior, then it follows that personal (including biogenetic) and environmental factors operate mechanistically and universally. However, this assumption is untenable. The current state of knowledge regarding drug use among adolescents has been derived largely from decades of research based primarily on non-Hispanic White or mixed ethnic populations. In other words, non-Hispanic Whites provided the reference group for empirical confirmation, but few comparative studies with other ethnic groups were conducted. Neither were cultural factors conceptualized as possibly additive or interactive to the effects of demographic and psychosocial risk factors. The past reliance on White non-Hispanics as a source of reference against which other groups were compared, along with the lack of cross-ethnic comparative studies, highlights our need for additional research designed specifically to extend our understanding of the role that risk factors play in substance use over the course of the maturational processes among ethnic groups.

Newcomb (1995), in reviewing several risk factor studies, including our own cross-sectional findings (Vega, Zimmerman, et al., 1993), reports that specific ethnic groups do not have consistent risk factor profiles in different studies. He concludes that variations in risk factor profiles within ethnic groups (intragroup) are as wide as those across different ethnic groups (intergroup). This finding could be interpreted as a rationale for avoiding comparative risk factor assessment. Although Newcomb's observation may be correct in some instances, we believe that the profound and patterned differences in social experiences that are the hallmark of a stratified, segregated society will inherently produce different contexts and profiles of risk among different racial and ethnic groups and, further, that these differences will become more evident with maturation. The lack of stability in ethnic group risk profiles accurately reported by Newcomb from previous studies, in our opinion, may be attributable to regional variations, the inadequacy of risk factors selected for inclusion in these studies, a failure to account for the differential importance or interaction of risk factors in the developmental process, and an inadequate data base of longitudinal studies using ethnically diverse samples. Presently, the information available is too limited to form any definite conclusions, and perhaps the only way to successfully overcome the aforementioned methodological problems is to conduct multisite collaborative studies using a common research protocol and a panel design.

Other general problems also constrain our understanding of risk factor effects on adolescent drug use. For example, in a number of studies, the risk factors related to substance use are sometimes identified without controlling for age. As a consequence, the effects of risk factors within specific developmental stages are confounded. Another weakness has been the failure to consistently compare the same dependent variables across studies, for example, lifetime, new use, high frequency of use, and addiction. If risk factor epidemiology is to become more useful in the development of carefully targeted programs of prevention and treatment for different ethnic groups, its precision must be improved. Therefore, as part of our efforts to produce more precise empirical data, we must pursue research that identifies culturally relevant risk factors for different racial and ethnic groups and, more specifically, research that identifies both common and unique risk factors. This is a different conceptual and analytical enterprise than that done previously (Phinney, 1996; Vega, 1992). This chapter provides an example of one approach using comparative risk factor analysis; that is, the data presented control for maturation as a basis for identifying ethnic group differences in pathways to early adolescent drug use.

Methodological Divergence in Risk Assessment

There are two descriptive techniques widely used in the study of risk factors for adolescent drug abuse. One method assesses the cumulative effects of individual risk factors on drug use. The second method involves the assessment of paired associations between individual variables and later drug use, for example, a risk factor occurring in childhood (e.g., conduct disorder) predicting illicit drug use in adulthood. Numerous studies of the first type have appeared in the literature (Newcomb, 1995)—including our own research (Vega, Zimmerman, et al., 1993)—using this cumulative risk factor technique. The findings from these studies, including those described in Chapter 5 in this volume, have consistently shown linear correlations between a variety of risk factors and substance use. However, the results of our research have demonstrated that the standard risk factors included in most other studies do not have equal value for predicting substance use among different racial and ethnic groups (Vega, Zimmerman, et al., 1993).

There are dilemmas in these individual variable, cumulative models of risk: for example, the potential confounding of cause and effect. Do risk factors cause drug use, or does drug use cause risk factors? And how do variables influence one another or combine? These problems appear in cross-sectional studies that have not controlled for bidirectional effects. One alternative is to rely on retrospective data, but this method accentuates problems associated with adolescent recall of distant events and behaviors in early childhood. A solution to this limitation is to use prospective design and time-ordered data to establish a clear ordering of events and drug use patterns, as illustrated by the example of pairing individual variables with outcomes at a different point in the life course. However, this method requires using longitudinal panel data covering many years, and these are increasingly difficult to secure due to cost factors. In this chapter, and Chapter 5, we use a longitudinal panel design to minimize recall bias and order confounds. Drug use is assessed after risk factor exposures have occurred.

Long-range assessment of paired-variable relationships suffers from reliance on early markers that must predict behavior occurring much later in the developmental process. The second law of biological maturation, formulated by Clarke and Clarke (1984, p. 197), is applicable: "regardless of age, the longer the period over which assessments take place, the lower the correlation is likely to be, that is, the greater the change in ordinal position of individuals within a group." Paired variables occurring closer in time will usually have stronger correlations than will distant ones. Consequently, early risk factors that are important because they create developmental vulnerabilities or heighten exposure to proximal risks may appear to be insignificant or go undetected. This is particularly important with early adolescents who are experiencing rapid maturational changes as part of the developmental process. However, despite these limitations, variable-level approaches are useful in screening possible predisposing factors, especially when used as part of a multimethod approach to knowledge development and hypotheses generation.

Life History Risk Assessment

A highly fruitful risk factor methodology is the person-centered longitudinal model that avoids the aforementioned confounds and the potential fallacy of attributing sample (population) characteristics to individuals who, indeed, do not live in "samples," but rather in communities with unique social and cultural characteristics. This approach is a life course perspective that is much more sensitive to the temporal and contextual idiosyncrasies of risk factor impacts on people as gendered, organic beings and not as statistical composites. As noted by Magnusson and Bergman (1988), the person-level approach overcomes two central weaknesses of the variable level of analysis: the existence of individual-level differences in growth curves, and the existence of nonlinearity and interactions between operating factors.

Person-centered longitudinal risk studies in the deviance field had their inception with the work of Sheldon and Eleanor Glueck, who pioneered the use of epidemiological panel designs to track long-term outcomes of delinquents and nondelinquents (Glueck & Glueck, 1968). More contemporary examples include the research of Smith and Fogg (1978), Robins (1980), Kandel (1978), Kandel, Davies, Karus, and Yamaguchi (1986), Kandel, Simcha-Fagen, and Davies (1986), Newcomb and Bentler (1988), and Jessor and Jessor (1977). Current research is advantaged by the availability of newer statistical techniques—event-history (Allison, 1984; Blossfeld, Hamerle, & Mayer, 1989), survivor data (Cox & Oakes, 1984), and latent class analyses (McCutcheon, 1987)—to accurately track developmental transitions in drug-using careers, including onset, type, frequency, persistence, and cessation of drug use, as well as cofactors associated with these transitions (Kandel & Yamaguchi, 1993).

As noted by Newcomb (1995), this research approach assumes that drug use is only an aspect or symptom of a cluster of behaviors and attitudes that reflect a lifestyle of problem behaviors and general deviance. However, an inherent limitation of pathway studies is that they require panels and event calenders covering multiple data points over long periods of time, often decades. As a result they are susceptible to attrition, inaccurate recall, and cohort effects that limit their external validity. In addition, they are expensive and require substantial funding. As a consequence of these design and logistical problems, researchers have tended to rely on short-term designs, without adequate ethnic stratification, for making clear-cut generalizations. There are historical influences (e.g., cohort effects) on drug use as a result of changes in drug availability, acceptability, popularity, and intensity of legal sanctioning.

Ultimately, person and variable approaches are both useful and potentially complementary. In Chapter 5, we rely primarily on an elaboration of the variable approach because our data set covers only the early adolescent period. However, we modified the variable approach somewhat in this chapter by utilizing a multi-variable, or patterned, method. We believe this approach offers more sensitivity for identifying ethnic group differences in risk exposures and comes closer to a person-level analysis in that individual multiproblem sets are used as risk constructs in a longitudinal analysis of risk.

Risk Factors as Multiproblem Factorial Domains

In this chapter, we assess longitudinal profiles of risk in early adolescence in a manner that highlights sociocultural differences among ethnic group adolescents. We attempt to improve upon the sensitivity of cumulative risk factor models by factor analyzing (using oblique rotations) individual risk factor combinations for each of the four ethnic groups in the sample. This method, we believe, more accurately reflects variations in the occurrence of risk factors and multiple problem situations in the lifestyles and social contexts of ethnically diverse adolescents. We refer to these risk combinations as "domains" to distinguish them from individual variables (e.g., risk factors) used in Chapter 5 or the usual paired association or cumulative risk models. Furthermore, a series of loglinear analyses were conducted in which the longitudinal effects of these domains for each ethnic group were assessed for marijuana use. The individual risk variables that compose the domains are fully described and documented in Chapter 5. These analyses yielded a saturated model whereby interaction effects for ethnicity were significant in every instance, thus supplying a statistically defensible justification for a more parsimonious domain approach.

Risk Domains, Ethnicity, and Marijuana Use

Risk Domains

The core supposition of the risk model is that domains are dynamic and changing rapidly in accord with the maturational processes occurring between early and midadolescence. Therefore, these domains were reassessed at each of three data points (T-1, T-2, T-3) that are, in fact, excellent proxies for the ages of respondents. At T-1, the average age was 11.6 years; at T-2 it was 12.6; at T-3, it was 14.3. As shown in Table 4.1, the individual risk factors were clustered into domains, and the sample was divided into immigrant Cuban, native-born Cuban, African American, and White non-Hispanic subsamples. All risk factor domains had Cronbach's alphas of .55 or greater.

The findings on T-1 risk domains indicated that all four ethnic groups shared a common psychosocial domain, even though foreign-born Cubans did not have parent derogation as a component as did the other groups. One very important interethnic difference was that African Americans did not share the drug/ delinquency domain found for the three other subsamples at T-1. This indicates that early alcohol and cigarette use were not linked to delinquent behavior (see Chapter 3) at T-1 for African Americans as they were for adolescents in the other three groups. However, at T-2, the drug/delinquency domain did appear for African Americans. Also at T-2, parent derogation appeared within the psychosocial domain for the foreign-born Cubans, and suicide attempts appeared for White non-Hispanics within the psychosocial domain. Therefore, the types and structures of domains were found to be increasingly similar among the ethnic groups by T-2, although White non-Hispanics had slight differences in the composition of the drug/delinquency domain.

Parenthetically, in another study using T-1 latent variables, we reported that while peer group associations were associated with early drug experimentation for White non-Hispanics, they actually served as protective factors against drug use among African Americans (Apospori et al., 1995). The maturational effect seems to be in the direction of changing affiliational patterns for African American adolescents. By T-2, African Americans who were experimenting with alcohol and cigarettes had more tolerant attitudes toward peers who were using drugs than did their nonusing counterparts.

At T-3, the domains were virtually the same for all groups, except for the inclusion of family drug use in the drug/delinquency domain and suicide attempts in the psychosocial domain among foreign-born Cubans. Therefore, the maturational effect on domains increased the homogeneity among ethnic groups over time, with the most evident change coming among African American adolescents who were the most dissimilar at 11 years of age and who became very similar by 14 years of age. The alphas also increased over time for all domains, suggesting greater stability. This may be one reason for later onset of experimental drug use among African Americans; it simply takes longer for their risk domains to coalesce, pattern, and become as coextensive as in other ethnic groups. This important issue is addressed more fully in Chapter 7.

Odds Ratios and Exposure to Risk Domains

The patterning of these domains, by itself, tells us nothing about their impact on illicit drug use. In order to discover the temporal effects of domains on first use

Table 4.1. Factors for Each Ethnic Group at Time 1, Time 2, and Time 3[a]

Time 1	Time 2	Time 3
U.S.-born Cubans		
Factor 1: Psychosoical, a = .69 Self-Esteem, Depression Symptoms, Parent Derogation.	Factor 1: Psychosocial, a = .74 Same as Time 1.	Factor 1: Psychosocial, a = .79 Same as Time 2.
Factor 2: Drug/Delinquency, a = .68 Disposition to Deviance, Major Deviance, Peer Drug Use, Peer Approval of Drug Use, Alcohol & Cigarette Use.	Factor 2: Drug/Delinquency, a = .75 Same as Time 1.	Factor 2: Drug/Delinquency, a = .76 Same as Time 2.
Foreign-born Cubans		
Factor 1: Psychosoical, a = .71 Self-Esteem, Depression Symptoms.	Factor 1: Psychosocial, a = .73 Same as Time 1, plus Parent Derogation.	Factor 1: Psychosocial, a = .76 Same as Time 2, plus reported suicide attempts.
Factor 2: Drug/Delinquency, a = .69 Disposition to Deviance, Major Deviance, Peer Drug Use, Peer Approval of Drug Use, Alcohol & Cigarette Use.	Factor 2: Drug/Delinquency, a = .71 Same as Time 1, except no Major Deviance.	Factor 2: Drug/Delinquency, a = .79 Same as Time 2, plus Family Drug Use Problems.
African Americans		
Factor 1: Psychosoical, a = .65 Self-Esteem, Depression Symptoms, Parent Derogation.	Factor 1: Psychosocial, a = .68 Same as Time 1.	Factor 1: Psychosocial, a = .67 Same as Time 1.
	Factor 2: Drug/Delinquency, a = .57 Disposition to Deviance, Major Deviance, Peer Drug Use, Peer Approval of Drug Use, Alcohol & Cigarette Use.	Factor 2: Drug/Delinquency, a = .64 Same as Time 2.
White non-Hispanics		
Factor 1: Psychosoical, a = .73 Self-Esteem, Depression Symptoms, Parent Derogation.	Factor 1: Psychosocial, a = .76 Same as Time 1, plus reported suicide attempts.	Factor 1: Psychosocial, a = .78 Same at Time 1
Factor 2: Drug/Delinquency, a = .69 Disposition to Deviance, Major Deviance, Peer Approval of Drug Use, Alcohol & Cigarette Use.	Factor 2: Drug/Delinquency, a = .75 Same as Time 1, plus Peer Drug Use.	Factor 2: Drug/Delinquency, a = .77 Same as Time 2.

[a]a = Cronbach's alpha.

of marijuana at T-3, we calculated odds ratios for three different intervals of exposures to risk domains for each ethnic subsample. The findings from these analyses are shown in Table 4.2. We also included an additional domain, low familism, because of empirical evidence that familism is exceptionally important for Hispanics (Keefe, 1984; Mindle, 1980; Vega, 1990). Low familism can be understood as a perception of weak family cohesiveness and unity and an absence of pride in family. This inclusion provided an indirect test of a hypothesis that low familism will have differential effects on first-time marijuana use across ethnic groups in the context of the other risk domains. We selected marijuana as the dependent variable because it increases in use in the transition from early to midadolescence for all ethnic groups in the sample.

Different exposure intervals were assessed. Long-range risk exposure included only T-1 effects on first marijuana use reported at T-3. Proximate risk exposures included only T-2 effects on T-3 marijuana use, and continuous risk exposures were those experienced at both T-1 and T-2. Presumably, in every instance, risk exposures preceded marijuana use because adolescents reporting marijuana use before T-3 were excluded from the analysis.

None of the long-range risk domains produced statistically significant odds ratios (OR) for marijuana use at T-3 for African Americans, and only the drug/delinquency domain was significant (OR = 1.8) for White non-Hispanics. The psychosocial domain had unique effects on foreign-born Cubans (OR = 4.6). This suggests that personal adjustment problems associated with immigration and resettlement may play a role in later marijuana use for some of these adolescents.

**Table 4.2. Odds Ratios of Risk Factor
Domains Predicting Marijuana Use at Time 3**

Risk factor domains	Cubans		African Americans	White non-Hispanics
	U.S.-born	Foreign-born		
Long range (T-1)				
Psychosocial	1.4	4.6***	1.4	1.7
Drug/Delinquency	2.3***	1.6	—	1.8*
Low family pride	1.9***	2.6**	1.2	1.3
Proximate (T-2)				
Psychosocial	1.5*	3.9***	1.3	1.7*
Drug/Delinquency	2.9***	4.0***	2.4**	2.6**
Low family pride	1.8***	2.7***	1.6†	1.7**
Continuous (T-1/T-2)				
Psychosocial	1.7**	3.8***	1.2	1.8**
Drug/Delinquency	2.0***	1.9**	—	1.5*
Low family pride	2.4***	4.5***	1.2	1.8*

$*p < .05; **p < .01; ***p < .001; †p < .06.$

U.S.-born Cubans were more similar to White non-Hispanic in that drug/ delinquency was associated with later marijuana use, but U.S.-born Cubans were similar to foreign-born Cubans in that low familism was a unique predictor of first marijuana use at T-3.

The effects of proximate domains on T-3 marijuana use were increasingly similar across groups, with the weakest effects found among African Americans. The psychosocial and low familism domains, although statistically significant predictors for all subsamples except African Americans, had their strongest effects among foreign-born Cubans. Similar results were obtained for the continuous exposure interval. Therefore, the most consistent and patterned temporal effects of risks on T-3 marijuana use involved low familism, low self-esteem, depressive symptoms, and parent derogation among Cuban adolescents undergoing social and cultural adjustments after immigration. The pattern for U.S.-born Cubans was similar to the foreign born but with weaker odds ratios for the psychosocial and low-familism domains.

These findings do not demonstrate that sociocultural adjustment issues are unimportant for U.S.-born Cubans. A more likely explanation is that sociocultural risk factors affecting their drug use were not included in the composition of the risk domains, thus remaining unmeasured in the analysis. In previous research, we found that acculturative stressors had different importance for native- versus foreign-born Hispanics. One study (Gil, Vega, & Dimas, 1994) assessed the distribution of five different acculturative stressors among foreign- and U.S.-born Hispanic adolescents. These stressors included language conflicts, acculturation conflicts, perceived discrimination, perceived acculturation gaps with parents, and low life chances. It was found that while immigrants reported a higher frequency of stressors, especially language conflicts, U.S.-born Hispanics reported higher levels of perceived discrimination. However, when self-esteem was regressed on these stressors it was found that more variance was explained for those born in the United States.

The same acculturation stressors were used to predict behavior problems in home and school settings (Vega, Khoury, Zimmerman, Gil, & Warheit, 1995) as measured by the Child Behavior Checklist (Achenbach & Edelbrock, 1983) and the Teacher Report Form (Achenbach & Edelbrock, 1986b). Among foreign-born Hispanics, only language conflicts were associated with both home and school problem behaviors. In contrast, both language conflicts and perceptions of a closed society (limited life chances) were associated with school behavior problems, but not with home-based problems. These studies show the importance of taking into account ethnic group specific variables that may affect risk for later drug use, or that might increase the likelihood that other risk factors will be experienced that are related to drug use in later adolescence. However, these acculturation strain risk factors are not shared by the non-Hispanic subgroups, so they were not included in the multigroup domain analysis. They do exemplify the importance of including risk factors that reflect unique lifestyle and situational conditions that add to a comprehensive understanding of the risk enhancement process. The acculturation effects on Hispanic adolescent drug use are reviewed more fully in Chapter 6, which is devoted to this topic.

What have we learned from this analysis? There are differences in the importance among risk domains for drug use within and across ethnic groups. In this instance, adolescents with lower acculturation had disproportionately high vulnerability to marijuana use when they experienced low familism or psychosocial risks. The hypothesis of different vulnerability due to low familism was confirmed most strongly for the foreign-born group and less convincingly for native-born Cuban adolescents. The relevant point for this chapter is that any assessment of risk factors has value only to the extent that adolescents of different ethnic groups share these risk factors, and that these factors have uniform effects on drug use. If these conditions are not met, the predictive model will be less sensitive.

One indication that this is occurring in our study comes from our assessment of African Americans that shows dissimilar patterning of risk domains in early adolescence, with increasing similarity over time. Nevertheless, the risk factors that compose the domains remain relatively weak predictors of first-time marijuana use in midadolescence. Of course, this does not preclude the possibility that the same domains will be better predictors of African American drug use in the latter stage of adolescence and that the early instability in patterning of risks for later marijuana use is due at least in part to unmeasured variables such as the presence of strong protective factors, compounded by very low base rates of early adolescent drug use. We have previously assessed the cumulative effects of individual risk factors on alcohol use at T-1 (Vega, Zimmerman, et al., 1993) and found that the "standard" subset of risk factors was inefficient for African American adolescents. Therefore, it seems appropriate to open up the pool of risk factors to additional ones that correspond to specific ethnic group experiences within appropriate developmental sequences. This process will, of course, create asymmetries in comparing ethnic group risk profiles, but it may produce more accurate, efficient models of risk, improved ethnic group epidemiology and theory, and a superior knowledge base for intervention research. In Chapter 7, we address these important differences as they pertain to African American adolescent males.

Protective Factors

Although there are many variations in approach, the notion of protective factors is usually addressed in one of two ways: as a residual of risk factors or as a discrete construct, or process, that insulates the adolescent from the pernicious effects of risk factors. The first approach simply turns risk factors on their heads by assuming that the opposite of risk is literally the "absence of risk," or protection (Jessor, Van Den Bos, Vanderryn, Costa, & Turbin, 1995). This approach, therefore, assumes that all risk factors are potentially protective. For example, if being delinquent is a risk factor for drug use, then not being one is a protective factor. The metric utility of this approach is self-evident because risk variables are used as thermometers; at the low end they are protective, and at the high end they are risk enhancing. In addition, this approach lends itself to statistical manipulation (Felix-Ortiz & Newcomb, 1992). Obviously, this is a nonspecific approach to understanding how risk is reduced and not very satisfying if the objective is to find intervention points or to model risk and protective factors.

Another approach is to assume that risk and protective factors are conceptually distinct (Rutter, 1987). This approach allows the use of specific factors that are known from previous research to reduce the effects of risk factors either directly (e.g., via linear effects) or through a more complex buffering process (e.g., interactive effects) (Hawkins et al., 1992; Luther & Zigler, 1991; Pellegrini, 1990). The salience of certain protective factors is well established. As Garmezy (1983) notes, there is a well-demonstrated triad of protective factors that derive from individual differences, characteristics of family functioning and support, and extrafamilial associations. Protective factors derived from any of these three domains may be protective against adolescent drug use, but, in a manner similar to risk factors, these protective factors may not function equally well for adolescents of diverse ethnic groups. Similarly, their effects may differ over the course of adolescence.

Empirical Assessment of Protective Factors

To gain some insight about this issue, we conducted three analyses. First, we tested the discriminate function of marijuana use, or nonuse, occurring between T-2 and T-3, or nonuse by T-3, among adolescents in our study. Four family domain variables were used as a block in the equation: familism, parent derogation, family cohesion, and family communication. For this analysis only, the entire Hispanic subsample was used to supply adequate cell sizes for meaningful statistical comparisons. Hispanics were partitioned by nativity, consistent with the groupings used throughout the book, and as our studies have demonstrated, the native–immigrant distinction is the most critical among the Hispanic adolescents in the sample.

The discriminant functions successfully identified 75% of marijuana-abstaining foreign-born (chi-square = 163.9, $p > .001$), and U.S.-born Hispanics (chi-square = 166.1, $p > .001$); 63.2% of African Americans (chi-square = 22.9, $p > .001$), and 62% of White non-Hispanics (chi square = 65.4, $p > .001$). The differences in chi-squares and percentages correctly identified in each ethnic subsample suggest that the domain of family factors has a general protective effect that is strongest among Hispanics. However, since the distribution of risk factors among the groups was unequal, a more definitive test of protective effects would require holding constant the number of risk factors experienced by adolescents in all ethnic groups.

Family Protective Factors and Psychosocial Risks

The results of our tests designed to determine the role of protective family functions in the context of the psychosocial risk factors are presented in Table 4.3. All adolescents included in this analysis had from 75% to 100% of all risk factors that composed the psychosocial domain at T-3 (see Tables 4.1 and 4.2). The family protective factors were created by simple mean split of each ethnic group distribution on the four scales that composed this domain. Those above the mean are identified in the left column as "high," and those below as "low." Marijuana use must have occurred between T-2 and T-3. Therefore, risk factors, protective factors, and marijuana use are contemporaneous.

Reviewing the aggregate results, we found that foreign-born Hispanic adolescents were more likely to receive strong protective effects from family factors than were the other ethnic subsamples. In fact, in all four bivariate comparisons there were statistically significant differences in proportions of T-3 marijuana users

Table 4.3.   Becoming a Marijuana User by Individuals with Psychosocial Risk Factors by Protective Factors

Protective factors	U.S.-born Hispanics	Foreign-born Hispanics	African Americans	White non-Hispanics
Familism				
Low	31.5	25.7	19.0	30.1
High	17.4*	10.0***	26.3	18.3*
Cohesion				
Low	29.5	25.3	20.5	26.4
High	25.4	6.7**	22.7	23.9
Family communication				
Low	29.8	26.4*	22.7	35.3
High	18.2	5.9	17.6	25.0
Parent derogation				
High	29.9	23.3	22.0	18.4
Low	20.8	2.4**	8.6**	5.1**

Note. All figures are percentages. In these analyses, subjects had 75% or more of the risk factors in the domain.
*$p < .05$; **$p < .01$; ***$p < .001$.

among foreign-born Hispanic adolescents who scored high or low on protective factors. Those who scored in the low range were between two and ten times more likely to use marijuana at T-3. The most consistently protective family factors across all ethnic groups were low parental derogation (e.g., acceptance rather than being put down by parents) and high familism. Both of these were statistically significant for White non-Hispanics. However, U.S.-born Hispanics and African Americans had just one protective factor each that was statistically significant, high familism and low parent derogation, respectively. These results point to important differences in protective effects of family functioning that are rooted in diverse cultural expectations and social experiences. Perhaps the most revealing contrast is the lack of importance of high family cohesion for all ethnic subsamples except foreign-born Hispanics, who were four times less likely than the other groups to have used marijuana. These results underscore the differential socialization of U.S.-born Hispanic adolescents and their family systems as they transform, thereby reducing the importance of family as a barrier against drug use.

Family Protective Factors and Delinquency Risk

The Table 4.4 analysis substitutes delinquency domain risk factors for psychosocial ones. Again, adolescents with 75% to 100% of all risk factors were included in the analysis. Since the delinquency domain includes early licit drug use

Table 4.4.   Becoming a Marijuana User by Individuals with Drug/Delinquency Risk Factors by Protective Factors

Protective factors	U.S.-born Hispanics	Foreign-born Hispanics	African Americans	White non-Hispanics
Familism				
Low	38.9	25.4	30.4	21.5
High	32.9	13.3**	31.0	16.7
Cohesion				
Low	37.4	23.3	37.9**	21.3
High	36.2	14.4**	14.8	17.4
Family communication				
Low	38.0	21.8	32.0	21.1
High	31.3	14.8	20.0	12.5
Parent derogation				
High	40.5	25.0	42.4	23.6
Low	34.4	17.3*	24.0*	6.3*

Note. All figures are percentages. In these analyses, subjects had 75% or more of the risk factors in the domain.
*$p < .05$; **$p < .01$; ***$p < .001$.

as a component, this test of family protective effects is more severe than the previous one. In this instance, the results followed a general pattern of lower proportions of marijuana use among those with protective family factors, regardless of ethnic group. However, the distribution of protective effects varied considerably. Logically, family protective factors were less potent in reducing marijuana use when the risk factors included alcohol and tobacco use. Again, family protective effects are most evident among foreign-born Hispanics. African Americans received protective effects from high family cohesion and low parent derogation. None of the protective factors were statistically significant among the U.S.-born Hispanics, and only low parent derogation was significant among White non-Hispanics, providing a four to one advantage in lower marijuana prevalence. This finding is consistent with others from our research with Hispanics that show family factors are protective against developing a disposition to deviance (Vega, Zimmerman, et al., 1993). However, these findings suggest that family protective effects were wearing down in the U.S.-born Hispanic group.

This bivariate assessment of differences in proportions of marijuana users based on uniform exposures to specific risks is useful for depicting the relative importance of family factors. Nevertheless, a multivariate analysis is required with tests of interactions between risk factors and family protective factors to determine if a buffering effect occurred. Table 4.5 presents this analysis using a marijuana

Table 4.5. Regression of Drug/Delinquency Risk Factors and Family Protective[a] Factor on Lifetime Marijuana Use Scale[b] for All Ethnic Groups

Protective factors	U.S.-born Hispanics	Foreign-born Hispanics	African Americans	White non-Hispanics
Cigarette use	.04	.06	.14**	.06
Alcohol use	.02	.03	.01	.01
Major deviance	.27***	.23***	.01	.10*
Disposition to deviance	.11*	.15**	.34***	−.01
Peer drug use	.14***	.16***	.06	.17***
Peer approval of drug use	.20***	.07*	.11*	.19***
Family protective factor	−.19**	−.37***	−.47***	−.03
Family protective × disposition	—	−.17**	−.37**	—
Family protective × major deviance	−.14*	−.20***	—	—
R^2:	.27	.19	.11	.16
F:	59.6**	33.6***	7.5***	13.8***

[a]Family protective factor consists of an index of the family protective factors used in the analyses in Tables 4.3 and 4.4.
[b]Marijuana use scale consists of number of times marijuana has been used in lifetime.
*$p < .05$; **$p < .01$; ***$p < .001$.

index of T-3 use as the dependent variable. All risk factors that composed the delinquency domain, along with a family protective factor index composed of the four individual family functioning scales, were entered into a multiple regression equation. The delinquency domain risk factors were selected because they represented the most severe test for protective effects. Separate stepwise equations were used for each ethnic subsample. The results are shown in Table 4.5.

The standardized betas for the family protective factors ranged from $-.03$ for White non-Hispanics, which is not statistically significant, to $-.19$ for U.S.-born Hispanics ($p < .01$), $-.37$ for foreign-born Hispanics ($p < .001$), and $-.47$ for African Americans ($p < .001$). The last two rows in Table 4.5 present the results of interactions. There was an interaction of family protective factors with disposition to deviance for foreign-born Hispanics and African Americans, both at $p < .01$. Decomposition of these interactions indicated that family factors reduced disposition to deviance in both groups, thus reducing marijuana use. There was also an interaction of family protective factors with major deviance for U.S.-born Hispanics ($p < .05$) and foreign-born Hispanics ($p < .001$). Decomposition into correlations indicated that, in the instance of U.S.-born Hispanics, family factors reduced deviance and this reduced marijuana use. However, among foreign-born Hispanics, family factors reduced deviance, thus reducing marijuana use, and family factors reduced marijuana use among those *who were already deviant*, yielding a true buffering effect. The multivariate analysis demonstrated the complexity and specificity of risk and protective factor relationships when viewed interethnically. However, it also confirmed the unique constancy of family protective factors for foreign-born Hispanics.

In summarizing this brief survey of protective effects, we are mindful of the central limitation of the approach. Risks and protective effects were assessed cross-sectionally. As a result, the direction of causation was imposed. It is possible, for example, that in some instances family factors could be rated unfavorably by adolescents who were sanctioned for their marijuana use. Conversely, those who had not used marijuana would not have had this type of negative family experience. Whether this is true or not, the diverse patterns among ethnic subsamples reinforces our belief that theory development for intervention should be informed by careful assessment of intergroup and intragroup variations. Adolescents of different ethnic groups have socialization experiences that vary systematically, and the social contexts and normative framework of family life underlying their development are diverse. In addition, their family structures and interaction patterns are dissimilar and so are their family arrangements that provide conduct supervision and emotional support to children. Perhaps, most importantly, in the transition from childhood to adolescence, children of different ethnic backgrounds may have very different expectancies about family characteristics and functioning. These are both interindividual and intergroup differences that need closer scrutiny.

Stages of Drug Use

The best known "blueprint" for progression, or stages, of drug use was advanced by (Kandel & Faust, 1975). It envisioned the stages of substance use as a monolithic, "stepping stone" process. Kandel's empirical findings essentially confirmed a gateway model that began with early experimentation with licit drugs, alcohol, and cigarettes. This was followed by a much smaller percentage of licit drug users becoming more intensive users of these substances and then progressing to the use of marijuana and other illicit drugs. Therefore, drug use was theorized to be a rigid chain of contingencies wherein there were fewer users advancing to the next step in the drug-using process. The progression was characterized as follows: (1) early experimentation with beer, wine, or tobacco occurred first; (2) heavier use of alcohol including hard liquor use followed; (3) marijuana experimentation began; and (4) use of illicit drugs such as cocaine, heroin, inhalants, and hallucinogens began.

Newcomb (1995) notes that this model is a probability one rather than deterministic, because it is unidirectional. However, arrival at any particular stage does not automatically presage advancement to the next stage. He also comments: "Unfortunately, most of the research on stages or sequencing of drug involvement has been conducted on white or combined samples of whites and other ethnic groups" (Newcomb, 1995, p. 108). There have been a few studies that have looked at variations in progression by ethnicity or race, and the results, broadly interpreted, have reaffirmed Kandel's model (Brook, Hamburg, Balka, & Wynn, 1992; Ellickson, Hays, & Bell, 1992).

However, there are several issues related to stages in drug use that remain poorly understood and underresearched. One is the failure to take into account developmental stages during adolescence as these condition the stability and probability values of the progression model. Another deficiency is the inability of the model to explain the causes and ramifications of ethnic groups preferences in drugs of choice. Hispanics disproportionately use inhalants; African Americans use crack; White non-Hispanics use methamphetamine and hallucinogens. The stages model also does not adequately account for differences in frequency of use as a variable that may moderate advancement in different ethnic groups.

It is almost axiomatic in drug research that early licit drug use is a robust predictor of illicit drug use. Perhaps the primary reason for this is that there is more time for progression to occur and a greater likelihood that risk factors are in place that maximize the probability of progression. However, the most glaring exception to this model is the inability to explain African American drug use, which is characterized by a trajectory of low prevalence of early licit drug use followed by a rapid acceleration after midadolescence leading to a near parity of lifetime illicit drug use with White non-Hispanics by early adulthood. In this instance, early licit use is not a satisfactory explanation for progression to illicit drug use, and the stages model would have to be recast to allow for later onset drug experimentation.

The metaphor of a funnel is perhaps more satisfying, albeit less rigorous, for understanding early adolescent drug use progression. At the top of the funnel, many adolescents enter; at the bottom, there is a drastic narrowing with a corresponding reduction of adolescents passing through to marijuana experimentation. From our data presented earlier in this volume and elsewhere (Khoury et al., 1996), we know that by 12 years of age, 40% of Hispanics and White non-Hispanics have used alcohol, approximately 20% have smoked, but less than 3% have used marijuana. By 15 years of age, the percentages of lifetime alcohol and cigarette users nearly double. But, during the same time frame, the percentage of lifetime marijuana users increases sevenfold for boys and even more for girls. Therefore, in the transition from early to midadolescence, the bottom of the funnel widens more rapidly than the top. To understand ethnic differences, we would have to imagine a much smaller funnel for African American adolescents, at both top and bottom.

A Longitudinal Scalogram Analysis

Moving from metaphorical to mathematical models, we examined the stages or sequences of drug use and the onset of regular use using Longitudinal Scalogram Analyses (Ellickson et al., 1992; Hays, 1991; Hays & Ellickson, 1991). This technique produces coefficients of reproducibility and scaling analogous to cross-sectional Guttman scaling. The goal of these analyses was to identify all longitudinal patterns consistent with a Guttman scale to select the pattern for each individual that is minimally different from observed scores. This is, of course, one of the central challenges of stages research since there are many possible permutations in careers of drug use, especially when one is contrasting differing racial and ethnic groups.

In a preliminary examination of first use of alcohol, cigarettes, marijuana, inhalants, pills (amphetamines, barbiturates, and tranquilizers), cocaine, and PCP, we identified the patterns for the total sample as well as for the four subsamples in order to compare them. The optimal total sample model yielded a longitudinal coefficient of reproducibility of .9661 and a scaling coefficient of .7571. Both of these values are above the minimally acceptable levels of .90 and .60, respectively. The model, or optimal, sequence of use to produce these coefficients was as follows: (1) alcohol, (2) cigarettes, (3) marijuana, (4) inhalants, (5) pills, (6) cocaine, and (7) PCP. High coefficients of reproducibility and scaling were also obtained for each of the four subsamples, but with some variations. The model had a better fit for the U.S.-born Cubans and the African Americans than for foreign-born Cubans or White non-Hispanics. Superior coefficients were secured for these two groups when inhalants entered before marijuana.

The next set of analyses modeled the sequelae of both first exposure and entry into regular use defined as three or more times during the past 30 days. These outcomes are displayed in Figure 4.1. These data represent the optimal model for the total sample fitted to the four ethnic categories. Again, the coefficients of reproducibility and scaling were well above the acceptable standard. For the total sample, the best model indicated a sequence of first use of alcohol, cigarettes, marijuana, inhalants, and pills. This was followed by regular use of alcohol and cigarettes, first use of cocaine and PCP, and regular use of marijuana and inhalants.

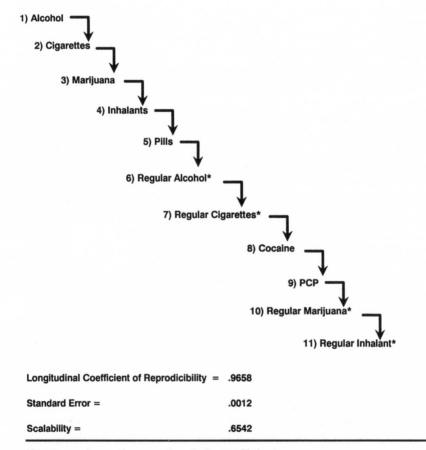

1) Alcohol

2) Cigarettes

3) Marijuana

4) Inhalants

5) Pills

6) Regular Alcohol*

7) Regular Cigarettes*

8) Cocaine

9) PCP

10) Regular Marijuana*

11) Regular Inhalant*

Longitudinal Coefficient of Reprodicibility = .9658

Standard Error =   .0012

Scalability =   .6542

*Denotes regular use (3 or more times in the past 30 days).

Figure 4.1 Stages of drug use for a multiethnic sample of early adolescent males.

Alternate models were tested for each of the four ethnic groups. While none provided a substantially different sequence, some alternative models fit as well or better than the overall model. For example, among foreign-born Cubans and African Americans, a model in which cocaine use preceded regular cigarette use fit slightly better. For African Americans, regular marijuana use appeared earlier and was best modeled as following regular alcohol use and cocaine use. Following marijuana use in this model was regular cigarette use; this was followed by PCP exposure. Among White non-Hispanics, a superior alternate model places cocaine exposure in the tenth, or next to last, position in the sequence.

These longitudinal analyses of stages of drug use in early adolescence strongly point to alcohol and cigarette use as a gateway to subsequent drug use, much as suggested by Kandel and Faust (1975). Either marijuana or inhalant use may follow these gateway drugs. Moreover, as alcohol was the most likely drug of first use, it was also the most probable drug to be regularly used and to precede use of cocaine and PCP. Somewhat earlier exposure to cocaine among foreign-born Cubans and African Americans was detected, as contrasted with later use among White non-Hispanics. However, more frequent use of alcohol and cigarettes did not necessarily precede use of illicit drugs.

Conclusions

We conclude, as did Newcomb (1995), that different ethnic adolescent groups have divergent trends "within a commonality" that signify different reasons for drug use and other forms of deviance. These diverse paths are only now being discovered by focusing more deliberately on the differences rather than the similarities among ethnic adolescent social behaviors and environmental contexts. This is a fundamental point. If you search for similarities in risk factors, etiologic processes, and critical mechanisms that increase or decrease risk in the developmental processes, you will find them. And this is the historical course of research in the drug field until very recently. However, if you start conceptualizing research with a fundamentally different assumption of ethnically patterned risk and causal processes, a different type of logical process ensues that permeates all aspects of research. We have presented only an overview and a starting point. The next phases of research should be exacting in their efforts to maintain the advantages of comparative research design while maintaining flexibility to explore the uniqueness and idiosyncracies of specific cultural groups. Careful empirical assessment will permit testing the relative value of these approaches against each other.

In the process of opening the aperture to new factors for inclusion in risk models, the next phase of studies should include neighborhood and school variables. Because American society is so stratified by class and residentially segregated by race and ethnicity, it is important to determine to what extent characteristics associated with race or ethnic or minority group membership are actually confounded by environment. That is, putative ethnic group differences in risk factors or drug use may actually be a reflection of neighborhood rather than group patterns. For example, adolescents of all backgrounds may have similar drug use rates in a given neighborhood, but there may be substantial variations in rates by ethnic groups citywide. In this instance, there is an ecological effect rather than a true group effect, and this is important to detect. Similarly, in the identification of protective factors, local availability of drugs and neighborhood practices around socialization of adolescents into use of various types of illicit drugs should be accounted for. Even neighborhoods that are saturated with drug use and drug-marketing activities have normative arrangements that increase or decrease the likelihood that specific adolescents will become involved in substance use. Regrettably, we did not have this type of information available in our own research, and this is basic to understanding the external validity of ethnic patterns of risks and drug use beyond individual studies.

Better risk and protective factor research also requires creating additional measures. This is especially true for measuring differences in family process, parenting styles, family structural arrangements and social support, and the modalities of family socialization and discipline around drug use. There are major variations among ethnic groups in family structures and environments, and these may influence drug use experimentation and progression. Although the risk and protective factor results certainly suggest the importance and complexity of family factors, we remain largely uninformed about how these factors are linked or transformed throughout maturation.

We believe that the strongest risk assessment approach is a comparative, person-level, life course model that follows ethnic group adolescents from childhood to early adulthood. The basic strength of this approach is that it permits one to determine both the precursors and consequences of drug use. The research reported in this book is designed to pursue this course of action. Extension of the original research reported in this volume is underway at the time of this writing. A subsample of adolescents from our original subsamples is being followed up with two additional, comprehensive, face-to-face interviews. These interviews will include the use of diagnostic measures to ascertain the presence of major psychiatric disorders, and they will contain life event and chronic stress inventories, in addition to the core variables used in the three earlier waves. Respondents will be between 18 and 19 years old at the time of the next data collection wave, and between 21 and 22 at the final wave. The panel will be stratified by ethnicity to retain adequate numbers for cross-ethnic comparisons, and special attention is being given to relocating and interviewing those that may be of greatest interest but most difficult to find, that is, school dropouts. This extension of our original study will address major issues of risk mechanisms in later adolescence among African Americans, the role of acculturation stress and cultural adjustment on drug use among Hispanics, and how risk factors and protective factors operate over time in all ethnic groups. We will also assess lagged relationships between drug use and psychiatric disorders, and their behavioral sequelae such as suicide attempts and crime. The availability of comprehensive data gathered from adolescents as they mature from early adolescence to young adulthood will make it possible to make more definitive statements about stages of drug use, addiction, and cessation.

In closing, we are cognizant of the fact that those who use risk and protective factor research findings in planning programs of prevention and treatment must have the most detailed and accurate information possible. We are also aware of their need for valid and reliable information regarding specific drugs; in addition, they need drug use information during maturational stages by different ethnic and gender groups. We also know that they must have an understanding of how risk factors are linked to each other and which ones can be modified.

Historically, most researchers have concentrated primarily on risk and protective variables derived from theoretically derived models, many of which are quite abstract in nature. Regrettably, the risk factors that lead to substance use among adolescents are most often imbedded in their lifestyles and social environments and, as such, they are not always captured by these abstract constructs. Those involved in prevention and treatment programs also know that there is a wide gulf between a general theory of deviance and the complex, multifaceted complex of problems manifested by the individuals they see as a part of their professional lives. Unless researchers can breach these differences, studies that identify risk and protective factors will fail to deliver what public health planners and human service providers need most desperately: clearly identified targets that are amenable to prevention and treatment activities.

5

Are Girls Different? A Developmental Perspective on Gender Differences in Risk Factors for Substance Use among Adolescents

Elizabeth L. Khoury

The goal of the previous chapter was to examine interethnic differences in patterning of risk factors, protective factors, and stages of progression. The primary focus of this chapter is to explore gender differences in risk factor patterns using traditional risk factor models described at the outset of Chapter 4. Research studies on gender differences in alcohol use conducted before the mid-1970s concluded that at all age levels males were much more likely than females to use alcohol (Cahalan, Cisin, & Crossley, 1969; Forslund & Gustafson, 1970; Maddox & McCall, 1964; Straus & Bacon, 1953). Over the past 20 years, however, a number of researchers have noted an increasing gender convergence in rates of adolescent substance use with prevalence rates for females increasing and approaching the higher rates of males (Downs & Robertson, 1982; Kaestner, Frank, Marel, & Schmeider, 1986; Prather & Fidel, 1978; Weschler & McFadden, 1976; White, Johnson, & Garrison, 1985; Wilsnack & Wilsnack, 1978). Several large epidemiological surveys comparing gender differences in prevalence rates of substance use initiation have documented similar proportions of alcohol and cigarette users among male and female adolescents (Bachman et al., 1991; Barnes and Welte, 1986). National studies of drinking problems among college students have raised concern about the frequency of heavy drinking among females (Weschler, Davenport, Dowdall, Moeykens, & Castillo, 1994). And a number of recent studies have reported that young adolescent girls are experimenting with all substances, including illicit drugs, at rates similar to those of boys (Farrell et al., 1992a,b; Khoury, Warheit, Zimmerman, Vega, & Gil, 1996; Murray, Perry, O'Con-

95

nell, & Schmid, 1987; National Center on Addiction and Substance Abuse, 1996; Swadi, 1988).

In seeking to account for this progressive increase in use of psychoactive substances among adolescent girls, one explanation has focused on the changing social role of females in American society (Baumrind and Moselle, 1985a,b). More specifically, such role changes include liberalization of traditional norms against substance use by females, rejection of traditional feminine roles by young women, increased female participation in the labor force, and an increase in the proportion of single and divorced adult women (Robbins & Martin, 1993). Single or divorced mothers may be more likely to encourage their daughters to assume less traditional gender roles (Barber & Eccles, 1992). Wilsnack, Klassen, and Wright (1985) provided evidence that changes in drinking behavior may be linked to nontraditional gender role orientation among females.

As a result of these alterations in the female social role, young women may be more likely to engage in increasingly greater risk-taking and adult-disapproved behavior. In fact, over the past two decades the rates of sexual experimentation, pregnancy, and out-of-wedlock childbearing have increased dramatically for adolescent girls (Rosenbaum & Kandel, 1990). Rates of delinquent behavior among adolescent girls have also increased significantly in recent decades, although still remaining much lower than those of boys (Federal Bureau of Investigation, 1966, 1986, 1990; Steffensmeier & Steffensmeier, 1980).

It is widely recognized that substance use among youth increases with age. National and local surveys indicate some drug use in the fourth and fifth grades and considerable increases from the sixth to the ninth grades (Grady, Gersick, Snow, & Kessen, 1986; Oetting & Beauvais, 1990; Segal, 1991). These findings suggest that there may be a critical period when young people are particularly vulnerable to initiation and experimentation with substance use. Several researchers have found that movement from a relatively protected elementary school environment to a larger, more impersonal middle school or junior high school in sixth or seventh grade was a particularly traumatic time for adolescents (Petersen, Sarigiani, & Kennedy, 1991; Simmons, Rosenberg, & Rosenberg, 1973). This period often corresponds with the onset of pubertal change in many adolescents. Therefore, the combination of these changes appears to contribute to the onset of substance experimentation and use.

As stated above, in this chapter the primary focus is on the exploration of gender differences in risk factors and patterns of drug use. We begin with the exploration of factors that may explain gender differences in substance use patterns as well as correlates of substance use. These differentiating factors may include developmental issues, gender role characteristics, reactions to life events, and coping styles.

Adolescent Development

Adolescence is a period of profound development involving complex interactions between the physical effects of puberty and psychosocial adjustments to changing roles. The focus of this development is ego identity formation and consolidation. This process results from the adolescent's experimentation with different lifestyles, adoption of socially appropriate gender roles, and emancipation from parental constraints (Baumrind & Moselle, 1985a,b; Erikson, 1959a).

During this period of transition adolescents may engage in a variety of risk-seeking behaviors such as experimentation with and abuse of illicit drugs, sexual activity, and delinquent behavior. The peer group becomes increasingly important as a source of socialization relative to the family, often leading to conflict with parents. The heightened consciousness of self and others that emerges during early adolescence produces both increased self-centeredness and an enhanced ability to understand the perspective of another (Baumrind & Moselle, 1985a,b).

Young adolescents may be especially vulnerable to stressful events occurring during this period of rapid changes because their coping strategies and competencies are in the process of development (Newcomb, Huba, & Bentler, 1986). A number of studies have reported that adolescence may have more negative psychosocial consequences for girls than boys (Allgood-Merten, Lewinsohn, & Hops, 1990; Hops, Sherman, & Biglan, 1989; Nolen-Hoeksema & Girgus, 1994; Petersen, et al., 1991; Rutter, 1986). Girls may have less positive reactions to the physical manifestations of pubertal changes than their male counterparts. And due to their adoption of less socially valued feminine gender role characteristics, girls may also develop lower self-esteem, less effective coping styles, and more depressive reactions to emotional distress.

Pubertal Changes

A number of researchers have reported gender differences in the developmental processes of adolescence beginning with the fact that females usually reach puberty earlier than males (Blyth, Simmons, & Zakin, 1985). In addition, puberty is likely to have different meanings for boys and girls. Several studies have found that the physical changes of puberty, which have positive meaning for boys, bringing increased size and strength, can have negative aspects for girls (Petersen, 1979; Petersen & Taylor, 1980). For example, girls must adjust to the rounder shapes and increased body fat characteristic of adult women when long, lean prepubescent shapes are idealized in modern fashion images (Faust, 1983; Petersen et al., 1991).

Gender Role Characteristics

As noted earlier, one of the primary tasks of adolescent development is the adoption of a socially appropriate gender role. The process of gender intensification begins in early adolescence when increasing socialization pressures from parents, peers, and media images lead boys and girls to adopt the personality characteristics of their respective gender roles. Markstrom-Adams (1989), in a literature review of research on gender role characteristics, found masculine attributes to be synonymous with assertiveness, independence, learned resourcefulness, and mastery. Feminine attributes were associated with better social relationships, nurturance, tolerance, and sensitivity. Research findings indicated that greater psychosocial well-being in adolescence was found for masculine males and androgynous females (Lamke, 1982; Wells, 1980). The masculine component of androgyny in females was most associated with positive social and psychological correlates (Markstrom-Adams, 1989; Stein, Newcomb, & Bentler, 1992). This suggests that greater societal value is placed on masculine traits and that self-esteem may be closely linked to characteristics that are considered typically male, such as dominance, independence, and assertiveness.

Stressful Life Events

Researchers have reported that during adolescence girls may face more negative experiences than boys, such as overcontrol by parents, vulnerability to sexual abuse and harassment, school and athletic problems, and controversies with intimates and friends (Burke & Weir, 1978; Compas, Davis, & Forsythe, 1985; Gore, Aseltine, & Colton, 1992). And adolescent girls have been found to rate negative life events as more stressful than boys rate them (Newcomb, Huba, & Bentler, 1986), perhaps because of a gender difference in coping styles. Petersen et al. (1991) indicated that pubertal change occurring prior to or around the time of transition from elementary to junior high school was a particularly stressful event and more likely to impact girls than boys because of their earlier onset of puberty.

Self-Esteem

A study of adolescent self-image, involving students in grades 3 through 12, found that compared with younger students, young adolescents (aged 12 and 13) exhibited heightened self-consciousness, greater instability of self-image, lessened self-esteem, and a less favorable view of the opinions held of them by their parents and teachers (Simmons et al., 1973). A gender difference in self-consciousness emerges during early adolescence with girls likely to be more aware of their inner states, more self-reflective, and more publicly self-conscious than boys (Rosenberg & Simmons, 1975). Allgood-Merton et al. (1990) reported that body image, a critically important aspect of self-esteem among young adolescents, is more salient to the self-esteem of girls than boys and that body dissatisfaction is an antecedent of depressive symptoms in adolescence. Adolescent girls have been found to have a more negative body image than boys (Brooks-Gunn, 1988; Girgus, Nolen-Hoeksema, & Seligman, 1989; Rierdan, Koff, & Stubbs, 1989; Simmons & Blyth, 1987).

Coping Styles

Whereas boys are culturally reinforced for learning active, instrumental behaviors, girls may not be and, as a consequence, are likely to develop a less active coping style and to perceive themselves as less resourceful and self-efficacious (Allgood-Merten et al., 1990; Dweck, Davidson, Nelson, & Enna, 1978). Many girls tend to develop a ruminative, self-focused style of responding to distressing events (Compas, Malcarne, & Fondacaro, 1988; Girgus et al., 1989). When individuals with this style of coping are faced with a stressful situation, they often dwell passively on their own distress rather than taking active steps to distract themselves or change the situation. This gender difference in coping with distress may contribute to the higher rates of depression found among adolescent girls and women (Nolen-Hoeksema & Girgus, 1994).

Expressions of Emotional Distress

Most studies of preadolescent children have found either no gender differences in depression rates or a somewhat higher prevalence among boys than girls (Nolen-Hoeksema, Girgus, & Seligman, 1991). However, around the ages of 13 to 14 girls consistently begin to show higher rates of depression than boys (Kandel & Davies, 1982; Nolen-Hoeksema & Girgus, 1994). The few studies focusing on the biological effects of puberty have failed to find a consistent causal relationship between hormonal changes and depressive symptoms in young adolescent girls (Brooks-Gunn & Warren, 1989; Susman, Nottelmann, Inoff-Germain, Dorn, & Chrousas, 1987).

Gender role theories of differences in styles of emotional expression indicate that females internalize their emotional distress, resulting in depression, whereas males express their distress through socially deviant behavior (Dohrenwend & Dohrenwend, 1976; Harris, 1977; Horvitz & White, 1987). Dornbusch, Mont-Reynaud, Ritter, Chen, and Steinberg (1991) found that the relationship between stressful events and deviant behavior such as stealing, physical aggression, or substance use was stronger among male adolescents.

Adolescent Substance Use

As has been stated in previous chapters, rates of adolescent substance use in the mid-1990s are on the upswing (Johnston et al., 1996), and experimentation with drugs seems to have become almost a rite of passage during the early teenage years. In fact, in the case of alcohol use, the adolescent abstainer has become the exception. Baumrind and Moselle (1985a) have suggested that the developmental stresses faced by adolescents in contemporary society may well predispose a majority of them to experiment with mood-altering and consciousness-altering substances.

Baumrind and Moselle (1985) contend that early adolescent involvement with drugs may interfere with the process of developing a stable ego identity and may contribute to alienation and estrangement from society. In addition, an understanding of the causes and correlates of substance use initiation is important because early experimentation can lead to problem use or addiction and may contribute to future psychological or health problems (Chassin, Presson, Sherman, & Edwards, 1990; Tschann et al., 1994).

Many researchers investigating the etiology of adolescent substance abuse have adopted a risk factor approach, recognizing that single factors are generally insufficient to explain the initiation to and continuation of drug use. In fact, a wide range of environmental, psychological, and social influences have been found to correlate with or causally influence substance use among adolescents (Bentler, 1992). The variable risk factor approach explained in Chapter 4 is based on the assumption that involvement in drug use is directly related to the total number of risk factors present for a given individual, rather than any specific combination of variables (Bry et al., 1982; Farrell et al., 1992a; Newcomb, Huba, & Bentler, 1986; Webb, Baer, McLaughlin, McKelvey, & Caid, 1991).

Gender Differences in Risk Factors for Substance Use

As a result of the gender differences in psychosocial responses to the changes of adolescence and socialization to different adult roles, gender can also be expected to moderate relationships among the antecedents of substance use. While there is a substantial body of literature on gender differences in pubertal adjustment and psychosocial affect among adolescent girls, research on gender differences in correlates of, or risk factors for, substance use has for the most part been sparse and inconclusive. Some questions that have not been definitively answered include the following: Are the substance use patterns of adolescent boys and girls similar over time? Are the risk factors for substance use similar for adolescent boys and girls? Do these risk factors differ by type of substance used (i.e., licit or illicit)? Is the increased emotional distress (i.e., low self-esteem, anxiety, depression) experienced by girls during adolescence a risk factor for substance use? With the acknowledged convergence in the rates of substance use between boys and girls, it is important to answer these questions in order to develop prevention programs that will be effective in stemming the increasing substance use among adolescent girls.

An additional element that must be considered is that risk factors for substance use among adolescents have been shown to vary by ethnic group (Felix-Ortiz & Newcomb, 1992). A study using a large representative sample of boys from four ethnic groups also found subgroup-specific patterning of risk factors and differential vulnerability to their combined effects (Vega, Zimmerman, et al., 1993). This was also shown in Chapter 4. It is therefore important to ascertain if the risk factors for substance use vary according to ethnic affiliation for girls as well.

In general, there has been little research that specifically examines both gender and ethnic differences in risk factors for substance use in adolescence. An extensive review of the literature on theories of experimental substance use found that none of the 14 multivariate theories specifically included gender or ethnicity as risk factors (Petraitis et al., 1995). The authors suggested that gender and ethnicity may moderate or interact with other causes of experimental substance use and, therefore, deserve more attention.

Several studies investigating psychosocial risk factors concluded that gender was not as salient as ethnicity and therefore combined boys and girls before doing further comparisons by ethnic group (Farrell et al., 1992b; Newcomb, 1986; Newcomb & Bentler, 1987). A study of 7,000 adolescents in the Southwest reported very similar patterns in correlates of lifetime substance use among boys and girls (Johnson & Marcos, 1988). A study comparing the influence of interpersonal and intrapersonal risk factor domains for predicting early adolescent substance use found differences and similarities in predictors of use according to gender and ethnicity (Flannery, Vazsonyi, Torquati, & Fridrich, 1994).

Risk Factor Analysis

Sampling

The analyses in this chapter were based on a subsample of students from four Dade County middle schools in which girls as well as boys were surveyed. These four schools were selected using stratified random sampling procedures so as to yield groups of nearly equal size with regard to ethnicity. Therefore, African Americans and White non-Hispanics were oversampled when compared to the actual ethnic composition of the Dade County schools.

There were 606 boys and 626 girls in this subsample at Time 1 (T-1) and 516 boys and 554 girls at Time 3 (T-3). When these two waves of data were matched, a total of 430 boys and 476 girls remained. To optimize the sample sizes of the ethnic groups examined in these analyses, it was decided not to utilize the smaller three-wave matched sample. Attrition analyses of the 116 girls who were in the sample at T-1 but not in the matched T-1–T-3 sample indicated that there were no significant differences in generational status or ethnic group distribution between them and the girls in the matched sample. Chi-square tests revealed that the girls who were not in the matched sample were more likely to report cigarette use at T-1 (seventh grade) than the girls who were in the matched sample. Use of other substances did not differ significantly for these groups of girls. Attrition analyses of the boys who were in the T-1 sample but not the matched T-1–T-3 sample showed no significant differences in generational status or substance use compared to boys in the matched sample. Inasmuch as the school dropout rate for the entire sample was extremely low, and because much of the sample attrition was due to matching problems, the investigators believe that there were no systematic biases between those students in and not in the study at all three data collection periods. All students in this subsample were in seventh grade at the T-1 data collection. The median age of both boys and girls was 12 years at T-1 and 14 years at T-3.

Table 5.1 presents the sample sizes by gender for the four ethnic groups examined in these analyses. Over 40% of the sample of boys were Hispanic with a nearly even division between those who were U.S.- and foreign-born. African Americans (24.9%) and White non-Hispanics (33.5%) made up the remainder of the male sample. The female sample was more evenly divided, with U.S.-born Hispanics composing almost 24.8% and foreign-born Hispanics making up 21% of the sample. African Americans were 28.6% and White non-Hispanics were 25.6% of the total sample.

Demographic Variables

For the purposes of this study, the sample was divided into four ethnic groups: U.S.-born Hispanics, foreign-born Hispanics, African Americans, and White non-Hispanics. Students from other ethnic groups were deleted from the analyses due

Table 5.1. Sample Sizes by Gender, Ethnicity, and Nativity

	Boys		Girls	
	N	%	N	%
U.S.-born Hispanics	91	21.2	118	24.8
Foreign-born Hispanics	88	20.5	100	21.0
White non-Hispanics	144	33.5	122	25.6
African Americans	107	24.9	136	28.6
Total	430	100.0	476	100.0

to their small numbers in this sample. Hispanics were not divided according to country of origin because although there were substantial numbers of Cuban-born students in this subsample, the other Hispanic students constituted an extremely heterogeneous group from Caribbean basin and South American countries. No single group had large enough numbers, however, to justify their inclusion in the analyses as a separate ethnic subgroup. In addition, previous analyses of this subsample (Khoury et al., 1996) and of the larger representative sample of boys (Warheit, Vega et al., 1996) found few significant differences between Cuban-born and other Hispanic students in prevalence rates of substance use. Nativity and length of time of residence in the United States (for those who were foreign-born) seemed to differentiate substance use rates of Hispanic groups more than country of origin (Warheit et al., 1996).

Selection of Factors

The risk factors used in these analyses (the same ones used in Chapter 4) are taken from a T-1 study conducted with the entire study sample of boys from which this subsample was taken (Vega, Zimmerman, et al., 1993). Ten risk factors were used, following the lead of Newcomb and colleagues, to maximize the predictive value of the profile for alcohol and illicit drugs (Newcomb, Maddahian, & Bentler, 1986; Newcomb, Maddahian, & Bentler, 1987). The risk factor approach emphasizes a multipath model of adolescent substance use with individual factors representing diverse variables from a number of different theories.

Each of the following risk factors was scored in a dichotomous manner, with a 0 assigned if the risk factor criterion was not met and a 1 if it was met. Scale scores for the total sample that were more than one standard deviation above the mean were assigned to the risk criterion group. This procedure differs from that used in the preceding chapter. In this instance total group means were used to calculate standard deviations that were used to establish risk thresholds. In the preceding chapter the threshold procedure involved using ethnic group specific means and standard deviations. In this chapter the primary focus was on gender comparisons, and there was no statistical justification, as occurred in Chapter 4, for using separate analysis. The use of one standard deviation as the threshold separation was below 20% for all risk factors except parent smoking. The risk factors used in this chapter, and described below, are the same as those used in Chapter 4.

Psychosocial Factors

A number of research studies have explored the relationship between adolescent substance use and psychosocial factors. Elements of emotional distress, such as poor self-concept, depression, and suicidal ideation, have been linked to substance use among adolescents (Aneshensel & Huba, 1975; Kaplan, 1975; Phil & Spiers, 1978; Tschann et al., 1994).

Low Self-esteem. Stacy, Newcomb, and Bentler (1992) found that adolescents low in self-acceptance or self-esteem may be more susceptible to social pressures to use drugs and may have a greater need for peer social approval. The authors suggested that greater self-acceptance may act as a buffer protecting individuals from social pressures to use hard drugs. As noted earlier, adolescent girls are much more likely to manifest lower levels of self-esteem than boys. The self-esteem measure used in this study consisted of a seven-item scale developed by Kaplan and colleagues (Kaplan, 1984b; Kaplan, Johnson, & Bailey, 1986). Scale questions included "I wish I could have more respect for myself" and "In general, I feel I am a failure." Items were scored from 1 to 4 with higher scores indicating lower self-esteem. Cronbach's alpha coefficients (Cronbach, 1951) of .83 were obtained at T-1 and .86 at T-3.

Depression. A recurring theme in the literature on adolescent substance use suggests that adolescents may use psychoactive substances to alleviate stress arising from depressive mood or distressing demands from the social environment. A number of researchers have found that adolescents experiencing elevated levels of emotional distress reported greater levels of substance use than their less-distressed peers (Brook, Whiteman, & Gordon, 1983; Huba, Newcomb, & Bentler, 1986; Pandina & Schuele, 1983; Paton, Kessler, & Kandel, 1977; Tschann et al., 1994). The association of depressive mood with drug use has been found to be stronger among girls than among boys (Newcomb, Chou, Bentler, & Huba, 1988; Novacek, Raskin, & Hogan, 1991; Paton and Kandel 1978; Robbins, 1989). Depression symptoms were measured in this study by a four-item subscale of the Center for Epidemiologic Studies Depression scale developed by Radloff (1977). Scale questions included "I felt sad," "I could not get 'going'," and "I felt depressed" and a question about poor appetite. Each item had a score range of 1 to 4 with higher scores indicating more frequent depressive symptomatology. Cronbach's alpha coefficients were .88 at T-1 and .87 at T-3.

Suicide. A study of older adolescents by Harlow, Newcomb and Bentler (1986) found that males may turn to drugs when experiencing psychic discomfort such as self-derogation and depression, whereas females may turn to suicidal ideation. In this study a single item, "Have you ever tried to kill yourself?" was used as a risk factor. The item was scored 0 if the student reported no attempts and 1 if the student indicated that attempts had been made.

Family Factors

Many studies have reported associations between parental behavior and adolescent drug use. Parents who are uninvolved with their children, hostile and rejecting, or too permissive or too harsh in their discipline may close avenues of communication between themselves and their adolescent children. Petersen et al. (1991) found that close relationships with parents may mediate the long-term effects of early adolescent changes on depressive mood by providing a source of security and comfort in the adolescent's rapidly changing world. Pandina and Schuele (1983) reported that parental control was a more important correlate of substance use for girls than for boys; girls who perceived greater parental control were likely to use substances more heavily than those who perceived more autonomy from parents.

Low Familism. Familism or affectual support was measured by a seven-item "pride" scale derived from the work of Olson (1986, 1989). Sample items included "We really do trust and confide in each other" and "We share similar values and beliefs as a family." Each item had a score range of 1 through 4 with lower values indicating less familism or affectual support. The Cronbach's alpha coefficient of this scale was .87 at T-1 and .91 at T-3.

Family Substance Abuse Problems. Parental modeling of substance use has also been shown to play a role in the substance use of adolescents (Hunt, 1974; Smart & Fejer, 1972; Kandel et al., 1978). Two items in this study tapped whether any family member had experienced problems due to the use of alcohol or drugs. These questions were phrased, "Has your immediate family (the people you live with) had problems because someone in your family uses alcohol?" The second question addressed drugs other than alcohol. Responses were "yes" or "no."

Parent Smoking. Two questionnaire items asked how often the adolescent's mother and father smoked cigarettes. The answers were scored from 1 to 5. The threshold for this risk factor was endorsement of a "sometimes," "often," or "always" response for mother or father.

Peer Factors

Peer factors have been identified as having the most powerful influence on adolescent substance use. Huba and Bentler (1980) reported that during the transition from seventh to ninth grade, both boys and girls perceive that an increasing number of their peers are using drugs. Swaim et al. (1989) found that having friends who used drugs and who encouraged drug use was directly and strongly associated with adolescent drug use. Kandel et al. (1978) reported that generalized peer influence can predict initiation to alcohol, cigarettes, and marijuana and that the influence of a best friend using drugs can lead to the initiation of other illicit drug use. Some researchers have suggested that females are more susceptible to social influences on substance use than males (Baumrind, 1985; Downs, 1985; Eagly, 1983). In addition, girls appear to be more influenced by peer attitudes toward substance use than by the attitudes of their parents (Kandel, 1985a).

Peer factors were measured by two scales from the Monitoring the Future Survey. These scales explored an adolescent's perception of peer approval of substance use and level of peer use of substances (Bachman, Johnston, & O'Malley, 1987).

Perceived Peer Approval. The peer approval scale contained four items asking adolescents how they thought their friends felt about people who use alcohol, cigarettes, marijuana, or cocaine. Responses ranged from disapprove a lot (1) to approve a lot (4). The Cronbach's alpha coefficient was .88 at T-1 and .87 at T-3.

Perceived Peer Use. The peer use scale asked how many of the adolescent's friends used alcohol, cigarettes, marijuana, or cocaine. The responses ranged from none (1) to all of them (4). The alpha coefficient was .90 at T-1 and .86 at T-3.

Deviance Factors

Deviant behavior has been found by many researchers to be one of the most salient correlates of adolescent substance use (Huba & Bentler, 1982; Kandel, 1982; Kaplan et al., 1985; Newcomb & Bentler, 1989). In fact, substance use has been linked to a general theory of deviant or problem behavior during adolescence (Donovan & Jessor, 1985; Jessor & Jessor, 1977, 1978; Osgood, Johnston, O'Malley, & Bachman, 1988). According to this theory, substance use may be but one manifestation of a constellation of norm-violating attitudes and behaviors such as low religiosity, rebelliousness, disregard for the law, precocious sexual involvement, and general delinquent behavior (e.g., fighting, vandalism, and petty theft) (Donovan & Jessor, 1985; Jessor & Jessor, 1977). A study of alcohol use and deviant behavior among high school students found few gender differences in the magnitude or patterns of association between alcohol use and deviance either cross-sectionally or longitudinally (Newcomb & McGee, 1989). Hundleby (1987) reported that cigarette use was more strongly correlated with delinquent activity for girls than for boys. Two measures of deviance, predisposition to deviance and delinquent behavior, were included as risk factors in this analysis.

Disposition to Deviance. A four-item scale, previously used in the replication of Kaplan's esteem enhancement model (Vega, Apospori, Gil, Zimmerman, & Warheit, 1996), measured disregard for conventional law-abiding behavior and hence disposition to deviance. Questions included "It is important to pay for all things taken from a store" and "It is okay to sneak into a movie or a ball game without getting caught." Response scores ranged from 1 to 4 with high values indicating a greater willingness to engage in law-breaking behavior. Cronbach's alpha for this scale at T-1 was .62 and at T-3, .79. The scale items and Cronbach's alpha for this scale are presented in the Appendix.

Delinquent Behavior. Involvement in serious types of delinquent behavior was measured by a seven-item scale developed by Kaplan, Johnson, & Bailey (1986). Scale items included "used force to get money or expensive things from another person" and "broken into or entered a home, store, or building." This scale had response scores ranging from 1 to 2 with higher values indicating that the adolescent had engaged in a particular delinquent behavior. The alpha coefficient was .77 at T-1 and .77 at T-3. The items in this scale are presented in the Appendix.

Outcome Variables

The outcome variables in this analysis were measures of alcohol, cigarette, marijuana, and other drug use. The student questionnaire included questions about ever in lifetime use, lifetime frequency, past 12 month frequency, and past 30 day frequency of alcohol, marijuana, and other drug use. These measures were taken from the Monitoring the Future project's annual survey of substance use among high school students (Bachman et al., 1991). Lifetime use was chosen as the best measure of substance use because of the relatively low rates of drug use in this early adolescent cohort. Lifetime prevalence of cigarette use was determined by an item that asked about frequency, regularity, and quantity of use. Indexes of lifetime use of other illicit drugs were developed from seven items that asked about use of any of the following substances: cocaine, crack cocaine, PCP, barbiturates/amphetamines, tranquilizers, inhalants, and LSD.

Median school grade level of first alcohol, cigarette, or marijuana use was determined by the question "In which grade did you first use (the particular substance)?" Possible answers ranged from "first grade" to "ninth grade" or "never have."

Statistical Procedures

T tests were used to determine whether there were gender differences in lifetime prevalence, more frequent substance use prevalence, or risk factor prevalence. Paired *t* tests were utilized to assess the significance of increases in substance use prevalence over time. Chi-square tests were used to compare gender differences in the prevalence of risk factors for substance use. Analyses were conducted by ethnic group and grade level. To avoid making a Type I error due to the large number of boy–girl comparisons, the Bonferroni method was used to adjust p values for multiple comparisons, such that $p \leq .001$ would denote a significant gender difference.

One-way analyses of variance (ANOVAs) using the Scheffé multiple comparison procedure were used to compare differences in lifetime prevalence and more frequent substance use across the different ethnic groups. One-way ANOVAs were also used to compare the prevalence rates of individual risk factors as well as the mean cumulative prevalence of risk factors among the four ethnic groups of boys and girls over time.

Magnitude-of-use scales were created for each type of substance: alcohol, cigarettes, marijuana, and other illicit drugs. These scales ascertained how many times an adolescent had used a particular type of substance in his or her lifetime. Correlations between the risk factor index and magnitude of substance use were computed separately for each substance by ethnic group within each gender group. To determine their significance, differences in correlation coefficients between boys and girls were examined with a correlation difference test for independent populations using an r-to-z transformation.

Logistic regressions were conducted separately for boys and girls to assess the effects of risk factors on alcohol, cigarette, marijuana, and other illicit drug use. The outcome, or dependent, variable, substance use, was coded with a value of 1 to indicate use of a substance and 0 to indicate no use. The predictor variables were all coded 0 or 1 to indicate the presence or absence of risks. The logistic regression categorical function was used for the ethnicity variable. Chi-square test statistics were used to estimate the statistical significance of the regression coefficients and of the fit of the models to the data.

Results

The lifetime prevalence rates of substance use over time are presented in Table 5.2 according to gender and ethnic group. With one exception, there were no significant gender differences in prevalence rates of alcohol, cigarettes, marijuana, or other illicit drug use in any ethnic group. The exception was for seventh-grade White non-Hispanics; seventh-grade girls had a significantly lower prevalence rate of lifetime alcohol use (29.5%) than seventh-grade boys (50.7%). Substance use prevalence rates for seventh-grade girls were generally lower than those of seventh-grade boys, but by ninth grade, these rates had begun to converge.

For boys and girls in each of the four ethnic groups, lifetime use of alcohol and cigarettes increased significantly between seventh and ninth grades. Among girls, prevalence rates doubled for alcohol use and tripled for cigarette use between seventh and ninth grades. And during this interval, lifetime prevalence of marijuana use increased significantly for all boys and for U.S.-born Hispanic and White non-Hispanic girls. However, for other illicit drug use, lifetime prevalence rates between seventh and ninth grades increased significantly only for White non-Hispanic boys and girls.

When substance use prevalence rates were compared by ethnic group, distinct patterns were evident. Among both boys and girls, U.S.-born Hispanics and White non-Hispanics had the highest prevalence rates of lifetime substance use. African American boys and girls generally had the lowest rates of ever in lifetime substance use of the four ethnic groups. And, foreign-born Hispanics had rates intermediate to the other groups.

The prevalence rate for lifetime use of a substance three or more times assesses usage that is less likely to be of an experimental nature. These rates are also presented in Table 5.2 by gender and ethnic group. For both boys and girls the prevalence of alcohol and cigarettes used three or more times increased significantly between seventh and ninth grades for all four ethnic groups. Prevalence rates of three or more time usages of marijuana and other illicit drugs increased significantly only for White non-Hispanic boys between these two grade levels. Among girls, there were no significant increases in prevalence of three or more time usage of marijuana or other illicit drug between seventh and ninth grades.

Table 5.3 presents the median school grade level of substance use for boys and girls who had ever used a particular substance. For boys in all ethnic groups, the median grade level of first use of alcohol was sixth grade. The median grade level of first use of cigarettes was sixth grade for foreign-born Hispanics and African American boys and seventh grade for U.S.-born Hispanics and White non-Hispanics. The median grade level for first use of marijuana was seventh grade for U.S.- and foreign-born Hispanic boys, and eighth grade for White non-Hispanics and African American boys. Other illicit drug use was not included in this table because this measure was a composite of seven drugs.

The girls in this sample started alcohol use later than boys, with the median grade level of first use being seventh grade for all ethnic groups. The median grade level of first use of cigarettes among girls was also seventh grade, except for U.S.-born Hispanics, who mainly started use in the eighth grade. Median grade level of marijuana use was eighth grade for U.S.-born Hispanic and African American girls. Foreign-born Hispanic and White non-Hispanic girls indicated later first use of marijuana in ninth grade.

To investigate developmental differences between boys and girls as they progressed through adolescence, a series of t tests was conducted contrasting mean scores by gender at Time 1 and Time 3 on a number of key variables. Results revealed that mean scores on many variables were similar for boys and girls at Time 1 but differed significantly at Time 3. A Bonferroni correction for multiple comparisons set the level at which a difference was considered significant at $p <$ .003. Girls reported significantly more depressive symptomatology and self-derogation than boys at Time 3. They were also more likely than boys at Time 3 to indicate that getting good grades in school was important. Conversely, boys were

Table 5.2. Lifetime Prevalence of Substance Use Over Time

	Ever used (%)				Used three or more times (%)			
	Boys		Girls		Boys		Girls	
	7th Grade	9th Grade	7th Grade	9th Grade	7th Grade	9th Grade	7th Grade	9th Grade
Alcohol								
U.S.-born Hispanics	47.3	75.8	39.0	79.7 c***	27.6	53.6 c**	23.7	53.3 c***
Foreign-born Hispanics	33.0	63.6 b*	34.0	71.0 d**	22.4	47.5 d*	21.3	42.7
White non-Hispanics	50.7 a*	81.3 a** b*	29.5	72.1 a***	36.1 a***	62.2 a***	20.7	58.0 a***
African Americans	31.8 a*	58.9 a**	27.2	48.5 a*** c*** d**	12.9 a***	27.0 a*** c*** d*	10.1	25.2 a** c***
Cigarettes								
U.S.-born Hispanics	23.1 c*	52.7 c***	10.2	48.3 c***	24.1 c*	48.4 c**	11.3	48.3 c**
Foreign-born Hispanics	12.5	35.2	9.0	34.0	12.9	36.4	9.5	38.0
White non-Hispanics	24.3 a**	44.4 a**	13.9	41.8 a**	25.7 a**	43.8 a**	14.0	41.8
African Americans	7.5 a** c*	22.4 a**	13.2 c***	23.5 a** c***	8.2 a** c*	26.2 a** c***	13.6	26.5 c**

Marijuana								
U.S.-born Hispanics	3.3	16.5	1.7	16.1	2.2	11.4	0.9	9.4
Foreign-born Hispanics	1.1	11.4 b*	1.0	7.0	1.1	7.0	1.0	4.0
White non-Hispanics	4.9	27.1 b*	1.6	15.6	1.4	16.3	0.8	6.6
African Americans	2.8	15.0	2.2	7.4	0.0	6.8	0.0	1.6
Other drugs								
U.S.-born Hispanics	11.0	16.5	7.6	15.3 c*	3.3	12.1	3.4	9.3
Foreign-born Hispanics	9.1	11.4	4.0	14.0	2.3	4.5	2.0	7.0
White non-Hispanics	6.3	22.9 a**	3.3	13.1	2.1 a*	13.2	1.6	7.4
African Americans	3.7	5.6 a**	2.9	3.7 a*	0.0	2.8 a*	0.7	2.9

Note. Same letters in a column denote pairs of ethnic groups that differ significantly within substances: a, White non-Hispanics and African Americans; b, White non-Hispanics and foreign-born Hispanics; c, U.S.-born Hispanics and African Americans; d, foreign-born Hispanics and African Americans.
*p < .05; **p < .01; ***p < .001.

**Table 5.3.   Median School Grade Level
of First Use of Alcohol, Cigarettes, and Marijuana**

	Alcohol use		Cigarette use		Marijuana use	
	Boys	Girls	Boys	Girls	Boys	Girls
U.S.-born Hispanics	6	7	7	8	7	8
Foreign-born Hispanics	6	7	6	7	7	9
White non-Hispanics	6	7	7	7	8	9
African Americans	6	7	6	7	8	8

more likely than girls at Time 3 to indicate more disposition to deviance and more involvement in delinquent behavior. Otherwise, boys and girls had similar mean scores on family pride, parent derogation, perception of peer substance use, and perception of peer approval for substance use. They also did not differ in the perception that they had the same chance to do well in life as others.

Table 5.4 presents the prevalence rates of 10 risk factors for substance use among boys and girls, comparing their rates in seventh and ninth grades. Boys' frequency of experiencing risk factors was significantly different from girls in only a few instances. For example, U.S.- and foreign-born Hispanic girls reported significantly higher prevalence rates of depression symptoms than boys. Ninth-grade U.S.-born Hispanic girls had significantly higher prevalence rates of family substance use problems than their male counterparts. And White non-Hispanic boys in seventh grade had significantly higher rates of disposition to deviance than their female counterparts. Otherwise, boys and girls did not differ significantly on prevalence rates of risk factors for substance use.

Ethnic group differences were most apparent for family substance use problems, with African American boys and girls in both seventh and ninth grades reporting the highest prevalence rates for this risk factor. The prevalence rates for perceived peer approval of substance use also differed significantly among the four ethnic groups of ninth grade girls. Significantly higher percentages of U.S.-born Hispanic (24%) and White non-Hispanic girls (25%) had this risk factor than foreign-born Hispanic (11%) and African American girls (9%).

The frequency of the total number of risk factors and the mean cumulative frequency of risk factors over time is presented in Table 5.5 for boys and girls in each of the four ethnic groups. The total number of risk factors was calculated by adding the number of risk factors present for each adolescent. The mean cumulative frequency of risk factors increased between seventh and ninth grades for all ethnic groups, with the exception of African American boys and girls. While gender differences were not significant, seventh grade girls' mean risk factor frequencies were higher than those of boys in all ethnic groups with the exception of White non-Hispanics. And, White non-Hispanic seventh-grade girls had a significantly lower mean cumulative frequency of risk factors than the other three

Table 5.4.   Prevalence of Risk Factors for Substance Use

	U.S.-born Hispanics		Foreign-born Hispanics		Non-Hispanic Whites		African Americans	
	7th grade	9th grade	7th grade	9th grade	7th grade	9th grade	7th grade	9th grade
Psychosocial factors								
Low self-esteem								
Boys	16.3	8.0	19.3	17.4	13.3	13.3	27.4	14.6
Girls	15.7	15.4	17.5	14.3	10.8	23.5	17.5	16.8
Depression symptoms								
Boys	11.9*	4.7*	9.5*	9.3*	15.0	9.1	15.5	10.2
Girls	20.2	23.1	22.1	28.0	15.8	22.1	14.0	20.0
Suicide attempts								
Boys	8.3	10.6	4.8	8.0	5.8	14.1	7.5	8.1
Girls	4.4	17.2	11.1	19.8	4.9	15.8	8.1	16.8
Family factors								
Low family support								
Boys	12.2	13.3	5.7	7.1	14.6	11.8	14.6	7.6
Girls	17.8	19.0	13.1	18.0	12.6	17.4	18.9	12.1
Family substance use problems								
Boys	12.1c	14.3*	11.4f	20.5	12.5a	18.1	27.1acf	21.5
Girls	18.6	33.1b	17.0	18.0	9.8a	15.6ab	30.1a	33.1a
Parent smoking								
Boys	33.0	37.4	36.4	30.7	23.6	26.4	29.0	30.8
Girls	37.3	42.4	34.0	32.0	25.4a	28.7	45.6a	41.9
Peer factors								
Perceived peer use								
Boys	11.8	17.9	1.3	17.4	6.5	10.5	6.7	15.3
Girls	9.7	18.3c	5.7	14.4	5.7	13.4	5.7	5.5c
Perceived peer approval								
Boys	19.8e	18.4	5.3e	18.4	11.0	22.0	9.4	14.0
Girls	11.6	24.1b	7.9	11.0d	4.9a	25.4ad	17.2a	9.2ab
Deviance factors								
Predisposition to deviance								
Boys	28.6	27.1	20.7	28.4	16.7*	16.2	20.0	26.8
Girls	25.4b	15.4	13.3	13.3	4.1ab	8.3	19.3a	10.8
Delinquent behavior								
Boys	10.6	15.6	4.9	11.6	6.4	14.7	11.4	9.8
Girls	5.4	8.6	2.2	5.0	2.5	6.7	8.2	5.9

*Boys significantly different than girls in that grade level, $p \leq .001$.
Same letters in a row denote racial/ethnic groups that differ significantly within grade levels, $p < .05$: a, non-Hispanic Whites and African Americans; b, non-Hispanic Whites and U.S.-born Hispanics; c, U.S.-born Hispanics and African Americans; d, non-Hispanic Whites and foreign-born Hispanics; e, U.S.-born Hispanics and foreign-born Hispanics; f, foreign-born Hispanics and African Americans.

Table 5.5. Frequency of Risk Factors for Substance Use

	Boys (%)		Girls (%)	
Number of risk factors	Seventh grade	Ninth grade	Seventh grade	Ninth grade
U.S.-born Hispanics				
0	33.0	36.3	31.4	21.1
1	25.3	26.4	28.0	31.4
2	22.0	9.9	19.5	15.3
3	8.8	9.9	6.8	7.6
4	2.2	9.9	6.8	8.5
5 or more	8.8	7.7	7.6	16.1
Mean	*1.59*	*1.61*	*1.64*	*2.14*
Foreign-born Hispanics				
0	37.5	30.7	41.0	32.0
1	34.1	31.8	23.0	25.0
2	13.6	5.7	16.0	16.0
3	9.1	13.6	7.0	12.0
4	2.3	11.4	7.0	6.0
5 or more	3.4	6.7	6.0	9.0
Mean	*1.15*	*1.67*	*1.37*	*1.70*
White non-Hispanics				
0	49.3	32.6	54.1	35.2
1	18.1	27.1	23.8	19.7
2	10.4	18.8	10.7	18.9
3	12.5	9.7	5.7	9.0
4	4.9	6.3	1.6	6.6
5 or more	4.9	5.6	4.0	10.6
Mean	*1.24*	*1.55*	*0.96*	*1.75*
African Americans				
0	28.0	23.4	20.6	19.1
1	31.8	34.6	33.1	33.1
2	15.9	21.5	20.6	24.3
3	15.0	12.1	11.0	14.7
4	5.6	5.6	8.1	4.4
5 or more	3.8	2.8	6.6	4.4
Mean	*1.53*	*1.51*	*1.77*	*1.68*

Note. Significant racial/ethnic differences in mean cumulative prevalence of risk factors found only among 7th-grade girls: non-Hispanic Whites different from African Americans, $p < .01$; non-Hispanic Whites different from U.S.-born Hispanics, $p < .05$.

ethnic groups of girls. Ninth-grade girls had higher mean numbers of risk factors than boys in all ethnic groups but, once again, differences were not significant.

The risk factor index, a composite of the 10 risk factors, was correlated with magnitude-of-substance-use scales for alcohol, cigarette, marijuana, and other illicit drug use in ninth grade (Table 5.6). Results are presented by gender within each ethnic group. Substantial and highly significant correlations between the risk factor index and magnitude of substance use were found for all substances in both Hispanic groups and for White non-Hispanic boys and girls. However, with one exception—alcohol use among boys—the risk factor index did not correlate significantly with substance use for African American boys and girls. There was only one significant difference in correlations between boys and girls: U.S.-born Hispanic males had a larger correlation between the risk factor index and mari-juana use (.64) than did females (.41).

Among U.S.-born Hispanic girls, the correlation between the risk factor index and magnitude of alcohol (.58) and cigarette use (.57) was significantly larger than the correlation for other illicit drug use (.36). Similarly, among White non-Hispanic girls, the correlation between the risk factor index and magnitude of cigarette use (.60) was significantly larger than for other illicit drug use (.35). These were the only significant differences in correlations between the risk factor index and specific type of substance use.

Table 5.6. Correlation between Risk Factor Index and Magnitude of Substance Use among Ninth-Grade Adolescents

	Specific drug substances			
	Alcohol	Cigarettes	Marijuana	Other illicit drugs[a]
U.S.-born Hispanics				
Boys	.44***	.49***	.64***	.46***
Girls	.58***	.57***	.41***	.36***
Z difference	−1.31	−0.77	2.22*	0.83
Foreign-born Hispanics				
Boys	.59***	.58***	.42***	.42***
Girls	.51***	.55***	.45***	.57***
Z difference	0.75	0.29	−0.25	1.35
White non-Hispanics				
Boys	.47***	.54***	.46***	.44***
Girls	.49***	.60***	.49***	.35***
Z difference	−0.21	−0.75	−0.24	1.08
African Americans				
Boys	.22*	.21	.15	−.10
Girls	.14	.07	.03	−.06
Z difference	0.62	1.07	0.90	0.30

[a]Other illicit drugs consist of cocaine, crack, barbiturates, amphetamines, and pills.
$*p < .05$, $**p < .01$, $***p < .001$.

Since marijuana use increased dramatically for both boys and girls from all ethnic groups, we assessed the relationship between risk factors and marijuana use separately for each gender. Figures 5.1 and 5.2 provide a visual depiction of these relationships. Number of risk factors and marijuana prevalence were both ninth-grade (T-3) measures. Among U.S.- and foreign-born Hispanic and White non-Hispanic boys and girls there was a general linear trend indicating that the more risk factors present the higher the prevalence rate of lifetime marijuana use. In fact, all boys (100%) in these ethnic groups with seven or more risk factors reported that they had used marijuana (Figure 5.1). Among foreign-born Hispanic and White non-Hispanic girls, all girls (100%) with seven or more risk factors reported that they had used marijuana, followed by 75% of the U.S.-born Hispanic girls with seven or more risk factors. In contrast, among girls with no reported risk factors, only 4% of U.S.-born Hispanics, 3% of White non-Hispanics, and no foreign-born Hispanics or African Americans had used marijuana (Figure 5.2). However, this linear trend was not found for African American boys and girls. And neither boys nor girls in this ethnic group had seven or more risk factors in ninth grade.

To determine the differential patterning of risk factors for substance use by gender, separate logistic regressions were conducted for each of the four types of substance use at Time 3 among boys and girls. Small sample sizes precluded conducting separate analyses for each ethnic group. Therefore, race/ethnicity is

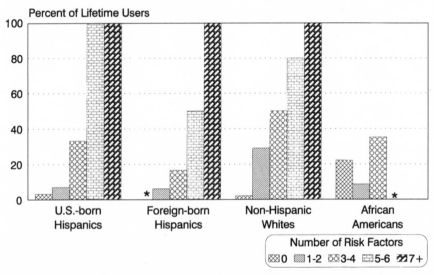

Figure 5.1. Relationship between number of risk factors and lifetime marijuana use among boys. A missing bar (*) means that there were no marijuana users in this risk factor group. No African American boys had seven or more risk factors.

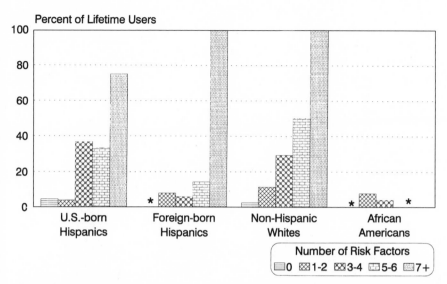

Figure 5.2. Relationship between number of risk factors and lifetime marijuana use among adolescent girls. A missing bar (*) means that there were no marijuana users in this risk factor group. No African American girls had seven or more risk factors.

included as a control variable in the regression equation for the total samples of boys and girls. Table 5.7 presents the results for boys and Table 5.8 presents the results for girls. Regression coefficients are provided in unstandardized form because they are especially useful for comparing the effects of the same variable in different samples (Menard, 1995).

When the significant risk factors for substance use were compared by gender, both similarities and differences between boys and girls were evident. For example, regarding the psychosocial factor of self-esteem, boys' and girls' results were in the opposite direction for alcohol use. For girls, low self-esteem was associated with significantly less likelihood of alcohol use ($p < .05$), whereas for boys, low self-esteem was associated with more likelihood of alcohol use, albeit marginally ($p < .10$). For marijuana use, lower self-esteem was a protective factor among both boys and girls, with the odds ratio approaching significance for boys. Low self-esteem was not significantly associated with other illicit drugs or cigarette use, for either boys or girls.

Depression was not a significant risk factor for any type of substance use among girls. Among boys, depression was a significant risk factor for alcohol use but not in the expected direction. In other words, boys who were less depressed were significantly more likely to use alcohol. Depression was not a significant risk factor for other types of substance use among boys.

Table 5.7. Logistic Regression of Risk Factors on Lifetime Substance Use among Adolescent Boys in Ninth Grade

	Alcohol		Cigarettes		Marijuana		Other illicit drug use	
	b	Odds ratio	b	Odds ratio	b	Odds ratio	b	Odds ratio
Low self-esteem	0.97†	2.64	0.26	1.29	-0.97†	0.38	0.46	1.59
Depression	-1.45**	0.23	-0.33	0.72	0.21	1.24	-0.06	0.94
Suicide attempt	0.77	2.15	1.36***	3.92	0.91†	2.48	1.15**	3.15
Low family support	1.68*	5.34	0.95*	2.58	0.66	1.93	0.25	1.28
Family substance use problems	0.98*	2.67	0.12	1.13	0.49	1.64	0.11	1.11
Parent smoking	-0.16	0.85	0.12	1.13	0.11	1.12	0.40	1.50
Perceived peer use	0.32	1.38	0.46	1.58	1.84***	6.32	0.84†	2.31
Perceived peer approval	1.02*	2.77	0.97**	2.63	1.89***	6.63	1.13**	3.11
Disposition to deviance	-0.07	0.94	0.33	1.39	0.76*	2.15	0.28	1.32
Delinquent behavior	0.58	1.78	1.14**	3.12	0.72	2.05	1.55***	4.73
Racial/ethnic group	0.50*	1.66 (3)	0.59**	1.81 (1)	-1.04**	0.35 (2)	0.90***	2.45 (3)
					0.99***	2.68 (3)		
Model chi-square	60.4***		81.8***		120.2***		81.7***	
Users correctly classified (%)	89.3		46.3		44.4		33.3	

Note. Values (*b*) shown are unstandardized coefficients, †$p < .10$, *$p < .05$, **$p < .01$, ***$p < .001$.
The independent variable "Racial/ethnic group" is a categorical variable for which deviation contrasts were used. The number in parentheses refers to the category that differs significantly from the reference category of African Americans: (1) U.S.-born Hispanics, (2) foreign-born Hispanics, and (3) White non-Hispanics.

Table 5.8. Logistic Regression of Risk Factors on Lifetime Substance Use among Adolescent Girls in Ninth Grade

	Alcohol		Cigarettes		Marijuana		Other illicit drug use	
	b	Odds ratio	b	Odds ratio	b	Odds ratio	b	Odds ratio
Low self-esteem	-0.77*	0.46	-0.44	0.64	-0.57	0.56	0.41	1.51
Depression	0.50	1.65	-0.28	1.32	0.39	1.47	-0.03	0.97
Suicide attempt	0.52	1.68	0.74*	2.11	0.35	1.42	0.15	1.17
Low family support	0.62	1.86	0.62†	1.86	1.20**	3.31	0.55	1.72
Family substance use problems	0.22	1.25	0.07	1.07	0.81	2.26	0.72†	2.05
Parent smoking	0.35	1.41	0.81***	2.25	-0.26	0.77	0.31	1.37
Perceived peer use	0.36	1.43	0.82*	2.28	0.96*	2.61	1.10**	3.01
Perceived peer approval	1.32**	3.76	1.30***	3.68	1.83***	6.21	0.77†	2.16
Disposition to deviance	-0.12	0.88	0.58	1.78	0.59	1.81	0.66	1.94
Delinquent behavior	1.06	2.89	1.81**	6.12	1.16*	3.18	1.73***	5.65
Racial/ethnic group	0.52*	1.69 (1)	0.38*	1.46 (3)	NS	NS	NS	NS
Model chi-square	74.90***		119.1***		99.3***		78.4***	
Users correctly classified (%)	88.0		50.9		34.7		24.0	

Note. Values (b) shown are unstandardized coefficients, $^{†}p < .10$, $^{*}p < .05$, $^{**}p < .01$, $^{***}p < .001$.
The independent variable "Racial/ethnic group" is a categorical variable for which deviation contrasts were used. The number in parentheses refers to the category that differs significantly from the reference category of African Americans: (1) U.S.-born Hispanics, (2) foreign-born Hispanics, and (3) White non-Hispanics. NS refers to no significant group differences.

A prior suicide attempt was a significant risk factor for cigarette use in both gender groups, more so for boys than girls. In fact, boys who had attempted suicide were almost four times more likely to smoke cigarettes than boys who did not have this risk factor. Girls who had attempted suicide were twice as likely to smoke cigarettes as girls who did not have this risk factor. A prior suicide attempt was also a significant risk factor for other illicit drug use among boys; they were three times more likely to use drugs than boys who had not attempted suicide.

Of the family factors, low family support (i.e., low familism) was a significant risk factor for alcohol use among boys. Boys with this risk factor were five times more likely to use alcohol than boys without it. Among girls, low family support was a risk factor for marijuana use. Girls with this risk factor were three times more likely to have used marijuana than other girls. Low family support was not a significant risk factor for other types of substance use among either boys or girls.

Family substance use was a significant risk factor for alcohol use among boys and marijuana use among girls. Boys and girls with this risk factor were more than twice as likely to use alcohol as their contemporaries. Family substance use was not a significant predictor of other types of substance use among boys and girls.

Parent smoking was not a significant predictor of substance use among boys. However, it was a significant risk factor for cigarette use among girls. Girls who had a parent who smoked were twice as likely to smoke cigarettes as girls whose parents did not smoke.

The peer factors were powerful predictors of substance use for both gender groups. Perceived peer approval for substance use was a significant risk factor for use of all four substances among both boys and girls. Boys and girls who believed that their peers approved of alcohol, cigarette, or other illicit drug use were two to three times more likely to use these substances than adolescents who did not perceive this approval. This risk factor was a particularly strong predictor of marijuana use. Boys and girls who believed that their peers approved of marijuana use were six times more likely to use marijuana than adolescents who did not have this risk factor.

Perceived peer use was a significant risk factor for marijuana use, more so for boys than for girls. Boys with this risk factor were more than six times as likely and girls more than twice as likely to use marijuana as their contemporaries. Perceived peer use was also a significant risk factor for cigarette and other illicit drug use among girls.

Among the deviance factors, disposition to deviance was not a significant risk factor for any type of substance use among girls. It was, however, a significant risk factor for marijuana use among boys but was not a significant predictor of other types of substance use.

Delinquent behavior was a significant predictor of cigarette and other illicit drug use among both boys and girls. Boys and girls who had reported some sort of delinquent behavior in the past year were three to six times more likely to have smoked cigarettes or used illicit drugs than adolescents who had not engaged in delinquent behavior. Delinquent behavior was also a significant risk factor for marijuana use among girls.

Ethnic group was a significant predictor of all types of substance use among boys and for alcohol and cigarette use among girls. Hispanics, both U.S. born and foreign born, and White non-Hispanics were more likely to use substances than African Americans.

To test whether there were significant gender differences in the risk factors for the four types of substance use, significance of difference tests between the betas for boys and girls were calculated for each risk factor. Only two significant differences were found and both concerned alcohol use. In the first instance, the betas for self-esteem were in the opposite direction for boys and girls such that having low self-esteem denoted more likelihood of alcohol use among boys and less likelihood of alcohol use among girls. In the second instance, the betas were again in the opposite direction, indicating that depression was a significant risk factor for less likelihood of alcohol use among boys and more likelihood of alcohol use among girls (although not significantly so).

Discussion

This investigation of gender differences in risk factors for substance use has resulted in a number of important findings. However, it must first be emphasized that, because this particular study subsample is small, caution must be used in generalizing findings beyond the sampled populations. Additional research using a population-based sample is needed to verify these observations.

An examination of the substance use patterns of boys and girls over time found that, in general, lifetime prevalence rates of substance use were lower for girls than for boys in the seventh grade. However, by ninth grade the rates for girls had begun to approximate or even exceed those of boys, particularly for alcohol and cigarette use. This finding was true both for lifetime and for three or more time usage.

These findings are surprising given that a number of other national and regional studies (National Center on Addiction and Substance Abuse, 1996) have reported that substance use, with the exception of cigarettes, is substantially lower among Hispanic females than Hispanic males (Bachman et al., 1991; Gilbert & Cervantes, 1986; Welte & Barnes, 1987). These differences may be due, in part, to the fact that many of the studies on gender differences in Hispanic substance use have utilized Mexican American samples, older age groups, or were conducted in the 1970s or early 1980s. The present study findings of gender parity in substance use among Hispanics, primarily from Cuba and South and Central American countries, may reflect changing patterns of gender identity and behavior, particularly among younger, more acculturated Hispanic adolescents.

For the most part, boys in this study started to use substances earlier than girls. Boys in all four ethnic groups reported their first use of alcohol in sixth grade, whereas girls reported first alcohol use in seventh grade. Boys who smoked began cigarette use in sixth or seventh grade, compared with girls, who began smoking in seventh and eighth grade. Boys who used marijuana first started use in seventh or eighth grade; girls reported first use in eighth or ninth grade. Such findings are consistent with the stage theory (see Chapter 4) of substance use documenting a progressive pattern of involvement in substance use from the more licit and ubiquitous alcohol and cigarettes to illicit drugs like marijuana and cocaine (Kandel & Faust, 1975; Kandel, Yamaguchi, & Chen, 1992; Kandel & Yamaguchi, 1993).

These results document the declining age at which adolescents today, and girls in particular, are beginning to experiment with substance use. In this study boys who used marijuana began when they were 12 or 13, and girls began when they were 13 or 14. In contrast, among adult men and women who had used marijuana, those 45 years or older started smoking marijuana during their middle or late twenties, while those 19 to 44 years old began around age 17 (National Center on Addiction and Substance Abuse, 1996). Early age of onset of any type of drug use predicts greater involvement in other types of drug use (Kandel, 1982; Rachal et al., 1982) and greater frequency of use (Fleming, Kellam, & Brown, 1982). These findings should serve to alert us of the need to renew prevention efforts for both female and male adolescents.

Exposure to the risk factors in this study did not differ significantly by gender, although girls in both seventh and ninth grades had a higher mean cumulative frequency of risk factors than boys. In fact, for all ethnic groups except African Americans, greater exposure to risk factors occurred with increasing age. The impact of the risk factor index on each type of substance use was measured by the correlation between them. There was only one marijuana gender difference in the correlation of the risk factor index with the magnitude of use of particular substances. U.S.-born Hispanic males had a higher correlation between the risk factor index and marijuana use than their female counterparts. This indicates that exposure to risk factor conditions had more impact on marijuana use among U.S.-born Hispanic males than among females. The fact that there was only one significant gender difference in the correlations between a risk factor index and magnitude of substance use indicates, once again, that the risk factors for substance use are relatively similar for boys and girls in this study.

An important research question concerned whether the increased emotional distress experienced by early adolescent girls constitutes a risk factor for substance use. Girls' lower rates of self-esteem and higher rates of depression relative to boys in the same age cohort have been cited in the literature and documented in this study as well. Results indicated that low self-esteem was related to alcohol use among girls but not in the expected direction. Girls with low self-esteem were about half as likely to use alcohol as girls who did not have this risk factor. A possible explanation for this contrary finding is that girls with low self-esteem may avoid or not be exposed to social situations where alcohol may be used by adolescents. This explanation may also account for the significant finding that boys who were depressed were one-fourth as likely to use alcohol as boys who were not depressed.

Depression was not a risk factor for any type of substance use among girls, in spite of the fact that close to 20% of the ninth-grade girls in this study indicated that they had a higher than average (for this group) level of depression symptoms. These findings contrast with those of a number of studies indicating that female adolescents use substances to lessen feelings of psychological distress (Mooney, Fromme, Kivlahan, & Marlatt, 1987; Newcomb et al., 1988; Novacek et al., 1991; Paton & Kandel, 1978). Other studies, however, have found no evidence that psychological distress leads to substance use among young adolescents, in general (Hansell & White, 1991), or among teenage girls, in particular (Flannery et al., 1994).

Further research on gender differences in risk factors for substance use is important in order to ascertain if the patterns described in this study are found as adolescents grow older and reach the ages where substance use is most wide-spread. Following a sample of girls from early to late adolescence could determine at what point depression becomes a salient risk factor for female substance use. It is also important to more fully investigate gender differences in risk factors for substance use among different ethnic groups. And, finally, the lack of correlation between the risk factor index and any type of substance use among African Americans in this study makes it imperative to establish culturally relevant risk factors that can be used to identify African American adolescents at high risk for substance use. (See Chapter 7 for an elaboration of this issue). What is clear from this preliminary study of gender differences is while the patterns of early drug use experimentation may show later onset for female adolescents, the rates of use become surprisingly similar by ninth grade, and the risk factors for use may be more similar than different.

6

Cultural Adjustment and Hispanic Adolescent Drug Use

William A. Vega and Andres G. Gil with Eric Wagner

Perhaps no single issue in the drug field is more illuminating and enigmatic than the relationship between culture and drug use. Epidemiological surveys in Latin America have consistently shown very low levels of adolescent drug use, even in countries that are primary producers and exporters of illicit drugs. The contrast of endemic American drug use and minimal use in Latin America points to the importance of investigating social and cultural factors to explain variations in drug use in the United States. There is something about American society that engenders experimentation and addiction at a much higher rate than experienced in other nations. Despite the obvious importance of this information for research and public policy, almost nothing has been done to systematically address this issue. One of the most obvious ways to search for answers is by investigating the effects of cultural adjustment on drug use among Hispanic adolescents.

Hispanic adolescents are an appropriate group for examining the culture–drug use relationship because they are coming from an ethnic group that has strong prohibitions against illicit drug use, they are highly familistic (Vega, 1990), and the population is heterogeneous, since it includes recent immigrants and families with multiple generations in the United States (Zimmerman et al., 1994). Therefore, we can anticipate a wide range of adherence to traditional cultural practices and behaviors that moderate drug-using behavior. There are two basic conceptual approaches pertinent to linking cultural adjustment to contemporary social psychological theories about drug use. These concepts are acculturation and acculturative stress (Berry, Poortinga, Segall, & Dasen, 1995; Triandis, 1994). Acculturation refers to the process of gaining new cultural information and either retaining or losing specific aspects of one's culture of origin (i.e., deculturation). Acculturative stress is a by-product of acculturation that is specific to personal exposures to social situations and environments that challenge individuals to make adjustments in their social behavior or the way they think about themselves. Although acculturation stress is impossible without acculturation, the intensity of psychological stress experienced during acculturation is variable, depending on the characteristics of the host society and the personal resources of individuals who are accommodating to a particular facet of that society (Fabrega, 1969; Favazza, 1980).

This chapter reviews the theoretical and factual bases of knowledge regarding acculturation and drug use among Hispanics and places acculturative stress in the context of the general deviance and social psychological stress theory. A multi-level empirical examination of the relationships between cultural adjustment and Hispanic adolescent drug use is conducted to illustrate key points. The design and measures used in this research were specifically designed to address these issues.

The Acculturation Process and Drug Use

Acculturation studies are not new. The contact of distinctive culture groups in an infinite variety of settings has always been the subject of lay and expert observation. Anthropology was the usual place where research about the ramifications of intercultural contacts were systematically investigated and recorded. The use of the term *acculturation* (Herskovits, 1938; Linton, 1940) was distinguished from assimilation, in that the latter is a component of the former. Acculturation was also distinguished from culture change in that acculturation represents only one modality of culture change (Redfield, Linton, & Herskovits, 1936). Acculturation has both group-level effects and individual psychological effects (Graves, 1967). As nicely described by Berry and colleagues (Berry et al., 1992): "population-level changes in social structure, economic base, and political organization frequently occur, while at the individual level the changes are in phenomena as identity, values, and attitudes"; further, "not every acculturating individual participates in the collective changes that are under way to the same extent or in the same way" (p. 272). Therefore, to comprehend relationships between culture contact and individual outcomes, population-level changes are implicated as is the level of participation by individuals in these populations.

From the outset of systematic research in this area it was evident that social ramifications for individuals experiencing acculturation were largely mediated by social factors such as differences in power, wealth, technology, and cultural or linguistic compatibilities between groups coming in contact with each other. Anthropological observation documented the impact on groups and individuals of superimposing one culture on another. These types of situations called forth the adaptive characteristics of subordinated cultures and the psychological resilience of culture group members. The classic studies of American Indians documented how massive shifts in cultural institutions and normative systems could bring about destabilization of groups and personal disorganization of individuals leading to extreme degrees of dysfunction (Kluckhohn & Leighton, 1946). In less agonizing situations, asymmetries of power and cultural incongruities in intergroup contact situations induced adjustments in the belief systems and behaviors of subjugated groups (Kluckhohn & Strodbeck, 1961). For example, cultural practitioners in the healing arts, religion, and government in subjugated groups often would modify their beliefs and alter practices in order to fit into the hegemony of a new cultural order. This situation created a cultural "borderland" of syncretisms, leading to new cultural behaviors that symbolized the intermediate status of ethnic groups in a more advanced stage of accommodation (Rosaldo, 1993). Such accommodations could take the form of cultural resistance or emulation, depending on the historical example. In the case of Hispanic adolescents, the range of cultural accommodations to American society is wide even within the same ethnic group, and is reflected in attitudes, behaviors, and in selection of ethnic identities (Rumbaut, 1994a).

The Chicago School sociologists (Burgess, 1926; Park, 1928, 1936; Wirth, 1928) had carefully studied the importance of prejudice toward newly arrived ethnic groups and social structural barriers that impeded economic mobility and resulted in de facto segregation, thus dramatically influencing group-level adaptation. Contemporary sociological studies have also produced new models for explaining modalities of social and economic incorporation among new immigrants. These models included factors such as circumstances and conditions that precipitated immigration, and the cultural and social compatibilities between immigrants and the society into which they were entering (Portes & Rumbaut, 1990). The importance of ethnic enclaves and their internal characteristics has also gained attention for several reasons. Kuo (1976) reported that Chinese immigrants living in ethnically similar residential areas had fewer mental health problems than those who lived in ethnically dissimilar areas. Portes (1995) developed a more comprehensive notion of enclave than merely an ethnically dense neighborhood. He includes the ethnic sphere of influence as it pervades the political, economic, and social life of an urban environment. When enclaves are highly developed they provide an alternate route to economic opportunity even when there is less than open access within the dominant society. In less favorable circumstances they do not, and then enclaves become synonymous with urban reservations for the underclass. Portes argues that three determinate factors are operating to control immigrant group accommodation: skin color, location, and mobility opportunities.

Social psychologists have struggled to describe how acculturation operates at the individual level. There are several overlapping approaches to conceptualizing and measuring acculturation in American social psychology: linear acculturation models (Rogler et al., 1991), cultural identity (Felix-Ortiz & Newcomb, 1995), and multidimensional models (Keefe & Padilla, 1987; Padilla, 1980; Szapocznik et al., 1978), including orthogonal models (Oetting, 1993; Oetting & Beauvais, 1991). It is universally acknowledged that acculturation is idiosyncratic, dynamic, and complex, and no singular approach can be completely satisfying. The field of acculturation measurement is unsettled, and no consensus exists on a best or most appropriate method for assessing acculturation. Multiple dimensional approaches are more comprehensive. However, culture is so vast a field that there must be limitations imposed based on the goals of the research.

Linear acculturation models have been widely used in health, mental health, and drug use research because they are easily operationalized in short scales (Cuellar, Harris, & Jasso, 1980; Marin, Sabogal, Marin, Otero-Sabogal, & Perez-Stable, 1987). These scales rely primarily on language behavior as a broad gauge of cultural orientation. Reliance on language behavior may appear simplistic when the goal of the research is to capture complex cultural changes at the individual level. However, the use of language behavior as the conceptual core of these scales is very powerful for depicting subgroup-level differences because embedded in language is cultural imagery, values, knowledge of customs, and access to a cultural group and its respective artifacts. In short, language use is a reference point for cultural allegiance and social expectations. Therefore, adolescents reporting speaking only Spanish to friends, family, and in school, will be much more likely than those speaking English to adhere to family practices and values that are consistent with Hispanic culture in contrast to American culture. Hence, lower drug use among unacculturated Hispanic immigrants has been attributed to the antidrug orientation of their culture of origin and their immersion in social networks that provide social control (Barrera & Reese, 1993). However, this illustrates the weakness of the unidimensional approach in that the protective factor in this example, retention of antidrug attitudes, is not directly measured but only inferred. The problem lies not in what was measured, but in what was missing.

Self-described identity as a basis of indexing acculturation is useful because it is multidimensional, and acknowledges the complexity of personality development. This means that acculturating individuals are unique composites of cultural characteristics, and they may think of themselves differently according to the demands of a social setting, or their cultural identity may change over time. For example, Hispanic adolescents may see themselves as very Hispanic in certain aspects of their values and behaviors, but very American in other aspects. Ethnic identity can be assessed globally or by adherence to specific cultural aspects or domains. An example of the latter can be found in the research of Felix-Ortiz and Newcomb (1995), who reported that Mexican American adolescents reporting high levels of ethnic activism and pride had lower drug use. At the global level, Hispanics that chose a certain ethnic identity may be revealing a "buy-in" to a cultural disposition. Failure to select a cultural identity may indicate a problem with social integration.

The multidimensional trait approach to acculturation presupposes that acculturation is idiosyncratic and piecemeal at the individual level. Keefe and Padilla

(1987) report that some features of early socialization may be retained, such as food preferences, but others may be forgotten because they are no longer practiced or functional, such as ethnic group history or use of the Spanish language. These dimensions of cultural orientation are numerous and operate with minimal interdependence. The social context of acculturation would have a preeminent influence in the patterning of these dimensions. Therefore, an adolescent could have little knowledge of ethnic group history yet still enjoy dancing to Latin music. This statement of the independent nature of acculturation dimensions resembles the orthogonal acculturation approach of Oetting and Beauvais (1991). They assume that aspects of cultural orientation are independent, and aspects of cultural knowledge and behaviors are retained in combinations that assist the adolescent toward a higher state of self-acceptance and functioning. Humans are creative, dynamic, adaptive, and capable of an infinite variety of cultural permutations. The implications for adolescent drug use are found in the identification of cultural and personal characteristics that are linked to drug use, and can include aspects of marginality wherein some individuals find themselves marginal to all cultural identifications, without any positive reinforcement for their identity formation from any ethnic group or defined cultural orientation.

The concept of segmented assimilation is very salient for understanding individual adaptation as well as group adaptation (Portes, 1995). Segmented assimilation is predicated on very distinctive socialization experiences of groups, and distinctive pathways into American society for individuals. The integration and underclass assimilation models virtually require extensive deculturation. The integration model requires social integration into dominant ethnic groups; the underclass model requires social integration into the street culture of disorganized inner-city ghettos. Both of these alternatives engender intergenerational conflicts between immigrant parents and children who were either born in the United States or immigrated when they were very young. Rumbaut (1995) refers to this type of individual adjustment as "subtractive" because it operates as a zero-sum: You must give up cultural knowledge and practices to acquire new ones. This is, in fact, the fundamental assumption of the linear gradient acculturation model discussed above. Over time everyone becomes Americanized to some mythical standard cultural form. The segmented assimilation concept provides for a second form of incorporation, a bicultural option of integration into ethnic enclaves. This requires a socialization process very similar to what Gibson (1995) calls "additive acculturation," which entails maintaining the core of cultural knowledge and practices but adding instrumental knowledge and skills of exogenous, and potentially dominant, ethnic groups. These variations in socialization experiences have very important ramifications for identity formation, perceptions of life chances, and potentially for drug-using behaviors and their sequelae.

This literature is fundamental for understanding the contemporary context of acculturation research. Culture contact and socialization among Hispanic adolescents is heavily influenced by the culture complex in which it is occurring. The identity and cultural adjustment selected by adolescents, although not totally volitional, has important ramifications for adherence to conventional behavior over the life course, including drug use. In the instance of immigrants, the more they conserve their culture of origin the less likely they are to be affected by American underclass culture, or by integration into middle-class American culture, both of which feature much higher levels of adolescent drug use than is found in their own subculture. Nevertheless, culture is dynamic, and acculturation to some degree is inevitable. We can expect that adolescents who immigrate early in their lives will have a higher likelihood of acculturating simply as a function of maturational level and length of exposure. This is precisely why acculturation studies are frustrating and challenging: Cultural orientation remains vulnerable to change along multiple dimensions over the life course. Some of these dimensions of acculturation and their relationship to drug use are explored empirically in this chapter.

Acculturative Stress and Drug Use

Acculturation theorists and researchers have advanced a number of theoretical models about the relationship between Hispanic cultural orientation and mental health (Rogler et al., 1991). These propositions are illuminating, if somewhat contradictory, and are based on two assumptions: (1) the process of acculturation can be conceptualized as a linear one and (2) the process is stressful but the intensity and types of stressors experienced vary systematically by level of cultural orientation. Hypothetically, at the population level, acculturative stress is disproportionately experienced among low-acculturation individuals because they lack the language skills, social knowledge, and personal resources to function adequately in a dominant culture system. High-acculturation individuals are at risk of stress because of greater exposure to definitions of self and one's ethnic group as different, stigmatized, and having unequal access to social, educational, and economic opportunity. Biculturalism is optimal for personal adjustment because it provides a bridging of cultures with dual skill levels in language and instrumental cultural knowledge. Presumably, this biculturalism leads to a more optimal state of psychological integration, lower cultural conflict, and greater self-acceptance.

The relationships between cultural orientation and acculturation level parallel those found in the additive acculturation model: One adds to one's original cultural base by acquiring new cultural information and social skills, but not at the cost of replacement. Low acculturation can be seen as stressful because of minimal societal integration and the constant threats posed to the individual to communicate effectively, especially for adolescents in school environments or adults in work situations. However, the disadvantages of low acculturation are somewhat offset by the protective effects of traditional culture. In contrast, high acculturation is seen as stressful because of the greater likelihood of exposure to U.S. underclass culture and internalization of minority status in American society. This framework is useful for hypothesis generation but we have limited empirical evidence to confirm the validity of this model, and contemporary researchers are convinced that the acculturation process, and acceptance or selection of ethnic identity, is nonlinear and multidimensional. Therefore, linear acculturation approaches represent an important foundation for theory construction and research, but advances in this field will require elaboration of existing theory. One purpose of this chapter is to make an empirical contribution to the acculturation discourse.

The standard reference in acculturative stress theory is Stonequist (1937) and his elaboration of the "marginal man" construct. Stonequist elaborated the marginal man ideas of Park (1928), who had himself written about intergroup cultural contact and adaptation with special heed to social context factors such as social status and culture. Stonequist focused his insights on describing psychological adaptive processes and consequences. His contribution was very powerful intellectually and has provided the basis for contemporary theory. In Stonequist's rendering of the acculturation experience, individuals who are of one cultural group but "condemned" to live in two societies that markedly differ in cultural content and may be antagonistic will be vulnerable to marginalization. Marginality is described as a situation created through social interaction, not as a psychological condition. Nevertheless, marginality has definite ramifications for personal functioning.

The link between contemporary acculturation theory and marginality theory is a clear one. Bicultural individuals are presumed to have the best opportunity for avoiding marginality because they have the personal resources to maneuver through social situations with differing cultural expectations, including bilingualism in the instance of Hispanics. This flexibility requires skills and cognitive flexibility. This is akin to Stonequist's description of adaptive marginality and should be associated with superior psychological coping. Higher-acculturation individuals are more likely to lose the protective effects of traditional culture, and thus have less resilience in the face of stressors. Low-acculturation individuals are not marginal but pay a price in social mobility for staying embedded in their ethnic group. This theory must be modified somewhat to fit the circumstances of Hispanic adolescents, especially those found in our study, because the sample included both foreign- and native-born adolescents. Acculturation may have very different effects in the two groups. These adolescents are young and receiving long-term exposure to English-language educational settings, but have a different start point for their socialization. Furthermore, the early circumstances of those born outside of the United States are very different. Presumably, immigrants grow up in a "stable" social milieu in which both they and their parents are exposed to the same cultural context. In contrast, the native-born adolescents have grown up in a "dual" or "multiple" cultural system, with different degrees of cultural conflicts depending on the level of acculturation of the parents.

The psychological requirement of living in two societies is stressful because of the incessant testing of cognitive and emotional control skills needed for negotiation in conflicting cultural situations. In other words, acculturating individual are under pressure to validate social and cultural expectations by selecting proper responses in each social situation. The "marginal man" fails to assimilate and functions at the edge of different cultural worlds, the result of either personal disposition or social strictures. This situation will lead to personal distress that can be resolved by reentrenchment in the culture of origin. If this does not occur, a marginal man or woman is produced who may be a confused individual with no cultural identification and an inferiority complex stemming from a sense of social inadequacy. However, Stonequist allowed for exceptions and believed that some marginal people could achieve superior social functioning with the added advantage of access to multiple cultural worlds. These individuals could be capable of greater interpersonal skills and creative expression, or even function as cultural ombudsmen.

The relationship between cultural orientation and drug use has been directly or indirectly tested among Hispanic adults in three large epidemiological surveys (Amaro et al., 1990; Burnam et al., 1987; Vega, Kolody, Hwang, & Noble, 1993). The results are consistent: High acculturation is associated with much higher drug use, especially illicit drug use. Furthermore, biculturalism was not found to be protective against drug use (Burnam et al., 1987), and low-acculturation individuals had much lower rates of drug use than biculturals (Amaro et al., 1990). However, these studies did not assess any acculturation or acculturative stressors beyond the use of language-based acculturation measures. Studies of Hispanic adolescents are needed that can overcome some of these limitations. It is important to distinguish between immigrant and native-born children in the study of acculturation and acculturative stress effects on drug use. Logically, immigrant children should be affected by acculturation in a fundamentally different way from the native born.

In these previous studies the acculturation process has been held responsible for higher levels of adult drug use among more acculturated Hispanics for three reasons. First, in contrast with their culture of origin, acculturating Hispanics are exposed to social definitions of drug use that either tolerate or encourage its use. Second, Hispanics experience frustrated levels of both social acceptance and expectations about achievement, especially those born in the United States. Third, immigrants may actually be a more robust population than the general population, so they would tend to have fewer health-degrading behaviors such as drug use (Burnan et al., 1987).

These studies point out the underlying weakness of research that attempts to explain Latino drug use using measures of acculturation. Acculturation measures are broad indicators of knowledge acquisition and behavioral practices, but do not actually assess group-level processes or their relationship to individual adaptation. In other words, acculturation measures have not directly assessed the effects of limited economic opportunity or language barriers, or satisfactory social adjustment. Researchers have been conducting population-level surveys that measure acculturation of individuals and inferring group-level explanations based on unmeasured variables to explain individual drug use. The approach is weak because it lacks a theoretical or factual basis of explanation.

An alternative approach presenting an explanation of Hispanic adolescent drug use that described acculturative stress mechanisms was found in the work on Cuban Americans by Szapocznik and his colleagues, and reported in numerous papers (1978, 1979, 1980, 1988). These researchers found that acculturation occurs more quickly among immigrant children than among their parents, and boys acculturate faster than girls. From clinical studies these investigators reported that this differential acculturation rate leads to differences in behavioral expectations intergenerationally. The immigrant parents, who are struggling to reestablish their lives and develop an adequate economic base, are bewildered and frustrated by their children, who quickly learn and emulate American cultural forms in demeanor, entertainment preferences, dress, and personal etiquette. This leads to conflicts over appropriate behavior. The parents are sensitive to losing control of their children in this new cultural setting and attempt to impose a tighter reign over adolescent conduct. The results are further deterioration in communication, association with delinquent peers, and potential delinquency and early drug experimentation. This is a very plausible model, drawn primarily from clinical research, which has a firm theoretical basis and is testable. Later in this chapter we evaluate this model using empirical data.

Our own research has focused on describing the distribution and effects of acculturative stress, specifically language conflicts, cultural incompatibilities, and perceived discrimination. We have found that immigrant adolescents actually report more total acculturation conflicts than U.S.-born Hispanics, but that the effects on self-esteem of these acculturative stressors are always greater on U.S.-born Hispanics. This suggests a difference in personal resources among the two groups. Immigrants are more likely to experience stress associated with language use, although the English language is acquired relatively quickly by immigrant children (Gil & Vega, 1996). U.S.-born Hispanics are more likely to report perceived discrimination as a primary source of stress. Whereas language problems are associated with problem behaviors at home and school for immigrants, consistent with the findings of Szapocznik, perceived discrimination and language problems are associated with problems at school but not at home for U.S.-born Hispanics (Vega et al., 1995). These findings confirm the impression that Hispanic adolescents born in the United States are more susceptible to internalization of minority status, and the behavioral component of this process, including deviancy, will be exhibited in school settings.

Other research using this data set, as noted in Chapter 5, confirmed the greater importance of familism for immigrant Hispanics as both a risk and protective factor. A study of family structure and change demonstrated that Hispanic immigrants are most susceptible to personal problems as a result of changes in family structure (Gil & Vega, 1997). Our previous research has also shown that immigrants are less likely than native-born Hispanics, African Americans, or White non-Hispanics to experience low levels of familism (Vega, Zimmerman, et al., 1993), and familism is inversely related to acculturation among immigrants but not among native-born Hispanics (Gil, et al., 1994). Therefore, acculturation (among immigrants) and U.S. nativity reduce familism and increase acculturation conflicts, and both factors are linked to subsequent delinquent behavior (Vega, Zimmerman, et al., 1993). It is evident that familism is especially important in mediating the effects of perceived discrimination on self-esteem among Hispanic adolescents (Gil et al., 1994).

In one study, acculturative stress levels reported by Cuban and Nicaraguan immigrants were compared, two groups that differed drastically in their social power in the Miami Hispanic enclave (Gil & Vega, 1996). Cubans, as noted in Chapter 2, are much better established in the political and economic life of the city. Nicaraguans as a group are much lower in income and educational levels, with some not having legal residency. Our findings showed that patterns of exposures, over time, to acculturative stressors were similar among Cubans and Nicaraguans. However, the prevalence of acculturative stressors is much higher among Nicaraguans than among Cubans. This includes both adolescents and their parents. Furthermore, Nicaraguan parent and child acculturative stressors predicted almost four times as much variance (32% vs. 9%) in their child's self-esteem as was the case with Cubans. Within both groups of parents, their acculturative stressors were a strong predictor of parent–child acculturative conflicts (i.e., variances explained 53% for Cubans and 58% for Nicaraguans). However, these findings leave unexplained the mediated relationships between parent and adolescent acculturative stress and drug use. In order to accomplish this it is necessary to link the acculturative stress construct to theories of deviance.

Empirical Tests of Acculturation and Drug Use

Based on the theoretical premises presented in this chapter, a series of hypotheses and questions exploring the relationship between acculturation factors and drug use were addressed. The first hypothesis tested the linear relationship between level of acculturation and drug use among Hispanics born in the United States and those who are immigrants. In the second hypothesis the relationship between marginality and drug use was tested, proposing that those with no clear cultural identity are more likely to use drugs. The third set of analyses examined gender differences on the effects of time lived in the United States and both levels of acculturation and ethnic identity. In the next analyses, we examined two hypotheses about the effects of intergenerational differences in acculturation levels on family conflicts and drug use.

Recalling that the Hispanic adolescents in this study were in their first year of middle school, consisting of sixth or seventh grade, at the time of first interview (Time 1), the distribution of boys and girls on acculturation was determined using a linear language behavior acculturation measure derived from Cuellar et al. (1980). This measure addressed language use in the contexts of home, school, friends, and personal preference. At the beginning of the study, 5% of the sample had lived in the United States less than 3 years, 7.4% between 3 and 4 years, and 12.1% between 5 and 7 years. The proportion of foreign- and U.S.-born adolescents was about evenly divided. We found that 7.7% were low acculturation, 25.4% bicultural, and 66.9% high acculturation. Two other variables were used to create a two-dimensional self-assessment of cultural identity. The items were "I consider myself to be a Latino (Hispanic)" and "I consider myself to be American." The response format for both was Likert-type level of agreement. The answers to these two questions were used to create a four-cell matrix with all possible sets of identities represented. For the overall sample, 51% rated themselves as equally Hispanic and American, 35.2% considered themselves Hispanic only, 11.7% considered themselves American only, and 2.1% did not strongly identify themselves as either Hispanic or American.

As noted earlier in the chapter, several studies have shown a positive relationship between drug use and linear acculturation for Hispanic adults. Therefore, to test this hypothesis among adolescents, we present in Table 6.1 self-reported

Table 6.1. Relationship between Level of Acculturation and Alcohol and Marijuana Use

Acculturation level	High alcohol use	T3 marijuana use	T3 marijuana initiation
All Hispanics			
Low acculturation[a]	7.1***	10.3***	6.3***
Bicultural	16.7	19.0	10.4
High acculturation	14.8	19.8	10.8
U.S.-born Hispanics			
Low acculturation[a]	25.0***	47.1***	35.3***
Bicultural	19.5	25.3	11.9
High acculturation	14.7	20.5	11.6
Foreign-born Hispanics			
Low acculturation[a]	5.6***	7.0***	3.7***
Bicultural	15.0	15.4	9.6
High acculturation	15.0	18.8	9.6

Note. All figures are percentages.
[a]Low acculturation significantly different from bicultural and high acculturation.
***$p < .001$.

acculturation rating and three forms of drug use assessed at Time 3—high alcohol use, marijuana use, and first marijuana use for those who were not previous users at Time 1 or Time 2. The measure for high alcohol use is derived from a scale that measures school grade at the time alcohol was used for the first time, lifetime alcohol use, number of drinks the last time alcohol was consumed, frequency of getting drunk, and whether alcohol use ever caused problems. High scores were those that were one standard deviation above the mean.

The first set of analyses in Table 6.1 are for the entire Hispanic sample. As shown, alcohol and marijuana use rates are lowest for the low-acculturation group, and increase in equal proportions for both the bicultural and high-acculturation subsamples. Therefore, the linear effect is limited to the contrast of low acculturation to bicultural for high alcohol use or marijuana use and initiation. Moreover, there are no important differences in drug use rates between bicultural and high acculturation for either U.S.-born or foreign-born Hispanics. However, there is a very important difference between low-acculturation U.S.-born and foreign-born adolescents. The foreign-born low acculturated have the expected increase in alcohol and marijuana rates that occurs between those that are low in acculturation and bicultural, whereas the U.S.-born low acculturated actually have the highest rates of alcohol and marijuana use, as well as new marijuana initiation. It appears that low acculturation is protective for immigrants, but not for the U.S. born. A similar finding was reported for Mexican American adults in Los Angeles by Burnam et al. (1987). The fact that U.S.-born adolescents who are low in acculturation have the highest drug use is consistent with our earlier research (Gil et al., 1994) that found this subsample to be most vulnerable to low self-esteem because they suffered the dual risks of both foreign-born (e.g., language problems and low life chances) and U.S.-born Hispanics (e.g., perceived discrimination and acculturation conflicts). This "double jeopardy" situation is unique, in part because of the absence of family protective factors found more frequently among the U.S. born. The U.S.-born adolescents appear to be socially marginal and isolated. They are 15 years old, born in the United States, and remain poorly skilled in the use of the English language in any social context. Although proportionately they are a small group, they are at very high risk for several negative outcomes as they mature. The implication of this finding for drug research is that foreign-born and U.S.-born Hispanics have a different developmental experience.

Table 6.2 presents information on cultural identification and drug use. The primary hypothesis tested by the table is the Stonequist-derived one: Those individuals who do not identify with either cultural reference group, or combination of groups, will have the worst outcomes—in this instance manifested as higher drug use rates. Indeed, we find this to be true for the combined Hispanic sample for high alcohol use and marijuana use or initiation at Time 3. It remains true in looking at the foreign born and U.S. born, respectively. However, the effects of marginality are strongest for the U.S. born, where nearly one-third are high

**Table 6.2. Relationship between Ethnic Identity
and Alcohol and Marijuana Use**

Ethnic identity	High alcohol use	T3 marijuana use	T3 marijuana initiation
All Hispanics			
Latino only	16.7	18.8	12.0
American only	12.6	18.8	10.0
Latino & American	13.2	18.2	9.2
Neither	24.6[a]***	30.4[a]***	22.8[a]***
U.S.-born Hispanics			
Latino only	28.6[b,c]**	32.4[b,c]**	22.2[b,c]**
American only	12.6	19.5	11.0
Latino & American	13.3	19.8	10.2
Neither	29.4[d]***	47.1[d]***	41.2[a]***
Foreign-born Hispanics			
Latino only	13.2	15.0	9.1
American only	12.5	16.4	6.8
Latino & American	13.1	15.5	7.5
Neither	22.5	23.1	15.0

Note. All figures are percentages.
[a]"Neither" different from all other categories.
[b]"Latino only" differs from "American only."
[c]"Latino only" differs from "Latino/American."
[d]"Neither" differs from "Latino only" and "American only."
**$p < .01$; ***$p < .001$.

alcohol users and one-half are marijuana users at Time 3. Interestingly, a clear-cut identification of Hispanic is no protection against drug use in either group, and is particularly problematic for the U.S. born. This may result from cultural conflicts and perceived discrimination in the same sense as we interpreted the results for the low acculturation U.S.-born Hispanics in Table 6.1. They are a nonnormative group of adolescents in their own social environment. Therefore, cultural identification and behaviors do have systematic relationships to adolescent drug use among Hispanics, but these relationships are obscured unless U.S.-born and foreign-born adolescents are analyzed separately.

Table 6.3 presents a comparison of the effects of time lived in the United States on acculturation level and cultural identity. This is the first of three illustrations intended to evaluate the adequacy of the Szapocznik model to determine its relative value for explaining Hispanic adolescent drug use. The central hypothesis is whether boys acculturate faster than girls. Among the U.S.-born the acculturation rate is similar for boys and girls. However, among the foreign born, girls with 3 to 7 years of residence have acculturated faster, probably because they are doing better in school. These results, combined with the cultural identity information, reinforce the findings reported by Rumbaut (1995) for Hispanics in California, in

**Table 6.3.   Effects of Time Lived in the United States
on Acculturation Level and Ethnic Identity by Gender**

Acculturation and ethnic identity	Time in the United States				
	Less than 3 years	3–4 years	5–7 years	8–12 years	U.S. born
Males					
Acculturation					
Low	68.1	26.1	5.8	2.7	1.1
Bicultural	24.8	52.2	42.5	19.9	19.8
High	7.1	21.7	51.7	77.4	79.1
Ethnic identity					
Latino only	69.1	70.8	57.6	44.1	18.6
American only	5.1	3.5	3.9	7.2	16.9
Latino and American	24.3	22.8	35.5	46.0	63.0
Neither	1.5	3.0	3.0	2.7	1.6
Females					
Acculturation					
Low	70.0	18.8	10.5	2.7	0.0
Bicultural	30.0	50.0	21.1	27.0	24.8
High	0.0	31.3	68.4	70.3	75.2
Ethnic identity					
Latino only	45.5	43.8	36.8	22.9	14.3
American only	0.0	6.3	10.5	8.6	21.4
Latino and American	36.4	37.5	42.1	62.9	62.5
Neither	18.4	12.5	10.5	5.7	1.8

Note. All figures are percentages.

that girls tend to select a cultural identification that is most normative, and least conflictive, from the standpoint of the dominant culture. In Table 6.3 we find that foreign-born girls are least likely to report being Hispanic only, and somewhat more likely to report being American only, then are boys. From the standpoint of the hypothesis of more rapid acculturation for boys, we do not confirm this finding.

In Figure 6.1 the hypothesis is tested that intergenerational differences, or gaps, in acculturation between parents and adolescent children produce family-based acculturation conflicts. The intergenerational differences were assessed using the linear acculturation scale with both parents and children, then calculating the differential across these two observations at Time 1 and Time 3. This allowed a comparison of low, bicultural, and high-acculturation parent–child dyad effects on acculturation conflicts in instances where they had acculturation gaps and when they did not. The findings are consistent with theory. Intergenerational acculturation gaps are associated with higher levels of adolescent acculturation conflicts, with the highest levels of conflicts reported among dyads where the acculturation

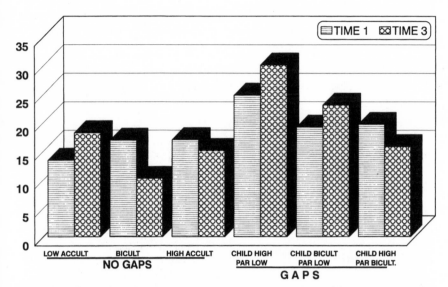

Figure 6.1. Effects of acculturation gaps on acculturation conflicts. Time 1 contrasts: child high/parent low significantly different from low acculturation at $p < .05$. Time 3 contrasts: child high/parent low significantly different from all no-gaps groups and child high/parent bicultural at $p < .01$.

level of adolescents is high and that of parents is low. These "maximum gap" dyads had the highest rate of adolescent acculturation conflicts at Time 1, and these increased even more by Time 3 as the adolescents matured. By Time 3 the "maximum gap" group was statistically different from all three "no gap" groups, as well as the groups with gaps where the child was high in acculturation, and the parent was bicultural. Few differences are evident in the "no gap" dyads. The hypothesis is confirmed that intergenerational acculturation differentials increase family conflicts.

In Figure 6.2 we tested the hypothesis that intergenerational gaps in acculturation are associated with higher drug use at Time 3. Using the same logic for comparing dyads as found in Figure 6.1, we profiled the prevalence rates for distinct classes of drugs. Drug use is least likely to be reported by parent–adolescent dyads when both are low in acculturation and there is no gap. Another dyad low in all types of adolescent drug use is a bicultural child and a parent low in acculturation. However, all other dyads are similar, regardless of whether there are intergenerational gaps or not. Specifically, the bicultural and high-acculturation dyad (no gap) has about the same prevalence of drug use as the high-acculturation adolescent–low-acculturation parent dyad (high gap). These findings make tenuous the inference that family conflicts lead to drug use in the context of intergenerational differences. Rather, our data suggest that acculturation of either

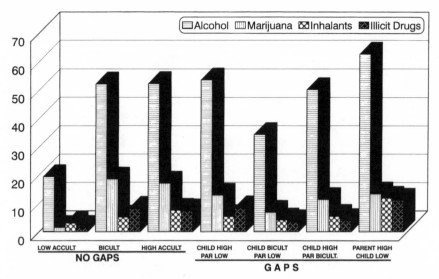

Figure 6.2. Relationship between acculturation gaps and substance use during Time 3. Alcohol: low acculturation different from bicultural, high acculturation, child high/parent low, and child high/parent bicultural at $p < .001$. Marijuana: low acculturation different from bicultural, high acculturation, child high/parent low, and child high/parent bicultural at $p < .01$. Illicit drugs: low acculturation different from child high/parent low at $p < .05$.

parent or child increases the likelihood of adolescent drug use. However, this does not preclude the possibility that over a longer period of time the conflicts resulting from the gaps could lead to problems associated with drug use. Finally, it is noteworthy that inhalant use was not affected by acculturation level.

Hispanics are believed to be very family oriented, with strong attachment and value commitment to family pride (*orgullo*) and respect (*respeto*) (Keefe & Padilla, 1987; Vega, 1990). Therefore, it is logically consistent that if conflicts result from acculturation differences, they will eventually wear down family members and degrade the quality of family life, thus creating negative feelings in the adolescent that may lead to rejection of family authority. This is very similar to the central mechanisms found in the self-esteem enhancement model of Kaplan and colleagues (Kaplan, Martin, & Johnson, 1986; Kaplan, Vega, Johnson, & Bailey, 1987; Vega et al., 1996). Personal distress brought on by parental disapproval produces either a change toward approved behavior or the development of a disposition to deviance. Over time this disposition will lead the adolescent toward association with deviant peers, and in this social context drug experimentation is experienced. Therefore, the deficiency of the Szapocznik explanation of Hispanic adolescent drug use resulting from intergenerational differences is the failure of the model to specify the additional mechanisms that must be in place. These mechanisms (i.e., intermediary variables) are complex and multidirectional and implicate a number of personal and social factors that unfold over the course of adolescence. Intergenerational acculturation differences are an important starting point for understanding communication problems in Hispanic families. However, it is very consequential to recognize that the bulk of drug use occurring during early adolescence cannot be explained by this model. This is because there are intermediary variables absent in this model, and because acculturation has divergent outcomes in foreign-born and U.S.-born adolescents due to the differences in their acculturation exposures, and the meaning of those exposures, during adolescent development. Indeed, as shown in Table 6.1, the highest rates of U.S.-born Hispanic drug use occur when the adolescent is of low acculturation.

These analyses are illuminating and point out the need for multivariate empirical models that account for important differences between foreign-born and U.S.-born adolescents. A model is proposed in order to provide incremental steps in understanding the complex effects of acculturation and acculturative stress on Hispanic adolescent drug use. We present an elaboration of the esteem enhancement model of adolescent drug use that locates the effects of acculturative stressors as antecedent to all other model variables in a self-rejection explanation of adolescent drug use.

This model is a logical extension of the empirical studies that we have conducted. Since the effects of family acculturation conflicts on drug use appear to be mostly indirect, and mediated by other factors, we use data collected at three data points to test causal relationships between explanatory variables in the context of acculturation stress.

Acculturative Stress, Self-Derogation, and Adolescent Drug Use

In a previous study we replicated the self-esteem enhancement model of Kaplan using the total data base from our Miami surveys (Vega et al., 1996). Furthermore, it was evident from the outset of this research that the Kaplan model was a very useful tool for exploring the effects of acculturative stress on personal distress, deviance, and drug use. As noted in citations of our earlier research, acculturative stress has been linked to the erosion of protective factors and to increased risk of delinquency and drug use. It is a logical extension of this work to seek the social psychological mechanisms that are triggered by acculturative stress. Negative and stressful experiences occurring in early adolescence provide a *prima facie* basis for the belief that personal distress and negative self-worth will be forthcoming. The acculturative stressors we used in this study included those that reflected negative social encounters of self, family, and friends, reported as problems resulting from either cultural or linguistic differences. In addition, we also included stressors involving intergenerational family acculturation conflicts, and perceptions of perceived discrimination attributed to being Hispanic. This spectrum of acculturative stress experiences, we believe, form a robust predictor of self-rejection, a key factor in numerous theories of personal and subcultural deviancy. This construct is represented in the model as "acculturation stress." The scales measuring acculturation stress are presented in the Appendix.

Most adolescent drug researchers concur that the pathways to drug use are diverse and multiple, and are adequately captured by the general theory of deviance that has emerged from the complementary work of numerous writers over the past 70 years. These theories are cast in social psychological modes of explanation that depict the adjustments of adolescents to specific environmental conditions. Our use of acculturative stress in this context is central to the key propositions of the general theory of deviance. Structured strain theory rests on the assumption of disjunctures between material artifacts and desired lifestyles, on the one hand, and the unequal access to these symbols of social status, on the other (Merton, 1938). The context of structured strain theory is a limited opportunity structure (Cloward & Ohlin, 1960), low social control due to weakened social institutions, inconsistent socialization, and the availability of adolescent and adult subculturals supporting deviant behaviors (Jessor & Jessor, 1977). Numerous theories have described how, under these conditions, deviant behavior can become an adaptive response and, within a reinforcing social context, can then be reframed as normative behavior (Becker, 1963; Reckless, 1967; Reckless et al., 1956). The differential association theory of Sutherland (1939) is the fundamental postulation of how social contexts replete with deviant subcultures operate to provide social learning opportunities and transform the basis for evaluating acceptable behavior. Once adolescents become attitudinally disposed toward deviance, their self-image may change in response to the negative sanctioning they receive from authority figures, thus weakening their commitment to conventional values and institutions and embedding them in deviant subcultures (Lemert, 1951).

From the outset, deviancy theorists have recognized the primary role of social psychological mechanisms in the decision-making process of adolescents in their struggle with conventional identity formation and adherence to socially approved conduct (Kaplan, 1975; Wells & Rankin, 1983). There was a need to depict a process with discernable stages that captured the internal conflicts, social pressures, and contested allegiance that adolescents experience and struggle to resolve and psychologically integrate. At the core of this process is the maintenance of an acceptable self-image, which is a tenuous, dynamic, and highly subjective entity. Biological and social imperatives during early adolescence are channeling individuals into learning new social roles, which is itself a stressful situation. Adolescents, especially American adolescents, are supported in experimenting with behaviors and testing the limits of acceptable behaviors. This stage of identity development involves ethnic identity formation and the internalization of images regarding ethnic group acceptability or social rejection, powerlessness, and boundary maintenance based on social class and skin color. Family social support, socialization into conforming behaviors, and forms of social control are critically important for adolescents during this period. Therefore, there are multiple sources for self-esteem enhancement or derogation, and adolescents' feelings about themselves are a product of the interaction of these influences.

The self-esteem enhancement model of Kaplan (1975) is based on a central behavioral premise. Adolescents will seek acceptance and approval for their behavior. Therefore, when their behavior is offensive to parents or teachers, it will provoke their negative sanctions and provoke psychological distress in the adolescent. The psychological distress will produce feelings of self-rejection, and these feelings must be resolved. The need to resolve this distress represents a contingency in the model. The adolescent can either change behavior in conformity with the expectations of parents or teachers, thus mitigating feelings of self-rejection, or take the opposite path of "rejecting the rejecters." However, this decision may involve very strong emotions and conflicts. Some adolescents may find themselves unable to change offensive behavior because they are receiving compensatory rewards from it. Deviant behavior may bring them a stature and social status among peers that may be unattainable in other ways, at least in the context of their present attitudes and beliefs. There may be poor communication and such an emotional breach with parents or teachers that winning their approval no longer seems a feasible or attractive alternative.

If adolescents who experience the distress of self-rejection cannot, or will not, assuage the sources of derogation by changing offensive behavior, then their adjustment may propel them toward withdrawing their emotional dependence on these sources of derogation, and more fully developing a disposition to deviance. Their deviant self-image is maturing, often reinforced by further negative sanctions and a drifting into deviant peer groups that will provide social reinforcement for deviant attitudes and a social context for learning or exhibiting specific forms of socially disapproved behavior such as drug use. In Kaplan's various iterations of his model with other colleagues (Kaplan & Fukurai, 1992; Kaplan & Johnson, 1991; Kaplan, Johnson, & Bailey, 1986, 1987, 1988b; Kaplan, Martin, & Johnson, 1986), he has used a three-wave longitudinal model covering early to midadolescence to empirically demonstrate the causal effects of Time 1 self-rejection on Time 2 disposition to deviance, negative social sanctions, and deviant or drug-using peers, and on Time 3 drug use (or deviant behavior). In his prediction of later drug use, Time 1 drug use was used as a control variable in the model. We elaborated the model by substituting drug-caused problems for negative social sanctions at Time 2, because we believed it was more specific for predicting drug use. We found similar, acceptable, statistical qualities in comparing path parameters between our model and Kaplan's work (Vega et al., 1996) using our full sample of adolescents. Below we proceed with a further elaboration of the model by the inclusion at Time 1 of the acculturative stress factor. Summarizing our logic, acculturative stress should be an important source of self-rejection based on conflicts and conduct problems at home and school (Vega et al., 1995), and presumes that the antecedent conditions are in place to produce structured strain effects on Hispanic adolescents.

Figure 6.3 presents the findings from the three-wave longitudinal model using a latent variable, structural equation analysis that included all Hispanic adolescents. The dependent variable at Time 3 is frequency of alcohol and marijuana use. As in our previous work, we used drug caused problems instead of negative social sanctions. The adjusted goodness of fit was adequate, if not optimal (.865), with a division of the chi-square over degrees of freedom of 4.51. In reviewing the structural model, all path coefficients are significant. The Time 1 path of acculturative stress to self-rejection is operating as anticipated by theory, with a standardized coefficient of .711, and there is an additional Time 1 path to Time 2 disposition to deviance with a coefficient of .247. Less important paths were estimated to Time 1 and Time 3 drug use, and Time 2 peer drug use. The strongest R^2 was for drug use among peers (.652). The reason for this was the strong coefficients from drug-caused problems and disposition to deviance. Another strong R^2 was for self-rejection (.512), which was caused by acculturation stress. This finding indicates

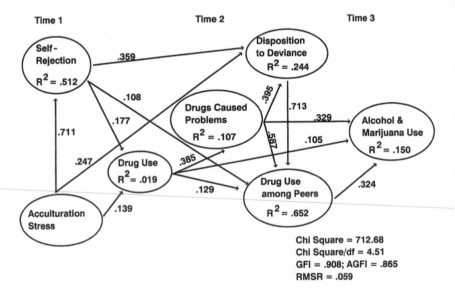

Figure 6.3. The esteem enhancement model in the context of acculturation stress for Hispanic adolescent males. GFI, goodness of fit; AGFI, adjusted goodness of fit; RMSR, root mean squared residual.

that the stressors associated with the acculturation process have powerful influences on self-concept among early adolescents. Furthermore, it is noteworthy that a large proportion of the explained variance for disposition to deviance derives directly from acculturation stress, as well as indirectly through self-rejection. These results indicate that at this early stage of adolescence acculturation stress has its strongest effects on self-derogation and disposition to deviance, thus explaining the relatively low proportion of variance explained for the dependent variable of alcohol and marijuana use. However, we suspect that with maturation, the strength of these associations to drug use will increase. This supposition will be tested in followup surveys with the panel.

These results provide evidence confirming a theoretical relationship that is central to our work on acculturation, deviance, and drug use. Acculturative stress experienced during early adolescence influences identity formation and self-esteem, then, operating through temporally dispersed mediating variables, increased later drug use. Acculturative stress increased personal distress and, over time, had direct and indirect effects (through T-1 self-rejection, T-1 drugs and T-2 drug-caused problems) on T-2 disposition to deviance. In turn, T-2 disposition to deviance has an important coefficient (.713) to T-2 peer drug use. Both drug-caused problems and peer drug use have the hypothesized relationships (.329 and .324, respectively) to T-3 drug use.

Our findings put into perspective several studies reported in the literature (Brynner, O'Malley, & Bachman, 1981; McCarthy & Hoge, 1984; Wells & Rankin, 1983) that failed to find any longitudinal effects of self-esteem on drug use (Petraitis et al., 1995). Our results suggest that acculturative stress contributes to low self-esteem and, in turn, that both factors have mediated relationships to later adolescent drug use. As Kaplan has noted, self-esteem measured globally incorporates external sources of derogation, which is a different construct than the more narrowly construed intrapsychic definition of self-esteem that is closer to demoralization. Although low self-esteem can be reversed and does not necessarily lead to later drug use, often a specific set of developmental and environmental conditions co-occur in the course of Hispanic adolescent development that leads to drug use or even frequent drug use in later years as a result of these early, unremitted cultural conflicts and adjustment problems.

Conclusion

The study of acculturation and acculturative stress effects on adolescent drug use is in its formative stages. Few research studies have been designed and conducted that were specifically intended to address etiologic issues. Therefore, we are left to conjecture about the interpretation and importance of statistical relationships between acculturation and drug use found in a few large cross-sectional studies of Hispanic adults. We know even less about acculturative stress and drug use. There has been a steady growth of research on the subject of acculturative stress. Most of it is theoretical, and recently a few studies have actually tested hypotheses about the correlates of acculturative stress, and its effects on personal distress. This chapter was conceived as a contribution to this literature and represents perhaps the only study to test hypothesized relationships using longitudinal data.

As we have shown, there are two important developments in the field at the present time. One is the growing sophistication in the conceptualization and measurement of acculturation and acculturative stress in social psychological studies. This is important because it simultaneously provides instrumentation for future research and analytical models for testing and elaboration. The second is the fast-growing research literature on social adjustment of immigrant children and families, reflected in the sociological and education literatures. Regrettably, this second literature has been partitioned from the first one. Great benefit would come from synthesis of these literatures because the sociological ideas are needed to provide a comparative framework for multigroup and multicontext research in the drug field. An additional advantage of merging these literatures is their fundamental compatibility with the general deviance and stress process literatures.

While we believe that the elaboration of the self-esteem enhancement model described above is very useful in explaining a fundamental set of developmental relationships that can increase the likelihood of Hispanic adolescent drug use, we cannot put aside the powerful observations of many researchers about family factors and drug use. As noted above, the intergenerational gap model of drug use is not satisfying, because it does not meet the basic standards of empirical validation and fails to specify intermediary variables and their temporal associations as is better demonstrated in the self-esteem enhancement model. Nevertheless, we believe intergenerational factors are very important because both parents and children are proceeding through the process of acculturation and experiencing acculturative stressors, and their mutually conditioned perceptions and behaviors will ultimately affect adolescent drug use (Gil & Vega, 1996). Therefore, researchers should test models that include both parental and child information about acculturation and acculturative stress and determine how these are related to other variables that increase risk, such as peer drug use, or provide protective effects, such as family social support. The importance of family factors is not new; it is axiomatic in the drug research literature that parental drug use, for example, increases adolescent drug use. Similarly, it is believed that the type of socialization about drug use provided by parents is critical for controlling early drug experimentation. Clear, unambiguous instruction about the unacceptableness of drug use is important for inhibiting adolescent drug experimentation.

Because the core construct we employ, acculturative stress, is rooted in stress process theory (Pearlin, Lieberman, Menaghan, & Mullen, 1981; Pearlin & Schooler, 1978; Thoits, 1985; Turner, Wheaton, & Lloyd, 1995; Warheit, 1979), it would be useful to summarize the assumptions implicit in our use of the concept. Chronic strains are an important source of negative outcomes on health behaviors and poor mental health. Environmental factors and interpersonal experiences occasioned in the process of cultural adjustment and social incorporation can increase perceived social stress. For example, being in an environment of limited opportunity, occupying unfavorable social statuses, and receiving negative information about self-worth in the context of a denigrated ethnic group membership are sources of systematic strain, especially during early adolescence when issues of social status, social definitions of biological characteristics, and ethnic group identification influence the identity construction process. However, these strains are important for adults as well, and Hispanic households serve as a social context for interpreting intercultural experiences. Although strains are potentially deleterious and may produce multiple negative health outcomes (Aneshensel, 1992; Aneshensel, Rutter, & Lachenbruch, 1991), the basic mechanism mediating the effects of strains on health and health-related behaviors are coping behaviors and personal resources. Chief among these for Hispanic adolescents is the family as a support system. Persistent strains are pernicious in their effects only when personal resources are overwhelmed and coping responses prove inadequate (Lazarus & Launier, 1978). In our research we have found that familism is the key construct mediating acculturative strains for both parents and adolescents. Hypothetically, familism should substantially reduce the effects of acculturation and acculturative strains on drug use. However, when familism is not present as a protective factor, especially among immigrant adolescents, this will serve as an additional stressor, and the risk of drug use is greatly increased. Acculturation influences drug use in two ways: by providing countersocialization to the antidrug norms of Hispanic culture, and by its complex effects on acculturative stress. Most contemporary models of acculturative stress effects have been too simplistic in their assumptions because they failed to take into account differences among immigrants and native-born Hispanics in familism, exposure to acculturative stressors, and the effects of those exposures.

Our operational assumption is that the social incorporation experiences of families, and their "segmented" socialization into American society, will produce differential levels of strain and exposures to social contexts of drug use behaviors. Therefore, intergenerational acculturation and acculturative stress factors operate in conjunction with social learning factors, and reinforce them (Vega, Zimmerman et al., 1997). The combined effects of these factors occur longitudinally. We believe intergenerational models are most useful for assessing the processes described and for future hypothesis generation about the selective effects of acculturation and acculturative stress variables on other model factors. Since we have already confirmed the powerful relationship of acculturative stress to key factors in the self-esteem enhancement model, especially to self-rejection, the most important linkage is made from stress theory to general deviance theory.

The next generation of research should demonstrate how social contexts moderate acculturative stress levels among Hispanic adolescents. The preliminary evidence that this is occurring is persuasive. Within some Hispanic ethnic groups, self-selected ethnic labels have become meaningful descriptors of personal attitudes and behaviors (Rumbaut, 1995). The notion of segmented assimilation assumes that three factors—color, location, and the ladders of opportunity—mediate the social adjustment of immigrant groups and personal adjustment of individuals (Portes, 1995). Color prejudice will create potential barriers to social acceptance, location provides a social context and mechanisms for regulating relationships between cultural groups, and the availability of ladders of opportunity facilitates economic incorporation. Therefore, depending on the match between cultural groups and environments, intergroup contact in American urban settings can lead to eventual integration, assimilation into underclass life in ethnic ghettos, or formation of ethnic enclaves that provide alternative channels for preservation of cultural forms and economic advancement among ethnic groups who have partially acculturated but sustain important cultural values and beliefs through group solidarity and social organizations.

Fordham and Ogbu (1987) have introduced the concept of involuntary minority status to describe adolescents who are embedded in social environments that are historically, and currently, oppressive for individuals with their specific racial and ethnic traits. This situation is also associated with adolescent oppositional identity formation and underclass status. Berry and his colleagues (1995) have also conceptualized acculturation as having multiple potential outcomes depending on environmental characteristics, including integration, separation, assimilation, and "marginalized," the latter being similar to involuntary minority status. The time is at hand for systematic research to compare the group- and individual-level effects of these diverse social contexts among different Hispanic ethnic groups and determine to what extent processes of marginalization, cultural conflicts, and limited opportunity are structuring the social and cultural adjustment of Hispanic adolescents in a consistent and predictable fashion, and to identify environmental factors that are protective in decreasing the likelihood of initial and persistent drug use or lessening the prospects that progression to drug-using lifestyles will occur.

7

Developmental Patterns of African American Adolescent Drug Use

Frank Biafora and Rick Zimmerman

Introduction

The Problems of Drug Use in African American Communities

Drug use continues to have a pervasive impact on American society, affecting all members directly or indirectly. The abuse of substances such as tobacco, alcohol, and illicit drugs has damaging short- and long-term consequences for both the individual and society. Some of the more obvious effects include excess morbidity and mortality, rising health care costs, decreased labor productivity, declining family stability, increased drug-related crime, and criminal justice–related expenses. Among the greatest costs of all, however, include the sustained loss of the human potential and the deterioration of the very social fabric that guides and holds together our nation's communities.

While the consequences of substance use and abuse in the United States are immense, the impact of drugs on African Americans in recent years has been particularly devastating. Evidence of this has been captured in a number of ambitious regional and national clinical and institutional studies designed to monitor the social and health consequences associated with substance abuse in the population. One example includes the Drug Abuse Warning Network (DAWN) of the National Institute on Drug Abuse (NIDA, 1988). One important function of DAWN is to monitor annual drug-related emergency room cases and drug-related deaths. Even though African Americans represent 12% of the population in the United States (U.S. Bureau of the Census, 1992), they accounted for 39% of the 160,170 drug abuse–related emergency room cases reported to DAWN. Of these cases, the most commonly abused drug is cocaine (57%), and 40% of admissions were of persons between the ages of 20 and 29 years. Of the 6,560 drug abuse–related deaths reported to DAWN by medical examiners, 30% were African American, an overrepresentation of about 2.5 their representation in the general population.

Reports from the Centers for Disease Control (CDC, 1989) also contribute to our knowledge of the issues. According to the CDC, the spread of HIV/AIDS due to intravenous (IV) drug use and the sex-for-drugs trade continues to be a severe problem facing African Americans. Currently, African Americans account for approximately 27% of all people with AIDS in the United States. Primary IV drug use is related to nearly half of these cases. Secondary transmission, that is, heterosexual contact with an IV drug using partner, is perhaps even more significant, as African Americans account for more than half of all AIDS cases who were heterosexual partners of IV drug users (CDC, 1989).

According to a report by the Task Force on African American and Minority Health (U.S. Department of Health and Human Services, 1985), drug use (i.e., inclusive of alcohol, tobacco, and illicit drugs) is one of the leading factors contributing to the significant 6-year gap in life expectancy that currently exists between African Americans and White Americans. Prior to World War II, reports on the rates of acute and chronic alcohol-related diseases among African Americans were typically lower than or similar to those of Whites (Ronan, 1986). Since that time, however, these rates have increased to near epidemic proportions (Beatty, 1994). Today, relative to Whites, African Americans are at higher risk for a variety of drug-related diseases such as alcoholic fatty liver, hepatitis, liver cirrhosis, heart disease, and cancers of the mouth, larynx, tongue, esophagus, and lungs (Jaynes & Williams, 1989). African Americans are also significantly more likely to experience a wide array of public health problems that are inextricably intertwined with drug and alcohol use, including drug-related injuries, criminal victimization and homicide (Gary, 1983).

Moreover, perinatal substance use has also been identified as a critical area of concern in the African American community (Ernest & Sokol, 1987; Ronan, 1986; Vega, Kolody, Porter, & Noble, 1997). Part of this may be accounted for by one of the more widely reported and consistent findings in the research literature on substance use that demonstrates that, while African American females are significantly more likely to report abstinence than White females, a greater proportion of African American females tend to report heavier drinking patterns than White females (Cahalan et al., 1969; Warheit & Auth, 1985). Cahalan and his colleagues found "two worlds" of orientation toward alcohol use among African American women. While a comparable percentage (21%) of heavy drinking existed among African American and White men, the rate of heavy drinking was three times higher for African American women (11%) than for White women (4%).

There exists no single explanatory framework for interpreting African Americans' experience with substance use or the related problems associated with use and abuse. The compounded issues of excess poverty, chronic unemployment, spatial isolation, and limited access to quality health care are typically cited as primary social structural correlates (Barr, Farrell, Barnes, & Welte, 1993). The multiplicity of these factors have led some experts to predict that substance abuse is and will continue to be a leading public health issue within the U.S. African American community (U.S. Department of Health and Human Services [USDHHS], 1993). Moreover, there is growing concern that if conditions in American inner cities worsen, the potential for drug-related problems may reach catastrophic proportions (USDHHS, 1985).

African American Youth and Drugs

Much of our current knowledge of the issues associated with substance use can be attributed to a fairly large and growing body of literature on African American adult populations, coupled with an emerging and corresponding literature concerning drug treatment among minority adults. Despite a commitment by several agencies within the federal government to maintain current funding for drug research projects that are inclusive of younger members of society, today there exists only a modest understanding of the nature of alcohol and other drug use among African American adolescents. Popular images and common stereotypes of African American youth have become commonplace and have tended to overshadow the limited empirical research that does exist.

While one might expect the scientific literature to be saturated with reference to substance use among African American youth, an extensive literature review revealed this was not the case. To date, limited epidemiological data exist that describe the prevalence and patterns of drug use among this group. Even less is known regarding the etiology of drug use among African American youth. This is due, in part, to methodological shortcomings that have impeded a great deal of comparative drug research in the past. Nonrepresentative samples, samples of persons in treatment, in jail, or in housing projects, or samples with too few African Americans to yield generalizable findings have been all too common.

A further reason for the paucity of knowledge regarding the predictors of African American drug use has been the result of a near absence of theory development in this area (Dawkins, 1996; Herd, 1987). To date, researchers have tended to draw on traditional sociological theories and models that view drug use either as part and parcel of general delinquency or as a form of pathology stemming from a state of social disorganization within the African American community. One common and limiting element of these theories has been their overemphasis on social structural forces to the neglect of psychosocial, cultural, and ethnic factors. Broader economic and structurally based factors may be related to the observed drinking and drug-taking behaviors among African Americans. However, interpretations of these factors have often led to what is commonly referred to in the sociological literature as the ecological fallacy, that is, making assertions about individual behaviors based on the examination of structural factors.

A third reason for this limited research may be related to the ubiquitous stereotypes associated with problems facing African Americans. Popular images of African American males getting drunk at the corner carry-out, the inner-city minority drug dealer, and violent youth gangs are very powerful and tend to overshadow the limited research that does exist. When stripped of stereotypes and media headlines, however, a very interesting picture of the epidemiology of African American early adolescent drug use emerges. When ethnicity and age are considered simultaneously, as they are in this 3-year panel study, a surprising picture of drug patterns surfaces. In point of fact, the data presented in Chapter 3 demonstrates that during the first and second years of the study, African American boys were significantly less likely than Hispanics or White non-Hispanic boys to smoke cigarettes, drink alcohol, or use marijuana or other illicit drugs (Warheit et al., 1995). This presents somewhat of a paradox when one considers that, relative to other ethnic groups, African American adults are at significantly higher risk for experiencing a disproportionate share of the negative health outcomes of substance abuse. By year 3 (i.e., eighth or ninth grade), however, our data showed important changes in the patterning of drug use as African Americans began to catch up to the lifetime usage levels of their White and Hispanic counterparts.

With respect to explaining the etiology of African American early adolescent drug use, our research over the past 5 years has been met with moderate success, and it has provided us with many more questions than answers. Evidence of this was demonstrated early on in one of our first attempts to build comparative risk factor models of experimental and regular drug use (Vega, Zimmerman, et al., 1993). While these risk factors, culled from current sociological and social psychological theory, differentiated between White and Hispanic lifetime users and nonusers of alcohol and marijuana, these same factors were considerably less predictive of African American use, with few exceptions. This was despite the finding that African Americans were significantly more exposed to the subset of risk factors under scrutiny. As it turns out, our research is not alone in this regard as other scholars have also reported puzzling findings that all but beg for researchers to huddle up and go back to the proverbial drawing board (Bachman et al., 1991). As Dawkins (1996) suggests, such obvious ethnic differences may indicate that the social and cultural contexts and conditions under which substance use occurs within African American populations are more important than simple African American–White comparisons in explaining outcomes of adverse consequences. We follow a similar line of thought in this research, arguing that early African American drug use and drug experimentation is patterned, normative behavior, and generally takes place within what Landrine and Klonoff (1996) remind us *is* an African American "culture" of drug use. This point is emphasized because

African Americans are often described as a racial group rather than an ethnic group with a distinctive culture. African American children acquire and participate in their own unique culture as well as the dominant European/Anglo American culture. Like the other Hispanic groups discussed throughout this text, African Americans also take part in a natural process of acculturation through which messages, symbols, and unique traditions are transmitted from generation to generation. Moreover, it is through this process that African American children acquire the prescriptions and proscriptions for the use, sale, and trade of drugs. We argue, along the same lines as Herd (1990), that gaining access to a more fruitful understanding of the correlates and processes of African American behaviors such as drug use requires a culturally sensitive eye and necessitates an in-depth exploration into this unique sociohistorical and sociocultural context.

Miami's African American Community

While reviewing the findings in this chapter we encourage readers to keep in mind some important and relevant points about the social and historical landscape of the study site. As discussed in Chapter 2, Miami has a long and unique history, one that in many ways has never before been experienced by an American city. For many years its familiar profile was that of a semitropical playground with entrenched southern-style race relations (Grenier & Stepick, 1992). Over the last quarter of a century, however, the established cultural venue of Miami has been radically transformed to meet the incredible challenges of the city. Massive immigration of persons of Hispanic origin and a corresponding out-migration of native Whites have characterized and dominated recent census counts.

The transformation from an ethnic community dictated by familiar Protestant norms, values, and traditions of the "Old South" to one that now resembles a cultural kaleidoscope provides particularly interesting and important contextual information for research into social deviance in general and drug use specifically. Also important from a sociological position for interpreting the nature of drugs within African American communities is the history of local rioting and civil unrest that has characterized metropolitan Miami over the last quarter century. Whether directly provoked or simply contextual, racial mistrust among young African Americans toward other ethnic groups is common (Biafora, Warheit, et al., 1993), and it has been shown to relate to law breaking and a willingness to engage in illegal acts (Taylor, Biafora, Warheit, & Gil, 1994).

The diversity among Miami's African American populations is itself particularly noteworthy and has been both a source of cultural excitement as well as a source of economic and political antagonism among the various dominant African American groups. Today Miami is home to several distinct groups that, when described in the aggregate, define themselves, or are socially defined as, "African

American." By far, the largest segment of Miami's African American population, consisting of over 300,000, is African American and traces its roots to West Africa. Still, several other groups of African Americans reside in the Miami area that are of Afro-Caribbean, Afro-Latin, Afro-Indian, Afro-European, and other descents. As a result of this heterogeneity, any effort to characterize the behavior of "African American" adolescents in Miami provides unique and difficult challenges. For purposes of this chapter, only those students who identified themselves as Black and not Hispanic, and who said they were born neither in Haiti nor on any other Caribbean island, were considered African American and included in the analyses presented in this chapter.

Despite its unique cultural history and heterogeneity of ethnicities, Miami is plagued with many of the same social and economic ills faced by most other postindustrial urban centers throughout the country. And as in most of these urban areas the ubiquitous challenges and problems are magnified if one is African American (Grenier & Stepick, 1992). As an illustration of the social and economic conditions facing African Americans in South Florida, consider the following census data for one of Miami's oldest and well known neighborhoods, Overtown. Referred to by many names, including Washington Heights and Culmer, during its more economically prosperous years, Overtown today is marked by very high unemployment (23%), low labor force participation (43%), low median income ($9,479), high dependence on public assistance (33%), and high percentage of single-parent, female-headed households (73%) (Overtown Neighborhood Partnerships, 1995). Fifty-nine percent of Overtown's children under 18 live below the poverty level and in single-parent, female-headed households. For comparative purposes, census data for all of Dade County demonstrate a 7.7% unemployment rate, 64.4% labor force participation rate, $26,909 median income, 10.0% dependence on public assistance, 26.3% female-headed households, and 13.7% under 18 living in poverty.

In the face of these economic stresses young African Americans growing up in communities like Overtown are surrounded by messages presented by corporate America of the elegance, power, and sensuality provided by alcohol. The pressures to consume alcohol are ubiquitous and have been marketed through athletics and celebrations of Black History. In *Marketing Booze to Blacks*, Hacker and his colleagues (Hacker, Collins, & Jacobson, 1987) describe how everything from schoolyard basketball tournaments to the annual meeting of the Congressional Black Caucus Foundation is sponsored by beer and liquor companies.

Data collected from the African American adolescents in our study and from a sample of their parents give us a snapshot of the social conditions of African American families in greater Miami from 1987 to 1990. During the first year of the study African American students' parents averaged 12.6 years of education, compared with 14.2 for Whites, 12.5 for Haitians, and 12.8 for other Caribbean Blacks. Average household income was $24,786 for African Americans, compared with $50,504 for Whites, $21,858 for Haitians, and $28,262 for other Caribbean Blacks. African Americans were least likely to be living with both mother and father (42.1% compared with 74% for Whites, and 53% for Caribbean Blacks), and were most likely to be living with mother only (29.9% compared with 11.7% of Whites and 22% of Caribbean Blacks) or with mother and other adults (18.1% compared with 9.2% for Whites and 18% for Caribbean Blacks). They were also most likely to say that they experienced "too much violence in their neighborhood," with 22% of African Americans saying this was "very true or often true," as compared with 6% for Whites, 14% for Haitians, and 10% for other Caribbean Blacks.

Epidemiology of Early African American Adolescent Drug Use Based on Findings from the Study Presented in This Book

Over the last two decades a number of large-scale epidemiological studies at both national and regional levels have been designed to monitor trends and patterns of drug use among adolescents in the general population. These studies were in response to the lack of adequate research on the extent of drug use in nonclinical populations and the limited theoretical understanding that existed with respect to the antecedents for drug experimentation, continuation, and cessation.

Two of the most widely known national studies to emerge in recent years to address these issues include the Monitoring the Future project, an annual survey of nationally representative samples of eighth- and twelfth-grade students (Johnston, Bachman, & O'Malley, 1984; Johnston, O'Malley, & Bachman, 1991), and the National Household Survey on Drug Abuse, a repeated cross-sectional household survey of persons 12 years and older (National Institute on Drug Abuse [NIDA], 1992). In addition to these important projects, other methodologically rigorous studies have been designed and conducted to obtain data suitable for making cross-cultural drug use comparisons and to identify specific sociocultural factors associated with these patterns (Herd, 1990; Oetting & Beauvais, 1991). Findings generated from these survey projects have also been supplemented in recent years by important institutional tracking systems capable of monitoring the health and social casualties of drug use across the country (USDHHS, 1985). Among these include the previously described DAWN project (NIDA, 1992) and the Drug Use Forecasting (DUF) of the National Institute of Justice (NIJ, 1992), which keeps track of drug use among arrestees in the criminal justice system.

Findings from self-report studies of school or general population samples consistently demonstrate that the lifetime prevalence of drug use is actually lower among African American early adolescents than most all other ethnic groups

(Bachman et al., 1991; Johnston et al., 1991; Kandel, Davies, & Davis, 1990; Maddahian et al., 1986).

When looking at average lifetime prevalences the ethnic patterns are fairly clear and consistent; Native American youth have the highest recorded prevalence rates, and Asian Americans have the lowest. African Americans have rates above Asians but below those found for Whites and Hispanics. Moreover, this general ethnic pattern holds for both males and females (Wallace & Bachman, 1991). With the exception of cocaine, Whites report higher rates of use than Hispanics. Studies that have reported differences between African American and White youth regarding specific drugs have also supported these findings. White youth smoke more cigarettes, have a higher prevalence of alcohol use and abuse patterns, and use marijuana and hard drugs more than African American adolescents (Landrine, Richardson, Klonoff, & Flay, 1994; Maddahian, et al., 1986; Warheit et al., 1995). Bachman and his colleagues (1991), in a longitudinal study of high school seniors from 1979 to 1989, also found that White non-Hispanic students use tobacco products more than African American students. This study found that the difference between African American and White cigarette smoking has become even greater since African American seniors' cigarette smoking from 1985 to 1989 decreased by two-thirds in comparison with the 1976–1979 time period.

The findings from our own longitudinal study in Miami, Florida, corroborate and extend the findings from studies of the general population and studies of high-risk nontreatment populations. As has already been shown in Chapter 3, African American sixth- and seventh-grade boys were significantly less likely to report lifetime use of licit drugs than either their White non-Hispanic counterparts or U.S.-born Hispanics. During our first year of the study (when students were in sixth or seventh grade), about one-third (31.5%) of the African Americans reported ever consuming alcohol, compared to 51.0% of the White non-Hispanics, 45.4% of the U.S.-born Latinos, and 35.0% of the immigrant Latinos. Even when the Hispanic immigrants and nonimmigrants were combined, with 40.2% reporting lifetime alcohol use, the African American prevalence was lower. The lower prevalences of alcohol use among African Americans persisted throughout the three waves of data collection during the middle school years (see Table 3.1). African Americans were also significantly less likely than these other groups to report drinking in the past month (see Table 3.3).

Rates of cigarette consumption followed these same general patterns as both U.S.-born and immigrant Hispanics and White non-Hispanics were nearly two and three times more likely than African Americans, respectively, to report ever smoking cigarettes by the sixth and seventh grades. At Time 3 of data collection, cigarette use among African Americans was lower than that of the other groups. Regular cigarette use was defined as smoking one pack or more per day. While this was relatively uncommon for all groups during the first data collection period, it increased dramatically by years 2 and 3 of the study, but again a much larger proportion of Hispanics and White non-Hispanics than African Americans reported regular use.

While the prevalence of lifetime cigarette and alcohol use demonstrated lower use of these "gateway" (Kandel, 1975) substances among African Americans during this developmental stage of their lives, the comparison of regular use and past month use is even more dramatic. These comparisons are based on the prevalence rates reported in Chapter 3. During the final wave of data collection, the ratios between the other three groups—U.S.-born Hispanics, foreign-born Hispanics, and White non-Hispanics—and African Americans for lifetime cigarette use were only 1.3, 1.2, and 1.4 to 1, respectively. However, the differences in regular cigarette use were much larger, with the regular use among White non-Hispanics being 6.6 times higher than that of African Americans; U.S.-born Hispanics were 7 times higher, and foreign-born Hispanics were 5.2 times higher.

The results with lifetime alcohol use and past month use during the third year of the study were also similar to the comparisons on cigarette use. For example, the prevalence of lifetime alcohol use during Time 3 among White non-Hispanics was 1.2 times higher than that of African Americans, compared with a difference that was 2.5 times higher for past month alcohol use. These findings indicate that although African Americans may be catching up on the lifetime prevalences of alcohol and cigarette use with the other groups (i.e., experimental use), at this stage in their lives "regular" use of these substances continues to be much lower than that of the other groups. This important issue of the catch-up effect of drug use among African American adolescents will be discussed in greater detail below.

Among females, lifetime cigarette and alcohol use is also lowest for the African American subgroup (see Table 5.2), and this is also the fact for heavier use of both substances during seventh and ninth grades.

Unlike the prevalence and patterns for alcohol and tobacco use, our data indicate relatively low prevalences across all ethnic groups for lifetime illicit drug use. Lifetime marijuana use was in the range of 1.8% to 2.1% for the three ethnic groups at Time 1, with no statistical differences among the groups. In addition, African Americans reported levels of inhalant use that were not statistically dissimilar from the White non-Hispanics or Hispanics at Time 1. Inhalant use ranged from 3.1% for the African Americans to 4.5% for the Whites, with Hispanic use one-half a percentage point lower than the Whites. It is important to note that when Hispanics are divided into those that are immigrant and those born in the United States, the prevalence of use among U.S.-born Hispanics (4.8%) is significantly higher than that of African Americans (3.1%). When we combined Time 1 lifetime use of cocaine, crack, angel dust (PCP), barbiturates, and tranquilizers into a composite other-drug-use measure, 1.8% of the African Americans reported ever using compared with 3.0% of the Hispanics and 2.7% of the Whites. Again, no statistically significant differences were found among the ethnic groups at Time 1.

The pattern of lower rates of substance use among African Americans is also reflected by the reported use of marijuana, other illicit drugs, and inhalants found in Chapter 3. By the end of middle school, marijuana use among African Americans is lower than that of Hispanics and White non-Hispanics, although there were no statistically significant differences in the comparison with foreign-born Hispanics, Similarly, past month marijuana use (Table 3.3) and scale scores on marijuana (Table 3.4) were lower for African Americans. The mean scores on a scale of lifetime marijuana use frequency (Table 3.4) were 1.0 for African Americans and double that for White non-Hispanics (2.1) as well as for U.S.-born Hispanics (2.0). Reported inhalant use was also much lower for African American adolescents. Lifetime inhalant use among White non-Hispanics and U.S-born Hispanics was more than double the prevalence for African Americans at the time of the third wave of the study. The difference between African Americans and immigrant Hispanics was not as large, but close to double (1.8 times lower), and statistically significant.

By the end of their middle school experience and the start of high school, African Americans were found to lag well behind Whites and Hispanics in terms of experimental illicit drug use. Looking first at the composite illicit drug use measure, African Americans were 2.5 times less likely to use than U.S.-born Hispanics ($p < .001$), 2.4 times less likely than foreign-born Hispanics ($p < .001$), and 3 times less likely to use than Whites ($p < .001$). The mean scores on a scale measuring illicit drug use were much lower among the African American group (Table 3.4).

Finally, the gender comparisons presented in Chapter 5 also show that among female adolescents illicit drug use is significantly lower among African Americans. For example, the ethnic differences in lifetime use of "other" drugs (Table 5.2) is even more dramatic among females, with the ratios of U.S.-born Hispanics, foreign-born Hispanics, and White non-Hispanics being 4.1, 3.8, and 3.5 to 1 for each group, respectively, when compared with African American females.

In summary, our study presents a picture in which African American early adolescents are less likely than other groups to have engaged in the use of cigarettes, alcohol, marijuana, inhalants, and other illicit drugs during the middle school years. The differences are even wider for frequent use than they are for lifetime use toward the end of middle school.

Another important factor to note with reference to the lower use of substances among African Americans is the fact that their rates of drug use are even lower than that of U.S. immigrants. This is a remarkable finding when we consider the fact that the African American adolescents have been exposed regularly to a society in which drug use and experimentation is much more common than in the nations from which most Hispanic adolescents and their families have immigrated. Broader societal influences on drug use have been demonstrated by the positive relationship between level of acculturation among Hispanic adolescents and increased drug use (see Chapter 6), as well as by the fact that U.S.-born Hispanics

have reported higher prevalences of substance use than their immigrant counterparts. Since African American adolescents report lower prevalences of substance
use than immigrant adolescents, we must consider the social factors and influences
in the African American community, as well as in African American family
networks, that may help to provide at least a temporary shielding mechanism for
early entry into drug use. The issues of protective factors for early African
American drug use will be explored below.

Ethnic Differences in Drug Use: Fact or Artifact

The finding that African American youth are less likely to experiment with
drugs or use them on a regular basis despite the overrepresentation of African
Americans in institutional samples has been referred to in the research literature
as a major paradox (Kandel, 1995). These findings are generally inconsistent with
numerous reports that indicate that African Americans, especially those in inner
cities, are arrested more often and are more often seen in emergency rooms for
drug-related problems than are Whites. Another paradox derives from the ethnic
distribution of other self-reported problem-related behaviors such as delinquency,
where African Americans are usually found to have disproportionate participation.

There is a long history of concern about the validity and reliability of self-
reported deviance. Thus, before concluding that there are real racial differences in
substance use among African American and other ethnic groups, it is appropriate
to consider possible alternative explanations for these differences. One of the most
difficult problems researchers face in trying to assess the validity of self-reports
of substance use is that there are seldom opportunities to collect "objective data,"
that is, concerning actual substance use, to which the self-reports can be compared.
As a result, a variety of indirect methods of assessing validity of self-reports have
been used.

In a summary article on this issue, Kandel (1995) presented three different
methodological explanations that may help to account for this ostensible inconsis-
tency. The first related to the possibility that self-reported drug use by African
Americans is subject to greater nondisclosure or intentional underreporting than
self-reports by other ethnic groups. One of the ways in which this question has
been studied is by analyses of inconsistent reporting patterns in repeated longitudinal panel designs. While such inconsistencies by African Americans in repeated
sample designs have been documented and reported in the literature (Johnston, et
al., 1984; Mensch & Kandel, 1988), it is unclear to what extent underreporting may
account for observed ethnic differences in drug use.

One plausible argument against the intentional underreporting proposition
could be developed from a consideration of findings from self-reported measures
of other types of social deviance. We know, for example, from our own analyses of

the project data that the prevalence of self-reported forms of minor and major delinquency is highest among the African American students in the sample. The delinquency indicators considered in the study ranged from misdemeanors such as petty larceny and trespassing to felonies such as breaking and entering and assault and battery. Taking a car for a ride without the owners permission was the only measure of delinquency considered in which the prevalence was lower for African Americans than Whites. As researchers, we can only conjecture why some African American students might be less willing to disclose information on drug use than on other delinquency behaviors.

In a further test of possible underreporting by African American respondents, we have compared African American and White respondents on self-reported honesty in completing the surveys. Our previous research (Zimmerman & Langer, 1995) has shown a strong relationship between self-reported honesty and discrepancies within surveys and across time for sensitive behaviors, including sexual behavior and substance use. We did find a considerably higher proportion of African American than White respondents in this study who indicated that they were "not very honest" or "not honest at all," 10.9% versus 1.2%. Further analysis indicated that this was related to cultural mistrust by African Americans, with a correlation of $-.28$; that is, those with greater mistrust of the majority group reported less honesty on the survey. After controlling for differences in self-reported honesty, however, prevalence of substance use for African Americans was still significantly lower than that for Whites in this study.

A second explanation for the paradox suggests that school-based surveys and household samples are unlikely to capture those who are at highest risk for drug use. Chronic absentees, dropouts, and incarcerated and homeless adolescents are among the groups most often cited. To account for dropouts, Johnston and O'Malley (1985) overweighted sample respondents who had completed questionnaires but said they were absent often, on the assumption that dropouts are in many ways similar to absentees. They concluded that prevalence rates for substance use would only have changed negligibly if the absentees had been present. We conducted a similar procedure for the data collected in the first wave of our project.

We used data from students in our sample who had been absent at an earlier questionnaire administration, but from whom data were later collected. By multiplying differences between these students and those present at the earlier occasion by 5, the differences between the racial groups remained very similar to those without weighting for absentees. Similarly, when additional weighting procedures were used to correct for students with low reading achievement scores and those enrolled in dropout prevention programs (both proportionately higher for African American than White students), differences in prevalence rates between the two racial groups did not change.

A third and possible explanation offered by Kandel (1995) suggests that this relationship between ethnicity and drug use may be spurious and other characteristics associated with these two factors account for the observed associations between them. Because of the strong relationship between social class and race in the United States, perhaps the most likely candidate variables to explain away the relationship between race and substance use are those related to social class: education, income, and occupation. The literature is quite consistent here, however: Even after controlling for possible differences in social class variables, African American adolescents report less substance use than White adolescents. We similarly collected data on parent education, income, and, in the third wave of data collection, household density, all indicators of social class. Statistically controlling for social class variables did not change the pattern of less substance use for African American than for White respondents. While self-reports of parent education, occupation, and income may not be particularly valid when given by 10- to 13-year-olds, when the parent-reported household income variable was used as the control variable, the results did not change.

Another kind of analysis that would validate differences in prevalence between the racial groups is parallel differences in variables that might be theoretically expected to relate to use: namely, attitudes and perceptions related to drug use. Bachman et al. (1991), in an analysis of data from the Monitoring the Future project, suggest that the substantial African American–White differences found in self-reports are "largely the result of genuine differences in drug use." Bachman found, for example, that African American seniors were more likely than White seniors to disapprove of drug use, and to perceive that drug use involves high risk. African American seniors were also more likely to report much less smoking, alcohol use, and illicit drug use by friends. Our data also show that Whites reported more cigarette and alcohol use and approval of those substances by their peers; African Americans did, however, report greater peer approval of marijuana. This difference may, however, reflect African American students' own awareness of greater media reports of African American substance use than that of Whites, as opposed to observation of greater marijuana use.

Before leaving this issue, it is important to note that our analyses also suggest that some portion of the racial difference in substance use may be due to methodological factors. Based on the relationship of honesty reports to prevalence, White students who were less honest may have *over*represented illicit drug or inhalant use. Based on risk factor analyses, it appears that some members of both groups of African Americans and Whites who were less honest may have underreported alcohol use, and some Whites who were not very honest may have underreported cigarette use.

African American Drug Use over the Life Course: Catch-up and Crossover Patterns

Research into the lower rates of licit and illicit drug use reported by African American youth is an area that has only recently received much needed attention by researchers and scholars. Nonetheless, our study, as well as others, provides ample evidence to suggest that a larger proportion of young African American youth than either Whites or Hispanics do, so to speak, say no to drugs, at least early on. Our findings attest to this factor, even when immigrant Hispanic adolescents are compared to African Americans. Whether low prevalences of experimentation with tobacco, alcohol, and other drugs is an imbedded cultural phenomenon or merely a brief cohort phenomenon that will soon disappear from the next generation of drug studies is yet to be determined. However, we believe that exploration and clarification of this phenomenon is not only critical for the understanding of African American drug use patterns, but that such understanding can provide very important information for drug prevention efforts for African American youth during late adolescence and early adulthood.

A comparison of reports on the prevalence of substance use across ethnic subgroups at multiple points along the age continuum provides two interesting and important observations. First, there is compelling evidence in the substance use literature to substantiate that while young African Americans are less likely than most other ethnic groups to use alcohol, tobacco, and illicit drugs, their aggregate patterns of lifetime use demonstrate what amounts to a "catch-up" effect by later adolescence. Data on the rates of cocaine use by age and ethnicity reported from the general household survey on drug abuse (NIDA, 1992) provide one specific illustration of these patterns. In this respected annual cross-sectional study, African American respondents aged 12–17, 18–25, and 26–34 reported lower rates of lifetime cocaine use than White non-Hispanic respondents. Importantly, in each progressive 5-year age cohort identified, the proportional difference in cocaine use between the groups decreased gradually; Whites 18–25 had rates two times higher than African Americans, whereas by age 26–34 this difference was reduced to only 1.25:1. More recent data (NIDA, 1995) suggest that marijuana and other illicit substance use by adolescents is on the increase; furthermore, African American and Hispanic adolescents' use may have especially increased over the last several years to be nearly at the same level as that of White teens.

A second common pattern can be discerned by adulthood. Here there is empirical evidence of an ethnic crossover, as African Americans currently report disproportionately higher levels of drug use than most other ethnic groups. Referring again to the data on lifetime cocaine use reported by the General Household Survey (NIDA, 1992), by age 35, the rate of lifetime use for African Americans was higher than that found for Whites. Specifically, by age 35+ the rate of lifetime cocaine use was 1½ times greater among the African Americans.

Corresponding patterns of an ethnic crossover have also been documented for intensive and abusive patterns of drug use. In a study of heavy drinking among a national sample of 1,466 African American and White males, Herd (1990) found important differences. Identified as consuming at least five drinks in one sitting at least once or more times per week, White males between the ages of 18 and 29 were more likely than their African American counterparts to be frequent drinkers (31%

and 16%, respectively). However, among the persons in the sample 30 years and older, 33% of the African Americans reported the heavy frequent drinking pattern, compared to 21% of the Whites.

Currently, these so called catch-up and crossover patterns have been identified from analyses of cross-sectional studies, by retrospective reports, and by merging together snapshots of data from disparate research (Vega, Zimmerman et al., 1997). Ultimately a major, ethnically diverse panel study designed to track the patterns of drug use of a single cohort from childhood into adulthood would be necessary to identify more precisely the timing and the mechanisms for these effects. As has already been mentioned, we are currently following a cohort from this study in order to examine the transition to young adulthood. Nevertheless, despite only a limited number of large panel studies, there is very little evidence to dispute that patterns of substance use and ethnicity are related to age in the manner illustrated.

While the epidemiological patterns relating to the transition from adolescent to adult drug use have been demonstrated and documented, one area that has not been adequately addressed to date in the research literature relates to the early development of these patterns. We witness the end product of an ethnic crossover in drug use from studies of adult populations and treatment studies. Likewise, findings from national and regional studies of the general population that are inclusive of persons ranging from young adulthood to adulthood support the aforementioned catch-up effect. However, gaps in the scientific literature currently exist in terms of the early developmental patterns of these important sociological observations.

The empirical questions that still need to be addressed include the following: (1) At what point in the earlier stages of the life course is the ethnic catch-up effect first evidenced? (2) Does this process begin with one specific drug or is it observed across drug categories? (3) What protective factors and mechanisms serve to assuage entry into substance use among African American youth? (4) What risk factors precipitate the catch-up effect among early adolescent African Americans? Whether risk or protective, it is important to identify the composition of these factors. Some of these may be social structural in nature and found in the broader socioeconomic environment of African American communities. Interpretations of social structural forces (e.g., poverty and joblessness) on African American problem behaviors are common in the sociological literature. Other factors may be, as suggested throughout this book, more closely aligned with the sociocultural norms, symbols, and messages that are transmitted among African American family members, among peers, and between teachers and African American students. Theories built around these psychosocial constructs are not as well developed in the substance use literature and remain more in the realm of anecdotal reports than empirically tested observations.

Findings from our three-year panel study were helpful in starting a scientific exploration on these issues. Presented initially are data related to questions 1 and 2.

**Table 7.1.   Past Year Incidence
of Substance Use during Year 3**

Substance	African Americans	Hispanics	White non-Hispanics
Alcohol	9.7	11.9	9.2
Cigarettes	12.5	12.8	12.0
Marijuana	7.8[b]***	10.4	13.1
Inhalants	1.3[a]***[b]***	5.1	5.6
Other illicit drugs	1.3[a]***[b]***	5.4	7.4

[a]African Americans significantly different from Hispanics.
[b]African Americans significantly different from White non-Hispanics.
***$p < .001$; Scheffe tests used for between-group comparisons.

Later, issues surrounding questions 3 and 4 will be discussed. Table 7.1 presents data on past year incidence of drug use among African Americans, Hispanics, and White non-Hispanics. Captured in this table are those students who at Time 2 reported they had never used a specific drug in question, but at a 1-year followup at Time 3 reported they had used the drug at least once. (Note: As a result of natural delays from Hurricane Andrew, the final data collection occurred more than one year from the prior collection period. See Chapter 2 for a more detailed discussion.)

One of the more important findings regarding early developmental patterns of African American drug use emerges from these data. Looking at the gateway drugs, notice first that the incidence of alcohol and cigarette use is statistically similar among all three groups. Just under 10% of the African American students reported their first drink of beer, wine, or hard liquor (not inclusive of religious observances or small tastes) between years 2 and 3 of the study. The incidence of alcohol use for White non-Hispanic students was 9.2% and for Hispanics, 11.9%. The incidence for cigarette use ranged from a low of 12.0% for the White students to 12.5% for the African Americans and 12.8% for the Hispanics.

One interpretation of these data relates specifically to the aforementioned catch-up effect. When coupled with the prevalence data discussed earlier, the combined data demonstrate that while young African American males are significantly less likely to report ever using alcohol or cigarettes at all three data collection periods, the rate of new use among this group, as demonstrated by past year incidence data, is similar to the other groups. It is important to note that given the lower prevalences among African Americans at Time 2, there was "more room" for them to catch-up to the other groups. On the other hand, their rate of new use could have just as easily been significantly lower than the other groups.

While the incidence of new alcohol and cigarette use was statistically similar among all three groups, the incidence of illicit drug use remained significantly lower for the African Americans. Just under 8% of the African American male students had tried marijuana for the first time within the 1-year period (Time 2 to

Time 3). This is compared to 13.1% ($p < .001$) of the White non-Hispanics and 10.4% of the Hispanics. The incidence of both inhalant and other illicit drug use was 1.3% for the African American boys in the sample. These rates were significantly lower than the 5.1% and 5.4% for the Hispanics and 5.6% and 7.4% for the Whites.

To summarize Table 7.1, there are signs of what appears to be a catch-up pattern among the later-using African Americans in our study. Our data demonstrate that this catch-up occurs during the early teen years around the ages of 13 and 14, and it begins with gateway substances. This finding closely parallels Kandel's (1975) important observation made over two decades ago that drug use occurs in sequential stages beginning first with licit drugs. Adolescents are very unlikely to experiment with marijuana without prior experimentation with one of the alcoholic beverages or with cigarettes. And very few try illicit drugs other than marijuana without prior use of marijuana (Kandel et al., 1992). Other analyses of our data indicate that alcohol and tobacco use were more closely related for African Americans than for Whites, and alcohol use at Times 1 and 2 was more significantly related to marijuana use for African Americans than for whites. Thus the gateway phenomenon may be stronger for African Americans than for Whites as they begin to catch up in their substance use.

We now proceed to questions 3 and 4 listed above, namely, what protective and risk factors serve first to maintain lower use of substances for African Americans and then to allow use to increase in what we have seen as the beginning of the catch-up effect? Thirty-eight risk and protective factors were assessed based on the research literature. These will be briefly described in six groups: family environment variables, mental health variables, deviance variables, school variables, peer variables, and societal perception variables. Unless indicated in the description as scales, most of these variables were measured with single, Likert-format items. For all of the risk and protective factors, in order both to capture the experience at T-1 and T-2 combined and to reduce missing data, the average of each of the predictor variables at these two points in time was used.

Fourteen variables assessed elements of the family environment: family cohesion (Olson, 1989); parent derogation (being put down by parents, Kaplan et al., 1987), family alcohol and drug problems, parent smoking, perception of fairness in rules and punishments, importance of talking with family members, importance of religious beliefs, frequency of attendance at religious services, desire to leave home soon, loyalty to one's family (three-item scale from Olson et al., 1985), older brothers' and sisters' use of drugs, parents being (or not being) divorced, parents' years of education, and living in a two-parent family (versus all other configurations).

Mental health variables included self-esteem (Kaplan et al., 1987), depressive symptomatology (a four-item scale based on the CES-D), suicidal ideation during the past year, and lifetime suicide attempts.

Deviance-related variables included belief in societal norms (Kaplan et al., 1987), frequency of disobeying at school; and major and minor deviance (scales from Kaplan et al., 1987). School variables included perceived derogation by teachers (Kaplan et al., 1987), doing poor school work, the perceived importance of grades, wanting to quit school soon, and reporting recent failing grades.

Variables relating to peers consisted of not being involved with peers, liking to be alone, perceived support from a good or best friend, use of substances (cigarettes, alcohol, and marijuana) by peers, and perceived approval of substances (cigarettes, alcohol, and marijuana) by peers.

Variables that tapped societal perceptions were perceptions of a lot of violence in one's neighborhood, perception of equal opportunity for all people in the U.S., African American racial awareness (Biafora, Warheit, et al., 1993), and cultural mistrust of the majority/white society (Biafora, Taylor, Warheit, Zimmerman, & Vega, 1993).

Differences in levels of risk factors between Africans and Whites are presented in Table 7.2. As shown, of the 38 risk factors, African Americans were at significantly higher risk on 12, significantly more protected on 10, and not significantly different on 16. African Americans were at greater risk due to low parent education, family substance use problems, not being from a two-parent family, high parent derogation, high teacher derogation, receiving failing grades, not being involved with peers, not having support from friends, greater perceived peer approval of marijuana, low self-esteem, violence in their neighborhood, and belief in unequal opportunities in our society, African Americans were more protected due to higher importance of religious beliefs, higher importance of talking in their family, grades being seen as important, not enjoying being alone, less cigarette and alcohol use, less perceived peer approval of cigarettes and alcohol, and lower prevalence of major deviance.

Several patterns of differences in risk and protection emerge from these findings. First, African Americans were more likely to feel put down, whether by self, teachers, or parents. Second, school variables put African Americans at greater risk, generally speaking, than Whites. Third, 4 out of the 10 differences where African Americans were more protected had to do with perceptions of peers: lower perceptions (accurately) of peer cigarette and alcohol use and peer approval of cigarettes and alcohol. African Americans, however (and inaccurately but consistent with cultural beliefs), were significantly more likely to say their peers approved of marijuana and somewhat more likely (but not quite significantly, $p = .06$) to think their peers used marijuana. Social perception variables showed African Americans to be at potentially greater risk for substance use.

Explaining Early Patterns of African American Adolescent Drug Use

We now attempt to synthesize a number of theoretical positions and our empirical findings into an emerging conceptual perspective on underlying mecha-

Table 7.2.   Differences in Levels of Protective and Risk Factors between African Americans and White Non-Hispanics

Risk factors	Significant difference	p value	Group with higher level of risk
Family environment variables			
Low family cohesion	Yes	.002	Whites
Low parent education	Yes	< .001	African Americans
Family substance use problems[a]	Yes	< .001	African Americans
Low importance of religious beliefs	Yes	< .001	Whites
Low attendance at religious services	No		
Divorced parents	No		
Not from two-parent family	Yes	< .001	African Americans
Low family loyalty[a]	No		
Punishments not fair at home	No		
Low importance of family communication	Yes	< .001	Whites
Older sibling substance use	No		
High parent derogation[a]	Yes	.002	African Americans
Parent smoking[a]	No		
Want to leave home	No		
School variables			
Poor school work	No		
Teacher derogation[a]	Yes	.02	African Americans
Failing grades	Yes	< .001	African Americans
Grades not seen as important	Yes	< .001	Whites
Want to quit school soon	No		
Peer variables			
Not involved with peers	Yes	< .001	African Americans
Like being alone	Yes	< .001	Whites
Have no support from friends	Yes	< .001	African Americans
Peer cigarette use	Yes	< .001	Whites
Peer alcohol use	Yes	< .001	Whites
Peer marijuana use	No		
Peer approval of cigarettes	Yes	.01	Whites
Peer approval of alcohol	Yes	.001	Whites
Peer approval of marijuana	Yes	< .001	African Americans
Mental health variables			
Low self-esteem[a]	Yes	.05	African Americans
Depressive symptomatology[a]	No		
Suicidal ideation	No		
Suicide attempts	No		
Social perception variables			
Violence in neighborhood	Yes	< .001	African Americans
Belief in unequal opportunities	Yes	< .001	African Americans
Deviance variables			
Low belief in norms[a]	No		
Disobeying in school	No		
Major deviance[a]	Yes	< .001	Whites
Minor deviance	No		

[a]Multiple-item scale

nisms for use of substances by African American adolescents. Since the turn of this century social scientists have articulated and advanced a number of theoretical perspectives in an attempt to better understand deviant behaviors and the multiplicity of rampant problems facing urban adolescents. Some notable theories have focused primarily on psychologically based antecedent factors (Abrahamsen, 1952; Aichorn, 1953), and others have emphasized the role of social structural or sociological variables (Cloward & Ohlin, 1960; Hirschi, 1969; Merton, 1938; Quinney, 1977; Shaw & McKay, 1942). There is also a large and growing body of literature that combines elements of both psychological and sociological perspectives. These theories of deviance can be distinguished from others by their central tenet: Deviance and the disposition to deviance emerge from the interface between self and society. More specifically, many of these theories attribute nonnormative behaviors, particularly among adolescents, to factors associated with psychosocial development. These include, for example, theories of differential association (Sutherland, 1947), reference group (Glaser, 1956), labeling (Becker, 1963; Lemert, 1951), peer group (Jessor & Jessor, 1977), social learning (Burgess & Akers, 1968), esteem enhancement (Wells & Rankin, 1983), and self-rejection (Kaplan, Johnson, & Bailey, 1986).

A review of this voluminous literature on social deviance is well beyond the scope of this chapter. However, readers are encouraged to visit Chapter 3, where a brief review of the cited theories is provided. This scholarship dates back to the early architects of the Chicago School of sociology and is important to the current discussion, not so much for the relevant insight this body of knowledge offers for interpreting African American drug use per se, but rather for what it collectively fails to offer.

A cursory review of these familiar sociological interpretations of social deviance reminds us of their historic importance for the emergence and growth of American sociology and its subdisciplines of criminology, juvenile delinquency, and to a lesser extent, medical sociology. However, a more detailed analysis of these theories taken from the vantage point of the adolescent drug researcher reveals important methodological shortcomings that effectively limit the applicability of these frameworks for understanding and predicting patterns of African American adolescent drug use. One of these relates to a general assumption that the theories of deviance advanced over the course of this century are, for the most part, adequate for explaining the etiology of drug use. A further limitation of this widely respected literature is that it tends to ignore the contributions of unique cultural processes and ethnic traditions that distinguish African Americans from other ethnic groups. Rather, discussions of race and ethnicity have usually been addressed more in the context of post hoc analyses.

The assumption that the processes and predictors of delinquency are more or less the same as those for other problem behaviors including drug use is not new to the deviance literature. Such a view is common as demonstrated by both classic and contemporary ethnographic accounts of inner-city life and by various attempts by social scientists to design prediction models for drug use based solely, or in part, on preexisting theories of delinquency. It is also obvious from the discussions by researchers and scholars who suggest that drug use is part of a broader constellation of delinquency and general problem behaviors among youth (Gottfredson & Hirschi, 1990; Jessor & Jessor, 1977). Related to these points is the fact that for decades, social scientists with varying interests have tended to tap the same "well" of deviance theory to explain a wide spectrum of issues ranging simultaneously from delinquency and precocious sexual behavior to truancy and suicide. This amounts to what might best be described as a one-size-fits-all philosophy.

It is not difficult to intimate the interrelationships among drug use, crime, and various other high-risk behaviors. Much of our research and our own personal experiences can attest to the multifactorial nature of deviance. Moreover, research has demonstrated that young people who exhibit various problem behaviors do differ along a number of common sociological and psychosocial dimensions, including, but not limited to, age, gender, region of residence, socioeconomic status, racial/ethnic group membership, attitudes and beliefs, self-esteem, and the existence of family problems (Dryfoos, 1990; Wallace & Bachman, 1991). Nevertheless, findings from our three-year longitudinal study suggest that it is problematic to conclude that the processes and predictors of drug use among African American youth are necessarily the same as the processes and predictors for other behaviors including delinquency. Such a leap also leads to the inevitable conclusion that the ethnic groups under study that are more likely to engage in delinquency are also more likely to engage in drug use. Analyses of data from the study have demonstrated that this is not necessarily the case. African American adolescent males, while considerably less likely than Whites to report drug use at all three time periods, were significantly more likely than Whites to report drug use at all three time periods, were significantly more likely to report involvement in nearly all other forms of social deviance, including breaking and entering a building, beating up someone for no reason, taking part in gang fights, damaging property, and theft. African Americans were also more likely to report a greater disposition to disobey and break the law than Whites.

A second shortcoming of the deviance literature relates to the panethnic nature of current theory. Specifically, most of these theoretical models were developed and founded on predominantly majority populations and, as such, have effectively relegated the importance of African American culture to an afterthought. A decade ago, Herd (1987) challenged researchers to broaden their theoretical scope and to "rethink African American drinking." Despite this challenge, the current level of knowledge of African American alcohol and drug use remains limited due in part to the general lack of theory development in this area. More recently, Wallace and Bachman (1991) point out that "in spite of fairly consistent findings of racial/ethnic differences in problem behaviors and drug use

specifically, relatively little research has been done to explain why these differences exist" (p.334). Again, our research provided compelling evidence that
African American drinking and drug use patterns, especially those patterns for
young adolescent African Americans, are quite distinct from larger American
patterns.

Why has African American culture been overlooked in the deviance and drug
use literatures? Herd (1987) suggests one possible explanation may be the common
perception that African American drinking and drug use patterns do not constitute
culturally distinct behavior in the same way that Irish, Jewish, or Italian patterns
were regarded. Instead, observed differences in African American drug use and
abuse rates appeared to be similar to those of other lower-class, White American
Protestants. Void of methodologically sound data and the absence of a culturally
relevant theory, most knowledge of African American drug use has been derived
instead from research on nonrepresentative samples viewed through existing
theoretical frameworks borrowed mainly from sociological theories already noted.

One of the more common themes of this traditional American scholarship
worthy of note relates to the ubiquitous assumption that social problems in the
inner cities are caused or determined primarily by environmental or social structural factors. The earlier writings of the Chicago School sociologists still resonate
today with familiar descriptions of how broad ecological forces such as urban
decay and social disorganization lead to social deviance (Shaw & McKay, 1942).
While not without critical comment, the work of researchers like Clifford Shaw
and Henry McKay and their analyses of official crime statistics over several
decades led to the now common assumptions that social deviance was more likely
to occur in areas of rapid industrialization and immigration, places in which
criminal values and traditions develop over time and ultimately supersede conventional ones (Shaw & McKay, 1942; Thrasher, 1927). Many a young child growing
up in these areas was as likely to see economic success and personal reputation
earned by criminal behavior as by school success and hard work in legal occupa-
tions (Miller, 1958). However, a life of crime is not for everyone, and other children
may decide to retreat or rebel from the stresses of inner-city life and resort to other
alternatives which most certainly included drugs (Merton, 1938).

One of the more commonly cited and controversial perspectives for interpreting the formidable challenges facing African Americans was introduced in the
1960s by the late Oscar Lewis (1969). Referred to as the "culture of poverty"
thesis, this view has many similarities with the sociological models just presented;
conditions where drug use occurred were viewed in the same manner as were the
concomitant problems related to drugs and crime. Yet the mechanisms by which
social disorganization led to problem behaviors were distinctive and gave rise to
several pejorative assumptions regarding African American culture. Central to this
thesis was the idea that the conditions under which poverty exists and are perpetuated in a class-stratified capitalist society constitute such powerful and enduring

constraints on a people that over time they develop a distinguishable culture of poverty, one that is crystallized and is passed on from generation to generation (Wilson, 1993). As Lewis (1969) put it, "By the time slum children are age six or seven, they have usually absorbed the basic values and attitudes of their subculture and are not psychologically geared to take full advantage of changing conditions or increased opportunities which may occur in their lifetime" (p. 188).

Applying this cultural transmission view to drug use, inner-city African Americans have been viewed as lacking the values of temperance and self-control that made drinking and drug use problems of little concern in middle-class White America. Moreover, the causes of drug use and other social problems were taken out of the realm of the social structural or political economy and placed, instead, on the individual and his or her immediate social networks. Family pathology and psychological dysfunction were combined with ghetto-specific practices, such as overt emphasis on sexuality, idleness, and public tolerance for drinking, drug use, and criminal activities, to provide a theoretical formulation that included both an identifiable cause and measurable effect. Critics of Lewis's position note that this negative view of inner-city life leads to increased pessimism on the part of social planners and the larger society because it suggests that not even reducing structural inequality would decrease the frequency of problem behavior or do much to improve the overall situation.

Not to be redundant, but the findings from our study of early drug use coupled with those from other researchers in the field today paint quite a different picture of African American drug use. Historical and ethnographic studies of drinking and drinking norms in the African American community, such as those provided by Herd (1985, 1987), show that, if anything, "African American attitudes are likely to be drier than those of Whites and that alcohol use traditionally and currently plays a much smaller role in home and family life. In addition, African Americans appear to use alcohol less frequently than Whites in many social situations (e.g., when entertaining friends at home or going out to bars or taverns)" (Herd, 1985, p. 151). This new literature calls for more rigorous explanatory models that take into consideration the wider sociology of African American life. Such a model would be more attuned to situational and social factors that govern the way drugs are perceived in the African American community while at the same time focusing on the social and cultural meanings of licit and illicit substances. Ultimately, a cultural model of African American drug use is warranted that not only steers clear of stereotypes and media headlines but is also less quick to accept that social pathology and psychological dysfunction are at the root of all inner-city problems.

Landrine and Klonoff (1996) offer another interesting view of the situation. These researchers point out that with the exception of African Americans, virtually every other group to immigrate to the United States has been realized as a distinct ethnic group with distinct customs, beliefs, and traditions. African Americans, on the other hand, have traditionally been characterized and distinguished not so much as an ethnic or cultural group, but rather as a racial or biological group. These writers argue further that the distinction between "African American" and "White" races has been widely adopted and perpetuated not so much for scientific reasons, but more for political purposes (Landrine & Klonoff, 1996, p. vii). This is not the forum to debate the validity of this charge. Nevertheless, some historians suggest that the African slave trade originated a process of deculturation by abruptly severing Africans from the unique customs and traditions of their homeland. Many of the remaining remnants of an African culture were eventually lost as the survivors gradually assimilated into the dominant White culture. While there is no discounting the horrifying tragedy of slavery on African people and their unique culture, the view that their history and traditions have been lost completely through generations of forced acculturation is not the only view. Family historians such as Herbert Gutman (1976, 1983) have demonstrated that throughout the period of slavery Blacks in the United States were able to retain traditional cultural norms and values, and that they used such traditions to adapt and survive the experiences of slavery.

Today a number of scholars in the social and psychological sciences are focusing their energies on deconstructing race and reviving, in a more positive light, discussions of African American culture. At the core of current discussions resides important beliefs and assumptions, among which are (1) that an African American culture can be identified and (2) that elements of this culture can be conceptualized and measured. Also believed is that African American behavior patterns and cognitive dispositions can be explained in part by these objective cultural mechanisms. These assumptions follow findings from research with other ethnic and minority groups including Cuban Americans (Szapocznik & Kurtines, 1980), Mexican Americans (Keefe & Padilla, 1987), and Native Americans (Hoffman, Dana, & Bolton, 1985), as well as other groups that show strong relationships between acculturation and an array of patterned beliefs and practices.

Such a view is also consistent with our own exploratory research of the relationships between ethnic-centered attitudes and delinquency (Biafora, Warheit, et al., 1993) and attitudes toward violating the law (Taylor et al., 1994) among the African American students in this study. Prior studies had demonstrated a link between perceptions of mistrust and prejudice by African American students and poor school performance (Terrell, 1980; Terrell, Terrell, & Taylor, 1981). Building on this research, we hypothesized that African American students who had acquired mistrustful attitudes toward the dominant White culture (either by direct experiences or by vicarious exposure) would be significantly more likely to act on their feelings by engaging in rebellious or reward-seeking behaviors that deviated from the accepted norms of the dominant group. This hypothesis was also consistent with Merton's (1938) notions that some individuals would seek out "innovative" alternatives to access opportunity structures when they perceived that their chances to legitimately access them were blocked. Bivariate analyses supported our hypotheses by demonstrating significant positive relationships between racial mistrust scores and conventional forms of delinquency. These findings also held in multivariate analyses in which a number of traditional predictors of deviance, including socioeconomic status, peer influences, family problems, family structure, and religiosity, were statistically controlled. Unexpectedly, cultural mistrust scores were found to be the most powerful predictor of both minor and major forms of delinquency in these analyses.

The concept of acculturation, while no stranger to research with most major ethnic groups in the United States, has only recently been applied to African Americans. Moreover, standardized instruments and scales to measure acculturation are in their infancy and require further validation. Despite current limitations, there is a general belief in this emerging literature that there exists a continuum of African American acculturation ranging from traditional to acculturated, with biculturated persons somewhere in the middle. Persons identified as traditional are those who remain immersed in many of the beliefs, practices, and values of an Afrocentric culture. At the other end are those who have more or less rejected the beliefs and practices of this traditional heritage in favor of those of the dominant White society or who have never acquired their own culture's traditions.

We also see an African American culture that is extremely dynamic and consisting of a variety of dimensions that researchers are only now beginning to empirically measure. With respect to problem behaviors such as early drug use, the expectation is that more acculturated persons would more likely use and use earlier in life than more traditional-oriented individuals.

The abstainers and less frequent users may include those who have a heightened sense of cultural awareness; who tend to maintain their own styles of food, dress and artistry; who uphold ethnic values toward childrearing, child care, extended familial relationships, and health practices; who regularly participate in African American festivities, cultural games, and traditional spiritual services; who engage in and understand rules of informal interaction and the use of cultural dialect; and who believe in and pass on superstitions (Landrine & Klonoff, 1996; McAdoo, 1983; Terrell, 1980). Our data, unfortunately, do not permit us to test this hypothesis.

The concept of African American acculturation is refreshing because, unlike a great deal of traditional sociological theory, this view provides researchers with a way to conceptualize and explain complex between-group and within-group behavioral differences without resorting to pathological or racist deficit explanations. When stripped of culture, behaviors such as drug use and delinquency are rarely viewed as normative and within the bounds of acceptability. On the contrary, such behaviors are usually described in terms of social deviance or social pathology and based on the normative behaviors displayed by the dominant, in this case, White, middle-class, culture.

We propose the following model for understanding both less drug and alcohol use among early African American adolescents and potentially more problematic drug and alcohol use in early to mid-adulthood. Early adolescent African Americans are afforded an environment significantly more protective with respect to alcohol and other drug use. As supported by our data on styles of discipline, parents use a more controlling style of parenting their children, resulting in greater fear of negative consequences and less problematic behavior; religion and its strong negative proscriptions against alcohol and drugs is a more pervasive force for African American than White youth; peers are generally perceived to be less approving of gateway drugs. In mid- to late adolescence, while these protective factors are largely still in place, negative influences of parental derogation, poor school performance, and persistent low income resulting from one-parent families increase as potential risk factors. The catch-up effects begin. Into young adulthood, the absence of perceived employment opportunities (with unemployment rates at 20% or higher in inner cities, three to five times higher than in other communities), increasing family substance use problems (as parents move into their thirties and forties) and continuing violence and drug-ridden neighborhoods increase risk to the point where, for an increasing proportion of young adults, drug use becomes an alternative related either to the generation of income or to coping with the comparisons of one's own community and oneself to the majority community. The greater, stricter external control placed on individuals by their parents in earlier life becomes ineffective when external controls are removed, values have been less internalized, and thus are more likely to be violated. This process of greater earlier protection and greater risk into young adulthood is depicted in Table 7.3.

While the model builds on previous theory and empirical research, it must be viewed as somewhat speculative and requiring longitudinal research focusing on testing the model. The proposed model does suggest a number of ideas with respect to interventions targeted at African American youth and young adults. First, interventions that strengthen the protective factors in early adolescence may further delay onset of substance use. Thus, increasing perceptions of peer disapproval, maintaining the importance of religion, and maintaining the exertion of greater parental control may all be effective in maintaining protective factors

Table 7.3. Factors Associated with Early Protection and Later Risk of Drug Use among African Americans

Early adolescence	Mid- to late adolescence	Young adulthood
Greater parental control	Greater parental derogation	Violence/drug-ridden neighborhood
Greater influence of religion	Poor school performance	Greater family substance use problems
Greater perceived disapproval	Less parental supervison	Strong awareness of unequal opportunities

over a longer period of time. Second, individual and family factors in mid- to late adolescence should be targets of intervention to delay or eliminate the catch-up effect for African Americans. School performance, parental supervision, and teacher and parent derogation might effectively be important targets of intervention during the period. Third, without social structural changes, the catch-up effect may never be eliminated. Unless the related problems of violence and drug dealing in neighborhoods, substance abuse problems of adults, and the lack of employment opportunities are addressed, even with the interventions suggested for adolescence, substance use and abuse are still likely to be problems for African Americans in young adulthood.

8

Prevention Implications and Conclusions

Introduction

The use of tobacco, alcohol, and drugs among adolescents has been a persistent problem in U.S. society for several decades. While there were some signs of decreases in substance use at the close of the 1980s, the initial optimism has faded with evidence of increases in drug use during the subsequent decade. There have been changes in attitudes about drug use, especially decreases in perceptions about the harmfulness of specific drugs such as marijuana since 1991 (Monitoring the Future Survey, 1994). The findings from the longitudinal study reported in this book, which took place between 1991 and 1993, also attest to substantial drug experimentation among adolescents during the middle school years.

Concurrent with the concerns about adolescent drug use has been the attempt to prevent drug use among future generations through various types of programs and initiatives at local and federal levels. Aside from a variety of legal measures, most of the contemporary prevention programs have emphasized interventions directed at psychosocial factors that are believed to promote substance use. A multitude of prevention programs have been school based, and many have followed the premise of rational behavior among adolescents (Botvin, & Botvin, 1992). Regrettably, most of these programs have proven to be ineffective in reducing the tide of adolescent drug use. We can conclude with certainty that isolated programs that only address circumscribed aspects of adolescents' lives will have marginal effects in preventing drug use.

Even if we discount the recent increases in the prevalence of adolescent substance use, the evidence is that drug use has become an integral part of U.S. society over the past 30 years. During that time there have been fluctuations in public concerns and efforts to address the problem of drug use. In some ways there have been improvements, as shown by the decline in youth drug use during the late

1980s and, correspondingly, a decline in media interest as well. However, even when declines in drug use were reported by the High School Survey in 1988, the authors warned that "it is still true that this nation's high school students and other young adults show a level of involvement with illicit drugs which is greater than can be found in any other industrialized nation in the world" (Johnston et al., 1988). After the declines in youth substance use in the late 1980s, the same high school surveys now report increases in drug use among students (Monitoring the Future Study, 1994). Furthermore, we know that students that drop out are more likely to use drugs (Wallack & Corbett, 1990), that dropouts also have rates of tobacco use estimated to be 79% higher than their high school peers (Pirie, Murray, & Luepker, 1988), and that those not planning to go to college have higher rates of drug use than the college bound (Wallack & Corbett, 1990).

The federal government has responded to the drug problem with initiatives such as the "War on Drugs" with expenditures of $12.7 billion in 1993 alone (Rosenbaum, 1996), and for primary prevention the investments have been estimated at $2.5 billion. With all of these financial efforts there is some evidence of success in the drug prevention arena. For example, the level of illicit drug use among 12- to 17-year-olds declined dramatically between 1979 and 1981, with use in any given month moving from 18% to 7% in this age group (Eigen, & Rowden, 1993). Furthermore, alcohol-related car accidents and fatalities among youth have been decreasing ("Making Prevention Work," 1997).

If the critical observer is removed from the periodic "drug crises" and "wars on drugs." then a disturbing picture emerges. It is a picture of a society that for the greater part of the century has had a high "baseline" of adolescent drug use in comparison to other industrialized nations. There are fluctuations in drug use, as well as programs and interventions that have helped abusers and have prevented others from becoming users. Nevertheless, drug experimentation has become a rite of passage for an alarming number of adolescents. Furthermore, the drug problem affects residents of low-income communities in different ways than those of higher socioeconomic status. Differences exist in the legal consequences of drug use, as well as in the availability of treatment programs for those that seek help for their drug use problems.

Drug use in our society is a broad social problem rather than solely a matter of individual choice or weakness. Insofar as the prevalence of drug use in the United States is very different from other industrialized countries, and very different from its own past history prior to the mid-1960s, then we must look at the social environment in our efforts to address the problem of youth drug use. Our own data dramatically show the influence of the social environment when immigrant Hispanic adolescents have lower prevalences of drug use than their U.S.-born counterparts but begin to catch-up as they are assimilated into the U.S. environment. Clearly the most important environmental factors that explain these differences are marketing and distribution systems of licit and illicit drugs, perceived social approval or barriers to drug experimentation, and the glorification and positive media images about drug use. The critical element for prevention efforts is the environmental context in which the individual makes decisions to use or abstain from drug use. While this may appear to be common sense to many, its implications require a shift that is difficult in a society committed to individual responsibility and mastery over hardships. Only in times of extreme crisis have we recognized the overwhelming influence of the social environment over the individual, with the major example being the period of the Great Depression during the 1930s. This society is rooted in a philosophy of free will and personal control, as contrasted with societies in which the individual is perceived as belonging, defined, and depending on the group, and where external forces are acknowledged as strong determinants of people's lives.

This is not to say that individuals are not a feasible target for prevention or treatment efforts. However, it is simplistic to ignore the social and economic system in attempts to explain and address adolescent drug use. The system fosters a clandestine economy, including the distribution and sale of drugs. Adolescent drug use is linked to the norms, values, and institutions in society, and thus it is in the broad context of society that prevention efforts must be focused.

There is no greater evidence of the nihilistic threat facing American society than the desperate search for "good" news on the part of the media and politicians. In the late 1980s the talk was about reductions in adolescent drug use; in the mid-1990s the talk is about decreases in crime in large urban centers like New York and Los Angeles. With this type of dialogue it is easy to forget the fact that despite these reductions in crime, this is the most violent Western democracy, and 30 years ago people would have been aghast if told that these reductions in crime would constitute "good news" in the 1990s.

Despite these apparent improvements, youth crime and drug use are endemic problems in American society. In 1950, .0004% of the underfifteen population in the United States was arrested for murder, forcible rape, robbery, and aggravated assault (Postman, 1994). This represented only 170 children or early adolescents. However, between 1950 and 1979 the rate of these crimes by this same age population increased 11,000%. Clearly, by any standard or any political persuasion, the "patient" is in very serious need of treatment.

Overview of Approaches to Substance Abuse Prevention

The continued concern about drug use and abuse as a social problem in the past quarter century has produced a variety of approaches to the prevention of drug use in the general population, many specifically directed at adolescents. Much has been learned during this period of time, and perhaps most importantly, there is a recognition that no single strategy has been absolutely successful (Bangert-

Drowns, 1988; Tobler, 1986). Most prevention approaches have focused on the reduction of demand through change in the attitudes of individuals. Simultaneously, the government has unsuccessfully attempted to diminish the supply of drugs through interdiction efforts, and through the involvement of the justice system.

Prevention approaches have focused on affecting the psychosocial factors associated with drug use (Schinke, Botvin, & Orlandi, 1991). Many prevention programs have consisted of educational formats, providing information about the harmful effects of tobacco, alcohol, and other drugs. "Affective" education targets self-esteem and responsible decision making. Such programs have largely proven ineffective in stemming the tide of adolescent drug use (Berberian, Gross, Lovejoy, & Parapella, 1976; Goodstadt, 1974; Schaps, Bartolo, Moskowitz, Palley, & Churgin, 1981). From the perspective of this book, it is not surprising that these programs have proven ineffective. First, they do not address the environmental factors leading to drug use and abuse. Second, they often do not address the psychosocial factors leading to drug use, such as peer pressure (Botvin & Botvin, 1992). Third, they often lack a developmental perspective that accounts for the particular idiosyncracies of adolescent thought processes and behaviors. In the following pages we summarize overlapping approaches that have been used in the prevention of adolescent drug use and their contributions and weaknesses.

Educational Approaches

Educational approaches that provide information about the nature and adverse effects of cigarettes, alcohol, and other drugs have been among the most common and earliest attempts to prevent drug use, going back to the early 1970s. These approaches have consisted of school-based programs in which students are provided with information about the harmful effects of drugs, or public information campaigns that have attempted to affect the attitudes of the public about drug use.

The other type of educational approach concentrates on "affective" education instead of factual information. These approaches are also usually school based, but they emphasize experiential activities with the goal of improving communication skills. The premise of these programs is that adolescents can be "trained" to be better prepared to reject the temptations and opportunities in their environment to experiment with drug use.

The evidence on the effectiveness of these strategies is mixed at best. It is clear that information is not a sufficient factor for the prevention of drug use among adolescents and youth, although it may be a necessary element. Human behaviors are complex and multifaceted; therefore, it is hardly surprising that increased knowledge does not automatically alter drug use behavior. The empirical evidence dating back to the 1970s indicates that affective education and approaches providing information have failed in preventing drug use (Dorn & Thompson, 1976; Kinder, Pape, & Walfish, 1980; Malvin, Moskowitz, Schaps, & Schaeffer, 1985; Schaps et al., 1981) and some education programs have had the paradoxical effect of increasing knowledge about drugs and related behavior, while also increasing usage (Mason, 1973; Rosenblitt & Nagey, 1973).

Despite this history of failure, educational approaches continue to be developed and evaluated because of their simplicity and ease of implementation, compared to those that are community based or environmental. Many of these programs become popular before there is any empirical evidence of their effectiveness, in part because the public needs to feel that something can be done about drug use in our society. The best example of this was the popularity of the DARE initiative a few years ago. Since 1990, DARE has received $8 million of federal funding and has been delivered to an estimated 25 million youth, and yet repeated evaluations have shown the program to be ineffective (Rosenbaum, 1996). A recent report documented the outcome of the program: "18% of 8th graders and 24% of 9th graders reported being heavy users of alcohol, meaning they drank more than 10 times or were drunk at least once in the past 30 days. Eighteen percent of 8th and 9th graders had used marijuana in the month before the survey and 5% reported being heavy users" (San Francisco Chronicle, Feb. 25, 1997). Nevertheless, the program continues to be popular and supported. President Clinton's drug czar responded to questions about the ineffectiveness of DARE by stating that the positive interaction between inner-city youth and police officers produced by DARE is a sufficient factor to continue the program.

Social Influence Approaches

Recently, there has been a shift in drug abuse prevention interventions away from informational or educational approaches toward programs that address psychosocial factors associated with the initiation of drug use (Botvin & Wills, 1985; Flay, 1985). The new emphasis, while still educational, focuses on making students aware of their exposure to social influences that can lead to drug use. Concurrent with this new approach are programs designed to enhance personal competence through life-skills training (Botvin & Botvin, 1992).

The general thrust of these approaches is to make participants aware of social factors that may influence their drug use; social skills training, including the teaching of social resistance skills; and correcting adolescents' misinterpretations of norms regarding drug use (Botvin & Botvin, 1992). Much of the research in this area is based on the smoking prevention work of Richard Evans and colleagues (1978). As a result, very few studies of the social influence approach have been conducted for other substances. However, McAlister and colleagues (1980) did demonstrate effectiveness in preventing alcohol and marijuana use, and others have demonstrated changes in attitudes and beliefs about drugs (Hops et al., 1986). Evans's approach was to increase adolescents' resistance to social influences for smoking by making them aware of the influences, and by preparing them with countermeasures to the social pressures for smoking. While these programs used varying methods and intervention intervals, the results have been generally positive in reducing smoking, ranging from 33% to 39% reductions (Botvin & Botvin, 1992). Follow-up studies have demonstrated the preventive effects of the programs to last up to 2 years, after which the effects begin to decay (Botvin & Botvin, 1992).

These psychosocial approaches represent a more sophisticated perspective on prevention than the earlier educational models (Schinke et al., 1991). The main difference is that psychosocial interventions, such as social skills training, and psychological inoculation take into account some of the complexities of human behavior and the multidimensionality of drug use behavior among adolescents. The main thrust of these perspectives is to strengthen adolescent resistence against the pressures in their environment to use drugs, using the logic of the medical model of preventive vaccination.

As has been the case with all forms of prevention efforts, the effectiveness of these psychosocial approaches has been mixed. As stated above, many studies have demonstrated reductions in smoking (Best et al., 1984; Botvin, Dusenbury, Baker, & James-Ortiz, 1989; Evans et al., 1981; Perry, Killen, Slinkard, & McAlister, 1980), and others have proven effective in preventing alcohol and marijuana use (Botvin, Baker, Botvin, Filazzola, & Millman, 1984; McAlister, Perry, & Maccoby, 1979). However, a large number of studies have failed to show important differences between experimental and control groups (Evans et al., 1978; Perry, Telch, Killen, Dass, & Maccoby, 1983). These inconclusive findings may be the result of methodological issues such as poor control and experimental group definition, or lack of specificity based on ethnicity and social class. The fact is that while these interventions constitute an advance from those based solely on education, they are not sufficient in addressing the etiologic complexities of adolescent drug use.

A factor that is critically important is that few studies have used this approach with adolescents who are at high risk to become tobacco or other drug users. In one notable exception, a prevention program was even more effective with students at high risk for cigarette smoking (Best et al., 1984). Nevertheless, despite the relatively long history of prevention programs using social influence approaches, there remains a shortage of information on the effectiveness of these approaches among various age groups, genders, ethnic groups, or social classes. We do not know the interaction of these demographic factors with specific program components. For example, there is evidence that boys and girls may be differentially influenced by peer-led programs, with girls more likely to be influenced than boys (Botvin & Botvin, 1992).

Social Skills Training Approaches

These approaches are derived from the social learning theory of Bandura (1977) and problem behavior theory (Jessor & Jessor, 1977). Under these theories, substance abuse is a behavior that is learned; therefore, prevention programs emphasize the learning of personal and social skills that would prevent substance use. Specific features include training for problem solving and decision making, skills for increasing self-control and self-esteem, assertive skills, and skills for resisting negative social influences, among others (Botvin & Botvin, 1992).

In reviewing 10 studies that used generic skills training approaches to drug abuse, Botvin & Botvin (1992) reported great variability in methods in terms of duration, sample size, target populations, dependent variables, and objectives. Most of the studies using this approach have concentrated on early adolescence. Botvin and Botvin reported that these studies have significant positive behavioral effects, and to a greater extent than social influence approaches. Botvin and Botvin (1992) summarize their positive reviews of these approaches, stating that "all these prevention approaches have produced measurable effects on a spectrum of mediating variables in a direction consistent with non-substance use" (p. 297). Despite these positive reviews, they recognize critical shortcomings that are highly relevant to the subject matter of this book. First, most of the studies using the social skills training approaches as well as the social influences approaches have been conducted with school populations, leaving unanswered the question of their effectiveness with dropouts or out-of-school populations (Swaim, Beauvais, Chavez, & Oetting, 1997). Second, little, if any, attention has been given to ethnic or racial minorities.

Positive effects of generic social skills training may generalize to several drugs and influence related behavioral domains as well (Pentz, 1983; Botvin, Baker, Botvin et al., 1994; Schinke & Gilchrist, 1983). Furthermore, interventions that consist of multiple synergistic components appear to be effective, as was shown with a school-based intervention among inner-city middle school students consisting of video materials, as well as consultation with nurses or doctors (Werch et al., 1996).

On the basis of the theoretical perspectives of social learning theory and problem behavior theory, Botvin and Botvin (1992) suggest two basic general prevention strategies. The first alternative proposes the elimination or reduction of environmental factors that promote or facilitate drug use. Such strategies would reduce the availability of drugs, alter social attitudes about the acceptability of drug use, or reduce the visibility of drug-using role models among other possible strategies. The focus of these strategies are macrosocial rather than individual or intrapsychic, and require the use of media strategies. Botvin and Botvin (1992) are basically pessimistic about such strategies, believing that they are costly, take too long to produce results, and "... because substance abuse occurs as a result of both environmental and social factors, it is unlikely that substance abuse could be prevented entirely using this strategy" (p. 294).

The second set of strategies proposed by Botvin and Botvin are based on social learning theory and problem behavior theory and call for interventions that attempt to reduce intrapsychic motivations. This is a familiar premise. Since the environment may not be malleable, the solution is to equip the adolescent with the tools to resist the temptations to use drugs.

Our contention is that prevention efforts need to be informed about the etiology of drug use in youth populations across the entire socioeconomic and ethnic spectrum. That is, an etiologic perspective provides the basic information about risk and protective factors that is fundamentally necessary for the implementation of broad prevention approaches. Moreover, despite the difficulties in influencing environmental factors, we believe that effective long-lasting prevention efforts require the cooperation and organization of communities. While Botvin and Botvin are correct in their assessment of the difficulties of environmental strategies, we believe that to do otherwise is shortsighted. This is an important issue that will be addressed later in this chapter.

Community-Based Approaches

Community-based approaches would seem to provide the greatest promise for sustainable efforts that can impact large segments of populations. However, these approaches present a number of theoretical and pragmatic challenges. Among the best-known community-based approaches have been organized parent groups, such as MADD (Mothers Against Drunk Driving), and the National Federation of Parents for Drug-Free Youth (NFP). The problem with these efforts has been the inability to produce stringent evaluations, largely because of the difficulties of separating the effects of these programs from other variables in the environment (Schinke et al., 1991). Theory about comprehensive community-based drug prevention is less well developed than social cognitive learning theories, and "off-the-shelf" models are not available, and would probably make little sense if they were, given the idiosyncracies of community settings, structures, and politics.

One of the best examples of a comprehensive community-based approach is that of Project STAR (Students Taught Awareness and Resistance), conducted in the Kansas City metropolitan area (Pentz, Cormack, Flay, Hansen, & Johnson, 1986). The theoretical bases of this program are psychosocial, integrating social learning theory (Bandura, 1977), a system-centered education model (Green, 1985), and multifaceted community organization (Rothman, Erlich, & Teresa, 1981; Watzlawick, Weakland, & Fisch, 1974). The program is implemented by combining school, family, media, and community advocacy. This approach has shown effectiveness in reducing marijuana use among participants.

There is little question that drug prevention efforts among adolescents are advantaged by a community focus. However, these approaches require time, patience, and sensibility to ethnic nuance in order to take root in a multicultural and ethnically fragmented community like South Florida. The tendency in this type of community is for those with the economic means to move elsewhere, leaving behind a population facing myriad structural barriers and racial tensions. An important factor in community-based approaches is that most fail to engage the communities that are at greatest need. The challenge is to implement community-based programs that allow communities to take ownership of the efforts. This is critical because we must recognize that in many inner-city communities in the United States there exists a state of anomie and lack of personal commitment to place. A common occurrence in a place such as South Florida, and Miami in particular, is that each ethnic group feels either disenfranchised or that they are transients, even if most members of the particular group remain in Miami for their entire lifetimes.

Mass Media Approaches

An honest examination of media approaches to the prevention of drug abuse must address the fact that media incentives to promote drug-using lifestyles compete with prevention messages. The fact of the matter is that television and films are commercial media. For example, in television, and increasingly in films, it is difficult to distinguish the "product act" from the "artistic act." Many films and television programs are long commercials for products, including alcohol, and television programs exist to create a commercial audience. Television programs are not canceled because of their poor quality, but rather because they fail to bring an audience for the advertisers.

Nevertheless, despite the countervailing pressure, there is evidence that media campaigns have been effective in reducing drug use. For example, in Sweden a ban on all beer and wine advertising in the mid 1970s resulted in a 20% per capita reduction of alcohol consumption (Romelsjo, 1987). In New Zealand, bans on cigarette advertising caused drops in consumption (Vickers, 1992), and in Norway, between 1975 and 1990 teenage smoking dropped from 17% to 10% after an advertising ban was imposed (Vickers, 1992).

One of the most comprehensive media efforts in the United States is the campaign mounted by the Partnership for a Drug-Free America, which has spent over $1 billion since 1987 in antidrug public service announcements (Partnership for a Drug-Free America, 1992). However, there has not been a systematic assessment of the effectiveness of this campaign, although there is some evidence that exposure to these types of media campaigns has some positive effects in convincing adolescents to stop using drugs (Reis, Duggan, Adger, & DeAngelis, 1992).

Advertising works, otherwise corporations would not be spending large amounts of money on it. Children in the United States are exposed to a constant barrage of advertising, at the rate of about 20,000 ads annually, which constitutes 360,000 by the time they finish high school (Strasburger, 1995). Children and adolescents view 25 to 50 alcohol commercials for every Partnership for a Drug-Free America ad they see (Strasburger, 1989). Studies have demonstrated that the most heavily advertised brands of cigarettes are the most popular among teenage smokers (Pierce et al., 1991). And 3 years after the introduction of the Joe Camel character, the preference for the brand among adolescents increased from .5% to 32% (DiFranza et al., 1991). Furthermore, alcohol commercials utilize some combination of rock music, attractive models, and sports figures (Strasburger, 1995). Clearly, cigarette and alcohol advertisers have paid a great deal of attention to the thought processes of children and adolescents, and they have devised very effective ways to influence their product preferences as well as their taste. The belief that teenagers are solely responsible for influencing trends and behaviors that are portrayed in the media is a myth, in view of the fact that the celebrities that teenagers emulate and admire are well past their teenage years.

The most critical factor about media campaigns is that none have approached the attractiveness, sophistication and pervasiveness of tobacco and alcohol advertising (Grube & Wallack, 1994). Antidrug campaigns are nothing more than drops in an ocean of direct and indirect advertisements that glorify the use of gateway substances like cigarettes and alcohol. Effective media campaigns need to be more systematic and comprehensive, and use more than one medium (Bauman, LaPrelle, Koch, & Padgett, 1991). Furthermore, the time slots provided by television stations for antidrug advertising are rarely aired during prime viewing hours or during very popular shows.

One conclusion on the use of media is that while it can be an effective tool for prevention, media advocacy efforts constitute minimalist efforts in contrast to the sophisticated use of advertising by the alcohol and tobacco industry (Atkin, 1993; Kilbourne, 1991; Strasburger, 1995). As we write this book, the liquor industry is attempting to end their voluntary restriction on television advertising, and the tobacco industry is contesting the right of the Food and Drug Administration (FDA) to regulate their products. Indeed, hard liquor ads have been shown on Spanish-language television stations in the United States.

Harm Reduction Approaches

Given the protracted nature of the drug use problem among American youth, it is not surprising that there has been a movement advocating harm reduction as an alternative to the "traditional" prevention goal of abstinence. Harm reduction education was conceived in the United Kingdom (Cohen, 1993). The goals of harm reduction are secondary prevention rather than primary. That is, children and adolescents are taught to deal with their drug use and that of their peers under the assumption that drug use among a large proportion of the youth population is present and inevitable. The harm reduction argument provides many valid elements that can inform prevention approaches, perhaps even those with a goal of abstinence. The most controversial element of harm reduction is the position that educational approaches should convey methods for avoiding abuse or accidents, rather than advocate complete avoidance of drugs. Responsible and moderate use of drugs is condoned. These advocates believe that it is possible to use drugs in a responsible way, and that use does not constitute abuse (Rosenbaum, 1996). We believe that there are dangers with this approach because it follows an overall trend in U.S. society of ascribing a degree of competency on the part of children and adolescents beyond their developmental capacities. If we assume that children and adolescents are prepared to assimilate the message of "responsible" drug use, then we may truly be arriving at Neil Postman's prediction of the disappearance of childhood (Postman, 1994).

Critics have vigorously opposed harm reduction approaches because of the fear that they undermine the social signal of prohibition (DuPont, 1996). Others believe that prohibition policies have worked (Musto, 1991), and that prohibition is a response to drug use increases in society rather than a contributor to the problem (DuPont, 1996). Even more poignant is the reality of disparate views on the acceptability of harm reduction. It is highly unlikely that harm reduction, as an absolute concept, would be culturally acceptable in African American and Hispanic communities where strong taboos exist about drug use.

The approach of harm reduction is a reaction to the stated failures of prevention efforts. While harm reduction as a strategy may lack support, advocates of this perspective make some important points. If drug use is unavoidable in American society in the foreseeable future, then it is logical that drug prevention policy should consider the goal of harm reduction instead of total elimination of use (Ching, 1981; Goode, 1993). However, whether drug use continues to be so widespread is a question that can only be answered by the passage of time. There must be sufficient political will to address primary determinants of drug use on a scale appropriate to the scope of the problem. Otherwise, harm reduction advocates will have a stronger position (Brecher, 1972).

While the harm reduction approach is extremely controversial, we believe that its premises provide fertile ground to address the need for integrative approaches to prevention. One of the most compelling premises of the harm reduction approach is the view that educational approaches have not worked in large part because they have exaggerated the harmful effects of drugs to an excessive point that is so unrealistic that often the messages are inconsistent with adolescents' experiences and observations (Moore & Saunders, 1991; Rosenbaum, 1996). The information provided for adolescents should be accurate and consistent with their experiences. If the information is inconsistent, then adolescents will dismiss the message and the messenger. As Rosenbaum succinctly states, "there are many concrete risks and dangers in the use of psychoactive substances. We must, however, separate the real from the imagined dangers of drugs and impart this information within the appropriate context" (Rosenbaum, 1996, p. 13). Furthermore, as a society, we minimize the harmfulness of certain substances like alcohol, and warn adolescents about terrible consequences of marijuana use, which they see as failing to materialize among their peers that are marijuana users.

As this review demonstrates, specific approaches to drug use prevention have shown some success, especially social skills training and interventions based on social influence theories. Educational approaches have become more sophisticated and have moved away from the tactics of scaring adolescents. Community-based and media approaches hold a great deal of promise. However, there has been less experience with community partnerships that address the environment, including structural factors that promote clandestine and sophisticated drug economies and subcultures in low-income communities. There is a clear need to reassess the problem of adolescent and youth drug use in the United States. Prevention efforts, if they are to have any effects at a macrolevel, must address personal and community risk factors and utilize an ecological perspective in the implementation of prevention efforts.

Toward an Integrative Contextual Prevention Approach

Before embarking on a plan for prevention strategies, it is critical to apply knowledge about the etiology of drug use. This is the most reasonable manner in which to develop programs and interventions that target specific behaviors or risk factors that may be associated with drug use. In this book we are concerned with drug use during early adolescence. Clearly, much of the drug use during this period of time may be experimental in nature, and circumstances leading to more serious drug abuse and addiction will differ across individuals and groups. One of the premises of this book is that there are important contextual circumstances that lead adolescents to drug use beyond the initial experimental phase. That is, experimentation may have very different consequences based on genetic, psychosocial, and environmental factors.

Inasmuch as drug use is the result of complex interactions between individuals and their environments, we find that there is a great deal of variability of determinants of adolescent drug use across individuals as well as ethnic groups. The failure of "traditional" approaches to drug use prevention based on factual information about the aversive effects of drugs should not be surprising given the content and variations in adolescent socialization in the United States.

The prevention strategy proposed is ecological and multilevel. That is, since the etiology of adolescent drug use is multidimensional, prevention efforts must simultaneously address the multiple elements associated with drug use behaviors. We believe that environments create vulnerabilities for populations. There are a variety of environmental factors that are associated with early drug use. One of the most evident is whether adolescents are residing in environments where drug use is widespread, perhaps even among parents, siblings, or peers (Botvin & Botvin, 1992). Drug use and related activities are far more visible in some communities than in others. Open street sales, gang distribution of drugs, and crack houses are obvious examples of drug-related behaviors that challenge conventional normative standards. In these settings there is a greater likelihood of exposure to important risk factors for drug use. Furthermore, social and cultural factors interact to create vulnerabilities in ethnic groups. For example, the high exposure to acculturation stressors and low familism among low acculturation, native-born Hispanic adolescents are implicated in their exceptional drug use, but immigrants have a different experience and outcome. Prevention programs should be grounded in an appreciation of these differences.

At the personal level, one of the most critical issues to be considered in the explanation of adolescent drug use is the influence of cognitive development on how adolescents see their world. The thinking of adolescents is markedly different from that of children. As development proceeds from childhood through adolescence, thinking becomes less rigid and concrete. Compared to the thinking of children, adolescents are generally better able to use abstract, hypothetical, and relative thinking (Piaget, 1932). Moreover, cognitive changes also lead many adolescents to believe that they are unique and somewhat indestructible (Elkind, 1967). Prevention approaches must account for this fact if they are to be effective in addressing skills training and the learning of resistance skills.

Another set of personal factors are beliefs about the harmfulness of drugs and attitudes about disapproval of drug use, which have been found to influence drug use among adolescents (Johnston, O'Malley, & Bachman, 1994). Low self-esteem, diminished personal control, greater need for social approval, impulsivity, and low assertiveness, among other factors, have also been found to be associated with adolescent drug use (Botvin & Botvin, 1992). Kaplan and colleagues have presented and tested their esteem enhancement model that links perceived self-derogation through peer associations and attitudes about deviance and deviant behavior to drug use (Kaplan, Johnson, & Bailey, 1986). This model has been replicated with a multiethnic sample composed of Hispanics, African Americans, and White non-Hispanics (Vega et al., 1996). In Chapter 6, the value of this model is demonstrated in the larger context of acculturation stress on self-rejection among Hispanic adolescents. Moreover, the esteem enhancement model illustrates how maturation structures etiological processes that, in turn, lead to different outcomes. For example, negative social sanctions intended to address misbehavior can, with maturity, result in the opposite effect of what was intended by provoking some adolescents further into delinquency.

Adolescence is a period of rapid and important changes physiologically, as well as socially. During this period the adolescent is neither a child nor an adult, and the adolescent begins to struggle with separation and individuation from parents and takes on new social roles. Erik Erikson (1968) suggested the necessity of a "moratorium" in order to allow adolescents to experiment and proceed with the formation of their identity. One of the most fundamental changes in the lives of adolescents is the increase in the importance and influence of peer interactions. Peers become the medium that adolescents use to test their convictions and to experiment. We know that parental influence may decline from early to late adolescence, while the peer group becomes more prominent (Cummings, 1995). This does not mean that parental influence disappears; many studies have shown that parents continue to be the primary source of identity and influence during adolescence (Schlegel & Barry, 1991). The values of peers are not necessarily divergent from those of parents in a highly stratified and ethnically segregated American society (Mussen, Conger, & Kagan, 1974). Nevertheless, these developmental factors can increase the vulnerability to drug use. It is therefore not surprising that the middle school years become critical for early experimentation with gateway drugs.

During early adolescence, conformity to group norms becomes paramount (Lerner, Petersen, & Brooks-Gunn, 1991). Our own study attests to the importance of peers for predicting drug use. The simple and often erroneous belief that one's peers use drugs, or that peers have positive attitudes about drug use, can facilitate adolescent experimentation with drugs. However, the social and developmental circumstances under which peers are influential vary across ethnic groups, as well as among individuals. For example, we find that peer associations actually protect against drug use among African Americans in the transition from childhood to adolescence.

The setting of the middle school is where the etiologic factors associated with drug use interact. Prior to middle school, the family holds the most influence on the child, albeit, increasingly, the media is influential throughout childhood. In essence, the school is the vessel in which family, environmental, and peer factors combine. It is in the middle school years when real and perceived structural barriers and social differences begin to crystallize, and minority status is recognized and internalized by some youth. Subcultures begin to form, and these provide a context for learning behaviors at variance with conventional values and beliefs about drug use. The school becomes the most vivid representation of the opportunity structures of early and midadolescence. Failure in the school arena predetermines to a great extent the future of adolescents, and they know it. Therefore, prevention efforts must recognize school experiences and preparatory opportunities as a central concern. Otherwise, adolescents may not become stakeholders in their own futures.

In the face of the relentless socialization favoring drug use, prevention programs have been piecemeal, addressing important etiologic factors and ignoring others. For example, school-based inoculation programs teaching resistance skills rarely address the different types of pressures, such as gang activity, that some children and adolescents confront across the social spectrum. Furthermore, while many of these programs may increase knowledge about drugs, they rarely change behavior (Rosenbaum, 1996). Attempts to change the behavior of children and adolescents in a vacuum fail to deal with negative environmental reinforcers and therefore are unlikely to be sustained over time (Brian, Daniels, & Cormack, 1990).

At this historical juncture the obstacles to the development of innovative drug prevention efforts are more a matter of social and political will than any given set of scientific or methodological barriers. Effective prevention is multileveled. There is a consensus in the literature that simple, unidimensional approaches have failed to produce satisfactory results. And even more discouraging, a review of 350 different school programs in 1988 showed that only 33 had valid evaluation data (Falco, 1992). Therefore, even with approaches that may be effective, we know little about their effectiveness (Rosenbaum, 1996). We need to integrate our knowledge about risk and protective factors into interventions that are coherent and that coordinate existing community resources and agencies.

Despite the long history and variety of approaches to the prevention of adolescent drug use, few youth have been exposed to these programs. Thus, beyond the arguments about the long-term ineffectiveness of educational and psychosocial interventions, these efforts have reached few of the inner-city children and adolescents passing through the public school systems during the past quarter century. Sussman and colleagues (1995) have provided evidence for this fact in their study of high-risk youth in "alternative" high schools. These researchers found that only 20% of students in "continuation" high schools reported ever receiving any drug abuse prevention interventions. Similarly, other researchers have concluded that prevention efforts have failed to reach other high-risk populations such as women whose children have entered foster care (Lewis, Leake, Giovannoni, Rogers, & Monahan, 1995).

An Ecological Approach to Prevention

Rappaport (1987) has written that prevention will not work in isolation from multilevel strategies for community change that have broad "buy-in" and active participation from neighborhood residents. A comprehensive approach to prevention of adolescent drug use must be ecological, based on a thorough understanding of community structure, assets, and agency and grassroots participatory mechanisms (Trickett, 1984). Repeated community assessments have demonstrated little correspondence between the focal concerns voiced by local residents and the focal concerns of "experts" who often define social problems and propagate programs to remediate them. Indeed, the recent summary of large-scale, and highly expensive, community interventions to reduce heart disease and smoking found that over time intervention communities had less favorable outcomes than control communities, especially after the termination of intervention activities. The explanation for these results was given as a failure to adequately appreciate and engage the multilevel community structure in the intervention process.

Drug prevention programs are often in much the same situation, isolated from those they seek to influence. School-based antidrug interventions are extended when accompanied by community-initiated action to remove drug dealers from local parks, mediate racial tensions among adolescents, reduce alcohol outlets, and organize against gun sales and saturation billboard advertising of cigarettes and alcohol products. Moreover, there is evidence of the effectiveness of school-based interventions extending to community-based, youth-serving organizations (Botvin & Botvin, 1992). As Norman Zinberg (1984) describes it, the context of drug use combines three essential elements: the pharmacology of the drug, the psychological state of the user, and the setting, which includes geography as well as the social group. While experimental drug use is widespread among America's youth, the trajectories from experimentation to abuse are influenced by these three elements that can also be thought about as modifiable risk variables.

The community is a system composed of multiple structural elements. Adolescents are not separable from their environments. Therefore, effectively reaching adolescents requires systematically changing the physical and social elements that local *community residents* deem necessary for alteration to foster a healthy environment. These elements should be addressed simultaneously so that they will be mutually reinforced. No doubt this is a shift from the intervention programs that have been so heavily supported in the past. However, the ecological framework of intervention is not new and is gaining very wide acceptance by public and private funders. What is often lacking is collaboration and flexibility in mechanisms to support coordination of multisectoral government and community agencies with neighborhood action groups. Even more fundamental is the necessity for public and private funders to invest for the long term in community change. Short interventions attempting social and behavior change of epic proportions will not work. Multilevel ecological change implicates schools, agencies, informal neighborhood networks, law enforcement, and many other community components that must first learn about each other, then slowly and deliberately develop fragile linkages for bringing about mutually desired changes. This type of fundamental planning and organization for action requires a time frame of decades, rather than the usual 3- to 5-year program intervention window. The Center for Substance Abuse Prevention has addressed this shift "toward a public health and preventive approach" in which community-based prevention activities must include the enhancement of efficiency and effectiveness of services in communities, improv-

Figure 8.1 A multilevel ecological perspective for adolescent behaviors.

ing collaboration among agencies, and coalition building and networking ("Making Prevention Work," 1997).

Figure 8.1 presents a general model of the ecological context that impacts on adolescent drug use. The model components influence adolescent behaviors and attitudes about drugs. The circles representing family and neighborhood or community have gone through major changes in the past 30 years, just as we have seen adolescent and youth drug use become a critical social problem in this society. We recognize that ecological models must fit the specific circumstances of the target communities. However, the overriding factor is the focus on person–environment connections.

Ecological perspectives have emerged in community psychology over the past decades (Altman, 1995; Barker, 1968; Kelly, 1968; Ogbu, 1978; Trickett & Birman, 1989; Wicker, 1986). These perspectives facilitate prevention intervention in complex communities in which there is a great deal of change and diversity. Ecological approaches provide the opportunity to address the issues of diversity presented in the multiethnic study in this book. As was described in Chapter 2, Miami and South Florida represent the view of the United States as culturally pluralistic (Sue & Moore, 1984) instead of the older vision as a melting pot.

The findings from the study funded by the National Institute on Drug Abuse, reported in this book and in multiple articles that have been published, attest to the dimensions of the efforts that will be required to address the problem of youth drug use. Experimentation with tobacco, alcohol, and multiple drugs increases during early adolescence in all ethnic groups and both genders. Risk and protective factors associated with drug use are both similar and different across ethnic groups. As we approach the new millennium, the United States is becoming an increasingly complex society that has not entirely addressed the changes of the past 30 years in institutions such as the family in its various forms. We can foresee an acceleration of changes and increased fragmentation among groups and institutions. Efforts in the public health arena must be in tune with these changes, otherwise we will continue to use limited resources on piecemeal efforts that, while helping some individuals, fail to address the larger problems.

We propose an ecological approach to adolescent drug use prevention with a central goal of reestablishing the community as a central source of meaning to families and individuals. The major differences between adolescents that progress to a world of drug use and abuse and those that do not are rooted in meaning acquired through their communities and families. Again, this does not mean the dismissal of individual personality and genetic factors, but unless we believe that genetic predisposition and personality factors have changed in a vacuum in the past 30 years, then we must recognize that changes in the conditions of communities and families have had profound effects on the experiences and choices of youth in the United States. Real and perceived structural conditions may be determined by the choices we make as a society, but those choices have direct and indirect effects on the conditions of persons and communities. There is a need to develop healthy communities that facilitate drug-free lifestyles; otherwise, prevention efforts will never reach the source of the problem.

From a public health perspective, little will change unless this cycle is interrupted, and this is critically important in view of the projected 21% increase of the population aged 12 to 20 years old between 1995 and 2010 (Current Population Report Series, 1995). Moreover, the multilevel approach to prevention is still required (Mrazek & Haggerty, 1994).

Figure 8.2 presents an ecological approach to adolescent drug use prevention that is an outgrowth of the many findings of our longitudinal study, and recognizes the multiple etiologic and environmental elements of adolescent drug use. This approach addresses all the elements that impact on the lives of adolescents simultaneously. Structural variables and constraints are considered, with the philosophy that the etiology of adolescent drug use calls for such an approach. In this model there is room for specific programs, such as drug education, but these interventions must be responsive to the contextual nature of adolescent drug use. That is, the approach can include educational interventions, community-based advocacy, media campaigns, and skills training, but each element must be integrated within an ecologically appropriate understanding of drug use in the social context of community. This proposed approach involves all the elements of basic

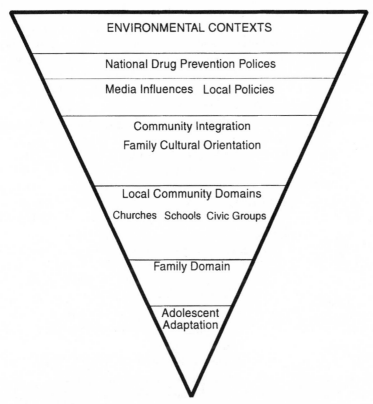

Figure 8.2 Representation of a multilevel prevention strategy.

prevention strategies recognized by the Center for Substance Abuse Prevention
(1995): raising awareness about drug use behaviors, promoting good parenting
skills, building academic and vocational skills, providing mentoring and positive
role models for adolescents and youth, building social skills, mobilizing communities to create environments that enhance personal development, and strengthening policies that promote healthy lifestyles. These elements of prevention must
function simultaneously at all levels, and the community must be allowed "ownership" of these efforts and become the focal point of implementation.

Organizations that are important to the target communities can be used as the
starting point for the implementation of the ecological approach to drug use
prevention. For example, in the African American community, the church or
religious organizations can be used to draw parents into efforts that can be
simultaneously generated in the schools. By coordinating school and church

activity it becomes possible to begin an effort of engaging parents and their children. But this is only a point of departure, because to address the problem of adolescent drug use, the entire community must eventually be "engaged." There is evidence that community coalitions can be a source of group mobilization (McMillan, Florin, Stevenson, Kerman, & Mitchell, 1995).

In the approach to prevention, we adhere to the general guidelines advocated by the Center for Substance Abuse Prevention, understanding the uniqueness of the target population, and the involvement of key individuals and organizations in the planning and implementation stages of prevention efforts ("Making Prevention Work," 1997). The National Structured Evaluation (NSE) of alcohol and drug abuse prevention recently completed by Substance Abuse and Mental Health Services (SAMHSA) (1995) support our premise that calls for an ecological model of prevention. The NSE analyzed 1,642 prevention efforts, finding that only 19% had rigorous outcome evaluations. Nevertheless, the evaluation concluded that "the delivery of a comprehensive, coordinated, and complementary set of strategies is likely to lead to levels of effectiveness that are much greater than could be achieved with single strategies carried out in isolation." (National Structured Evaluation of Alcohol and Other Drug Abuse Prevention, 1994; National Drug Control Strategy, 1995). The focus of this report is clearly in the direction of community-directed change that decreases the probability of drug use and strengthens communities that help children and adolescents develop the social skills and positive self-image to avoid drug use.

The findings from this book attest to the important differences in the patterns of drug use, as well as risk and protective factors, among groups of African American, White non-Hispanic, and Hispanic adolescents. These differences are rooted in sociocultural variations in the experiences of these adolescents, and they point to the basic requirement of prevention strategies to address multiple levels simultaneously, and devised in a manner that is appropriate for the contextual experiences of adolescents and their families. Prevention of adolescent drug use must recognize social, cultural, and ethnic variations in the connection between individuals and the collective, and there is evidence that community-based approaches are a viable conduit for public health promotion (Trickett, Watts, & Birman, 1993; Kaftarian & Hansen, 1994).

Appendix

Items and Alphas for Scales

Delinquent Behavior Scales

Major Delinquency (alphas: T1 = .77, T2 = .78, T3 = .77)
  Taken between $2 and $50 when you weren't supposed to.
  Taken part in gang fights.
  Used force to get money or expensive things from another person.
  Broken into and entered a home, store, or building.
  Taken a car for a ride without the owner's permission.
  Taken something worth more than $50 when you weren't supposed to.
  Beaten up someone for no reason.
Disposition to Deviance (alphas: T1 = .62, T2 = .78, T3 = .79)
  It is okay to sneak into a movie or ball game without paying.
  It is okay to steal a bicycle if one can do it without getting caught.
  It is important to pay for all things taken from a store.
  It is important to try to follow rules and obey the law.
  I don't care about other people's feelings.
  I would like to quit school as soon as possible.
  I would like to leave home.
  The kids who mess around with the law seem to be better off than those who
    always follow the law.

Acculturative Stress Scale

Language Conflicts (alphas: T1 = .63, T2 = .67, T3 = .70)
  How often has it been hard for you to get along with others because you don't
    speak English well?

How often has it been hard to get good grades because of problems in understanding English?

Perceived Discrimination (alphas: T1 = .58, T2 = .63, T3 = .68)

How often do people dislike you because you are Latin?

How often are you treated unfairly at school because you are Latin?

How often have you seen friends treated badly because they are Latin?

Acculturation Conflicts (alphas: T1 = .61, T2 = .66, T3 = .70)

How often have you had problems with your family because you prefer American customs?

How often do you feel that you would rather be more American if you had a choice?

How often do you get upset at your parents because they don't know American ways?

How often do you feel uncomfortable having to choose between non-Latin and Latin ways of doing things?

How often do you feel that you would rather be more American if you had a choice?

References

Abrahamsen, D. (1952). *Who are the guilty: A study of education crime.* New York: Holt, Rinehart and Winston.

Abramson, H. J. (1981). Assimilation and pluralism. In S. Thernstrom (Ed.), *Harvard encyclopedia of American ethnic groups* (pp. 150–160). Cambridge, MA: Harvard University Press.

Achenbach, T. M., & Edelbrock, C. S. (1983). *Manual for the Child behavior checklist and revised child behavior profile.* Burlington: University of Vermont, Department of Psychiatry.

Achenbach, T. M., & Edelbrock, C. S. (1986a). *Manual for the youth self-report profile.* Burlington: University of Vermont.

Achenbach, T. M., & Edelbrock, C. S. (1986b). *Manual for the teacher's report form and teacher version of the child behavior profile.* Burlington: University of Vermont, Department of Psychiatry.

Acuña, R. (1981). *Occupied America: A history of Chicanos.* New York: Harper & Row.

Aftermath of Hurricane Andrew. (1992, September 24). *Miami Herald,* p. A1.

Aichorn, A. (1953). *Wayward youth.* New York: Viking Press.

Akers, R. L. (1984). Delinquent behavior, drugs, and alcohol: What is the relationship? *Today's Delinquent, 3,* 19–47.

Akers, R. L. (1994). *Criminological theories: Introduction and evaluation.* Los Angeles: Roxbury Publishing.

Akers, R. L., Krohn, M. D., Lanza-Kaduce, L., & Radosevich, M. (1979). Social learning and deviant behavior: A specific test of a general theory. *American Sociological Review, 44,* 636–655.

Allgood-Merten, B., Lewinsohn, P. M., & Hops, H. (1990). Sex differences and adolescent depression. *Journal of Abnormal Psychology, 99,* 55–63.

Allison, P. D. (1984). *Event history analysis: Regression for longitudinal event data.* Beverly Hills, CA: Sage.

Altman, D. G. (1995). Sustaining interventions in community systems: On the relationship between researchers and communities. *Health Psychology, 14,* 526–536.

Amaro, H., Whitaker, R., Coffman, G., & Heeren, T. (1990). Acculturation and marijuana and cocaine use: Findings from HHANES 1982–84. *American Journal of Public Health, 80,* 54–60.

American Almanac: Statistical Abstract of the US: 1993–1994. (1995). Austin, TX: Reference Press.

Aneshensel, C. S. (1992). Social stress: Theory and research. *Annual Review of Sociology, 18,* 15–38.

Aneshensel, C. S., & Huba, G. J. (1975). Depression, alcohol use, and smoking over one year: A four-wave longitudinal causal model. *Journal of Abnormal Psychology, 92,* 134–150.

Aneshensel, C. S., Rutter, C., & Lachenbruch, P. A. (1991). Social structure, stress, and mental health: Competing conceptual and analytic models. *American Sociological Review, 56,* 166–178.

Apospori, E., Vega, W. A., Zimmerman, R. S., Warheit, G. J., & Gil, A. G. (1995). A longitudinal study of the conditional effects of deviant behavior on drug use among three racial/ethnic groups of adolescents. In H. B. Kaplan (Ed.), *Drugs, crime and other deviant adaptations: Longitudinal studies* (pp. 211–230). New York: Plenum.

Atkin, C. K. (1993). Alcohol advertising and adolescents. *Adolescent Medicine: State of the Art Reviews, 4,* 527–542.

Bachman, J. G., Johnston, L., & O'Malley, P. (1987). Monitoring the future: Questionnaire responses from the nation's high school seniors. Ann Arbor, MI: Survey Research Center.

Bachman, J. G., Wallace, J. M., O'Malley, P. M., Johnston, L. D., Kurth, C. L., & Neighbors, H. W. (1991). Racial/ethnic differences in smoking, drinking, and illicit drug use among American high school seniors, 1976–1989. *American Journal of Public Health, 81,* 372–377.

Bandura, A. (1977). *Social learning theory.* Englewood Cliffs, NJ: Prentice Hall.

Bangert-Drowns, R. L. (1988). The effects of school-based substance abuse education: A meta-analysis. *The Journal of Drug Education, 18*(3), 243–265.

Barber, B. L., & Eccles, J. S. (1992). Long-term influence of divorce and single parenting on adolescent family- and work-related values, behaviors, and aspirations. *Psychological Bulletin, 111,* 108–126.

Barker, R. G. (1968). *Ecological psychology.* Stanford, CA: Stanford University Press.

Barnes, G. M. (1990). Impact of the family on adolescent drinking patterns. In R. L. Collins, K. E. Leonard, & J. S. Searles (Eds.), *Alcohol and the family: Research and clinical perspectives* (pp. 137–161). New York: Guilford Press.

Barnes, G. M., & Welte, J. W. (1986). Patterns and predictors of alcohol use among 7–12th grade students in New York State. *Journal of Studies on Alcohol, 47,* 53–62.

Barr, K. E. M., Farrell, M. P., Barnes, G. M., and Welte, J. W. (1993). Race, class, and gender differences in substance abuse: Evidence of middle-class/underclass polarization among black males. *Social Problems, 40,* 314–327.

Barrera, M., & Reese, F. (1993). Natural support systems and Hispanic substance abuse. In R. S. Mayers, B. L. Kail, & T. D. Watts (Eds.), *Hispanic substance abuse* (pp. 115–130). Springfield, IL: Charles C Thomas.

Bates, M. E., Labouvie, E. W., & McGee, C. R. (1986). The effect of sensation seeking needs on alcohol and marijuana use in adolescence. *Bulletin of the Society of Psychologists in Addictive Behaviors, 5,* 29–36.

Bauman, K. E., LaPrelle, J., Brown, J. D., Koch, G. G., & Padgett, C. A. (1991). The influence of three mass media campaigns on variables related to adolescent cigarette smoking: Results of a field experiment. *American Journal of Public Health, 81,* 597–604.

Baumrind, D. (1985). Familial antecedents of adolescent drug use: A developmental perspective. In C. L. Jones & R. J. Battjes (Eds.), *Etiology of drug abuse: Implications for prevention* (Research Monograph No. 56, pp. 13–44). Rockville, MD: National Institute on Drug Abuse.

Baumrind, D., & Moselle, K. A. (1985a). A developmental perspective on adolescent drug use. *Advances in Alcohol and Substance Use, 5,* 41–67.

Baumrind, D., & Moselle, K. A. (1985b). A developmental perspective on adolescent drug abuse. In B. Stimmel (Ed.), *Alcohol and substance abuse in adolescence* (pp. 41–67). New York: Haworth Press.

Beatty, L. A. (1994). Issues in drug abuse prevention intervention research with African Americans. In A. Cazares & L. A. Beatty (Eds.), *Scientific methods for prevention intervention research.* Research Monograph No. 139, pp. 25–32). Rockville, MD: National Institute on Drug Abuse.

Beck, R. (1996). *The case against immigration.* New York: W.W. Norton.

Becker, H. S. (1963). *Outsiders: Studies in the sociology of deviance.* New York: Free Press.

Bellah, R. N., Sullivan, W. M., Swidler, A., & Tipton, S. A. (1985). *Habits of the Heart: Individualism and commitment in American life.* New York: Harper and Row.

Bentler, P. M. (1992). Etiologies and consequences of adolescent drug use: Implications for prevention. *Journal of Addictive Diseases, 11,* 47–61.

Berberian, R. M., Gross, C., Lovejoy, J., & Parapella, S. (1976). The effectiveness of drug education programs: A critical review. *Health Education Monographs, 4,* 377–398.

Berry, J. W., Poortinga, Y. H., Segall, M. H., & Dasen, P. R. (1992). *Cross-cultural psychology: Research and applications*. New York: Cambridge University Press.

Best, J. A., Flay, B. R., Towson, S. M. J., Ryan, L. B., Perry, C., Brown, K. S., Kersell, M. W., & d'Avernas, J. R. (1984). Smoking prevention and the concept of risk. *Journal of Applied Social Psychology, 14*, 257–273.

Biafora, F. A., Taylor, D. L., Warheit, G. J., Zimmerman, R. S., & Vega, W. A. (1993). Cultural mistrust and racial awareness among ethnically diverse black adolescent boys. *Journal of Black Psychology, 19*, 266–282.

Biafora, F. A., Warheit, G. J., Zimmerman, R. S., Gil, A. G., Apospori, E., & Taylor, D. (1993). Racial mistrust and deviant behaviors among ethnically diverse black adolescent boys. *Journal of Applied Social Psychology, 23*, 891–910.

Blau, G. M., Gillespie, J. F., Felner, R. D., & Evans, E. G. (1988). Predisposition to drug use in rural adolescents: Preliminary relationships and methodological considerations. *Journal of Drug Education, 18*, 13–22.

Blossfeld, H. P., Hamerle, A., & Ulrich Mayer, K. (1989). *Event history analysis: Statistical theory and application in the social sciences*. Hillsdale, NJ: Erlbaum.

Blyth, D. A., Simmons, R. G., & Zakin, D. F. (1985). Satisfaction with body image for early adolescent females: The impact of pubertal timing within different school environments. *Journal of Youth and Adolescence, 14*, 207–225.

Botvin, G. J., & Botvin, E. M. (1992). Adolescent tobacco, alcohol, and drug abuse: Prevention strategies, empirical findings, and assessment issues. *Developmental and Behavioral Pediatrics, 12*(4), 290–301.

Botvin, G. J., & Wills, T. A. (1985). Personal and social skills training: Cognitive-behavioral approaches to substance abuse prevention. In C. Bell & R. Banges (Eds.), *Prevention research: Deterring drug abuse among children and adolescents* (Research Monograph No. 8, pp. 1–22). Washington, DC: National Institute on Drug Abuse.

Botvin, G. J., Baker, E. M., Botvin, E., Filazzola, A. D., & Millman, R. B. (1984). Alcohol abuse prevention through the development of personal and social competencies: A pilot study. *Journal of Studies on Alcohol, 45*, 550–552.

Botvin, G. J., Baker, E. M., Renick, N., & Filazzola, A. D. (1984). A cognitive behavioral approach to substance abuse prevention. *Addictive Behaviors, 9*, 137–147.

Botvin, G. J., Dusenbury, L., Baker, E., & James-Ortiz, S. (1989). A skills training approach to smoking prevention among Hispanic youth. *Journal of Behavioral Medicine, 12*, 279–296.

Bowlby, J. (1982). *Attachment and Loss*: Vol. 1. *Attachment* (2nd ed.). New York: Basic Books.

Bowlby, J. (1988). *A secure base: Parent child attachments and healthy human development*. New York: Basic Books.

Brecher, E. M. (1972). *Licit and illicit drugs*. Mt. Vernon, NY: Consumers Union.

Brian, R. F., Daniels, S., & Cormack, C. (1990). Effects of program implementation on adolescent drug use behavior. *Evaluation Review, 14*, 448–449.

Brook, J. S., & Cohen, P. (1992). A developmental perspective on drug use and delinquency. In J. McCord (Ed.), *Advances in criminological theory*: Vol. 3. *Crime facts, fictions, and theory* (pp. 231–251). New Brunswick, NJ: Transactions Publishers.

Brook, J. S., & Newcomb, M. D. (1995). Childhood aggression and unconventionality: Impact on later academic achievement, drug use, and workforce involvement. *Journal of Genetic Psychology, 156*, 393–410.

Brook, J. S., Whiteman, M., Gordon, A. S., & Brook, D. W. (1983). Fathers and sons: Their relationship with personality characteristics associated with the son's smoking behavior. *Journal of Genetic Psychology, 142*, 271–281.

Brook, J. S., Whiteman, M., & Gordon, A. S. (1983). Stages of drug use in adolescence: Personality, peer, and family correlates. *Development Psychology, 19*, 269–277.

Brook, J. S., Hamburg, B. A., Balka, E. B., & Wynn, P. S. (1992). Sequences of drug involvement in African-American and Puerto Rican adolescents. *Psychological Reports, 71,* 179–182.

Brook, J. S., Whiteman, M., & Finch, S. (1992). Childhood aggression, adolescent delinquency, and drug use: A longitudinal study. *Journal of Genetic Psychology, 153,* 369–383.

Brook, J. S., Whiteman, M., & Cohen, P. (1995). Stage of drug use, aggression, and theft/vandalism: Shared and unshared risks. In H. Kaplan (Ed.), *Drugs, crime, and other deviant adaptations: Longitudinal studies* (pp. 83–96). New York: Plenum.

Brook, J. S., Whiteman, M., Cohen, P., Shapiro, J., & Balka, E. (1995). Longitudinally predicting late adolescent and young adult drug use: Childhood and adolescent precursors. *Journal of the American Academy of Child and Adolescent Psychiatry, 34,* 1230–1238.

Brook, J. S., Whiteman, M., Finch, S., & Cohen, P. (1995). Aggression, intrapsychic distress, and drug use: Antecedent and intervening processes. *Journal of the American Academy of Child and Adolescent Psychiatry, 34,* 1076–1084.

Brooks-Gunn, J. (1988). Antecedents and consequences of variations in girls' maturational timing. *Journal of Adolescent Health Care, 9,* 365–373.

Brooks-Gunn, J., & Warren, M. P. (1989). Biological contributions to affective expression in young adolescent girls. *Child Development, 60,* 372–385.

Bry, B. H., McKeon, P., & Pandina, R. J. (1982). Extent of drug use as a function of number of risk factors. *Journal of Abnormal Psychology, 91,* 273–279.

Brynner, J. M., O'Malley, P. M., & Bachman, J. G. (1981). Self-esteem and delinquency revisited. *Journal of Youth and Adolescence, 10,* 407–444.

Bureau of Business and Economic Research (1995). *Florida Census Handbook.* Gainesville, FL: University of Florida.

Burgess, E. W. (1926). *The urban community.* Chicago: University of Chicago Press.

Burgess, E. W. (1927). The determination of gradients in the growth of a city. *Publications of the American Sociological Society, 21,* 178–184.

Burgess, E. W. (1954). Economic, cultural, and social factors in family breakdown. *American Journal of Orthopsychiatry, 24,* 462–470.

Burgess, R., & Akers, R. (1968). A differential association-reinforcement theory of criminal behavior. *Social Problems, 14,* 128–147.

Burke, R. J., & Weir, T. (1978). Sex differences in adolescent life stress, social support, and well-being. *Journal of Psychology, 98,* 277–288.

Burnam, A., Hough, R., Karno, M., Escobar, J., & Telles, C. (1987). Acculturation and lifetime prevalence of psychiatric disorders among Mexican Americans in Los Angeles. *Journal of Health and Social Behavior, 28,* 89–102.

Cahalan, D., Cisin, I. H., & Crossley, H. M. (1969). *American drinking practices: A national study of drinking behavior and attitudes* (Rutgers Center of Alcohol Studies, Monograph No. 6). New Brunswick, NJ: Rutgers Center of Alcohol Studies.

Centers for Disease Control. (1989, September). *HIV/AIDS surveillance.* Atlanta, GA: Department of Health and Human Services.

Chassin, L., Presson, C. C., Sherman, S. J., & Edwards, D. A. (1990). The natural history of cigarette smoking: Predicting young-adult smoking outcomes from adolescent smoking patterns. *Health Psychology, 9,* 701–716.

Chavez, E. L., & Swaim, R. C. (1992). An epidemiological comparison of Mexican-American and White non-Hispanic 8th and 12th grade students' substance use. *American Journal of Public Health, 82,* 445–447.

Child, I. L. (1943). *Italian or American? The second generation conflict.* New Haven, Conn: Yale University Press.

Ching, C. L. (1981). The goal of abstinence: Implications for drug education. *Journal of Drug Education, 11*(1), 13–18.

Clarke, A. D. B., Clarke, A. M. (1984). Constancy and change in the growth of human characteristics. *Journal of child psychology and psychiatry, 25*, 191–210.

Cloward, R. A. (1959). Illegitimate means, anomie, and deviant behavior. *American Sociological Review, 24*, 164–176.

Cloward, R. A., & Ohlin, L. E. (1960). *Delinquency and opportunity*. New York: Free Press.

Cohen, J. (1993). Achieving a reduction in drug-related harm through education. In Nick Heather, A. Wodak, E. A. Nadelman, & Pat O'Hare (Eds.), *Psychoactive drugs and harm reduction: From faith to science* (pp. 52–74). Liverpool: Healthwise.

Cohen, P., & Brook, J. S. (1987). Family factors related to the persistence of psychopathology in childhood and adolescence. *Psychiatry, 50*, 332–345.

Compas, B. E., Davis, G. E., & Forsythe, C. J. (1985). Characteristics of life events during adolescence. *American Journal of Community Psychology, 13*, 677–691.

Compas, B. E., Malcarne, V. L., & Fondacaro, K. M. (1988). Coping with stressful events in older children and young adolescents. *Journal of Consulting and Clinical Psychology, 56*, 405–411.

Covello, V. T., & Mumpower, J. (1985). Risk analysis and risk management: An historical perspective. *Risk Analysis, 5*, 103–107.

Cox, D. R., & Oakes, D. (1984). *Analysis of survival data*. London, New York: Chapman and Hall.

Cronbach, L. J. (1951a). Coefficient alpha and the internal structure of tests. *Psychometrica, 16*, 297–334.

Cronbach, L. J. (1951b). *Essentials of psychological testing*. New York: Harper.

Cross, W. E., & Fhagen-Smith, P. (1996). Nigrescence and ego development: Accounting for differential Black identity patterns. In P. B. Pederson, J. G. Draguns, W. J. Lonner, & J. E. Trimble (Eds.), *Counseling across Cultures*. Thousand Oaks, CA: Sage.

Cuellar, I., Harris, L. C., & Jasso, R. (1980). An acculturation scale for Mexican American normal and clinical populations. *Hispanic Journal of Behavioral Science, 2*, 199–217.

Cummings, R. (1995). *Adolescence: A developmental perspective*. New York: Harcourt Brace.

Current Population Reports (1995). Washington, DC: US Department of Commerce, Bureau of the Census.

Dade County district and school profiles (1990–1991). Miami FL: Dade County Public School System, p. 13.

Dade kids face hardships. (1993, November 19). *Miami Herald*, p. A1, A25.

Dade schools on notice. (1995, October 12). *Miami Herald*, p. A1, A10.

Dawkins, M. P. (1996). The social context of substance use among African American youth: Rural, urban, and suburban comparisons. *Journal of Alcohol and Drug Education, 41*, 68–86.

De La Rosa, M. R., & Recio-Adrados, J. L. (1993). *Drug abuse among minority youth: Advances in research and methodology*. Rockville, MD: National Institute on Drug Abuse.

Dembo, R., Williams, L., LaVoie, L., Getreu, A., Berry, E., Genung, L., Schmeidler, J., Wish, E., & Kern, J. (1990). A longitudinal study of the relationships among alcohol use, marijuana/hashish use, cocaine use, and emotionally/psychologically functioning problems in a cohort of high risk youths. *International Journal of the Addictions, 25*, 1341–1382.

Demos, J. (1975). Myths and realities in the history of American life. In H. Grunebaum & J. Christ (Eds.), *Contemporary marriage: Structure, dynamics, and therapy* (pp. 9–36). Boston, MA: Little, Brown.

DiFranza, J. R., Richards, J. W., Paulman, P. M., Wolf-Gillespie, N., Fletcher, C., Jaffe, R. D., & Murray, D. (1991). RJR Nabisco's cartoon camel promotes Camel cigarettes to children. *Journal of the American Medical Association, 266*, 3149–3153.

Dohrenwend, B. P., & Dohrenwend, B. S. (1976). Sex differences and psychiatric disorders. *American Journal of Sociology, 81*, 1447–1454.

Donovan, J. E., & Jessor, R. (1985). Structure of problem behavior in adolescence and young adulthood. *Journal of Consulting and Clinical Psychology, 53*, 890–904.

Dorn, N., & Thompson, A. (1976). Evaluation of drug education in the longer term is not an optional extra. *Community Health, 7,* 154–161.

Dornbusch, S. M., Mont-Reynaud, R., Ritter, P. L., Chen, Z., & Steinberg, L. (1991). Stressful events and their correlates among adolescents of diverse backgrounds. In M. Colton & S. Gore (Eds.), *Adolescent stress: Causes and consequences* (pp. 157–180). New York: Aldine de Gruyter.

Downs, W. R. (1985). Using panel data to examine sex differences in causal relationships among adolescent alcohol use, norms, and peer alcohol use. *Journal of Youth and Adolescence, 14,* 469–486.

Downs, W. R., & Robertson, J. F. (1982). Adolescent alcohol consumption by age and sex of respondent. *Journal of Studies on Alcohol, 43,* 1027–1032.

Drug education's results questioned. (1995, February). *San Francisco Chronicle,* p. A6.

Dryfoos, J. G. (1990). Religiosity, beliefs, normative standards and adolescent drinking. *Journal of Studies on Alcohol, 41,* 662–671.

DuPont, R. L. (1996). Harm reduction and decriminalization in the United States: A personal perspective. *Substance Use & Misuse, 31,* 1929–1945.

Durkheim, E. (1951). *Suicide.* New York: Free Press.

Dweck, C. S., Davidson, W., Nelson, S., & Enna, B. (1978). Sex differences in learned helplessness: II. The contingencies of evaluative feedback in the classroom. III. An experimental analysis. *Developmental Psychology, 14,* 268–276.

Eagly, A. H. (1983). Gender and social influence: A social psychological analysis. *American Psychologist, 38,* 971–981.

Eliot, D. S., & Huizinga, D. (1984). *The relationship between delinquent behavior and ADM problems.* Boulder, CO: Behavior Research Institute.

Eliot, D. S., Huizinga, D., & Ageton, S. S. (1985). *Explaining delinquency and drug use.* Newbury Park, CA: Sage.

Eliot, D. S., Huizinga, D., & Menard, S. (1989). *Multiple problem youth: Delinquency, substance use and mental health problems.* New York: Springer-Verlag.

Elkind, D. (1967). Egocentrism in adolescence. *Child Development, 38,* 1025–1034.

Elkind, D. (1978). *A sympathetic understanding of the child: Birth to sixteen* (2nd ed.). Boston: Allyn & Bacon.

Elkind, D. (1995). *The ties that stress: The new family imbalance.* Cambridge, MA: Harvard University Press.

Ellickson, P. L., Hays, R. D., & Bell, R. M. (1992). Stepping through the drug use sequence: Longitudinal scalogram analysis of initiation and regular use. *Journal of Abnormal Psychology, 101,* 441–451.

Ensminger, M. E., Brown, C. H., & Kellam, S. G. (1982). Sex differences in antecedents of substance use among adolescents. *Journal of Drug Issues, 38,* 25–42.

Erikson, E. H. (1959a). Identity and the life cycle. *Psychological Issues, 1,* 1–171.

Erikson, E. H. (1959b). *Identity and the life cycle.* New York: International Universities Press.

Erikson, E. H. (1963). *Childhood and society* (2nd ed.). New York: Norton.

Erikson, E. H. (1968). *Identity: Youth in crisis.* New York: Norton.

Ernest, A., & Sokol, R. (1987). Incidence of fetal alcohol syndrome and economic impact of FAS-related anomalies. *Drug and Alcohol Dependence, 19,* 53.

Evans, R. I., Rozelle, R. M., Mittlemark, M. B., Hansen, W. B., Bane, A. L., & Havis, J. (1978). Deterring the onset of smoking in children: Knowledge of immediate physiological effects and coping with peer pressure, media pressure, and parent modeling. *Journal of Applied Social Psychology, 8,* 126–135.

Evans, R. I., Rozelle, R. M., Maxwell, S. E., Raines, B. E., Dill, C. A., Guthrie, T. J., Henderson, A. H., & Hill, P. C. (1981). Social modeling of films to deter smoking in adolescents: Results of a three-year field investigation. *Journal of Applied Social Psychology, 8,* 126–135.

Fabrega, H. (1969). Social psychiatric aspects of acculturation and migration: A general statement. *Comprehensive Psychiatry, 10*, 314–329.

Fagan, J., & Hartsone, E. (1984). *Dilemmas in juvenile corrections: Treatment interventions for special problem youth.* San Francisco, CA: URSA Institute.

Falco, M. (1992). *The making of a drug-free America.* New York: Times Books.

Faris, R., & Dunham, H. (1939). *Mental disorders in urban areas.* Chicago: University of Chicago Press.

Farrell, A. D., Danish, S. J., & Howard, C. W. (1992a). Risk factors for drug use in urban adolescents: Identification and cross-validation. *American Journal of Community Psychology, 20*, 263–286.

Farrell, A. D., Danish, S. J., & Howard, C. W. (1992b). Relationship between drug use and other problem behaviors in urban adolescents. *Journal of Consulting Clinical Psychology, 60*, 705–712.

Faust, M. S. (1983). Alternative constructions of adolescent growth. In J. Brooks-Gunn & A. C. Petersen (Eds.), *Girls at puberty: Biological and psychosocial perspectives* (pp. 105–127). New York: Plenum.

Favazza, F. R. (1980). Culture change and mental health. *Journal of Operational Psychiatry, 11*, 101–119.

Federal Bureau of Investigation. (1966). *Crime in the United States: Uniform crime reports, 1965.* Washington, DC: U.S. Government Printing Office.

Federal Bureau of Investigation. (1986). *Crime in the United States: Uniform crime reports, 1985.* Washington, DC: U.S. Government Printing Office.

Federal Bureau of Investigation. (1990). *Crime in the United States: Uniform crime reports, 1989.* Washington, DC: U.S. Government Printing Office.

Felix-Ortiz, M., & Newcomb, M. D. (1992). Risk and protective factors for drug use among Latino and White adolescents. *Hispanic Journal of Behavioral Sciences, 14*, 291–309.

Felix-Ortiz, M., & Newcomb, M. D. (1995). Cultural identity and drug use among Latino and Latina adolescents. In G. J. Botvin, S. Schinke, & M. A. Orlandi (Eds.), *Drug use prevention with multiethnic youth* (pp. 147–165). Thousand Oaks, CA: Sage.

Flannery, D. J., Vazsonyi, A. T., Torquati, J., & Fridrich, A. (1994). Ethnic and gender differences in risk for early adolescent substance use. *Journal of Youth and Adolescence, 23*, 195–213.

Flay, B. R. (1985). Psychosocial approaches to smoking prevention: A review of findings. *Health Psychology, 4*, 449–488.

Flay, B. R., Hu, F. B., Siddiqui, O., Day, L. E., Hedeker, D., Petraitis, J., Richardson, J., & Sussman, S. (1994). Differential influence of parental smoking and friends' smoking on adolescent initiation and escalation of smoking. *Journal of Health and Social Behavior, 35*, 248–265.

Fleming, J. P., Kellam, S. G., & Brown, C. H. (1982). Early predictors of age at first use of alcohol, marijuana, and cigarettes. *Drug and Alcohol Dependence, 9*, 285–303.

Florida officials to meet with city manager. (1996, December 4). *Miami Herald*, p. A1, 2.

Florida statistical abstract (1995). Bureau of Business and Economic Research. Gainesville, FL: University Press of Florida.

Fordham, S., & Ogbu, J. U. (1987). Black student's school success: Coping with the burden of 'acting white.' *Urban Review, 18*, 176–206.

Forney, M. A., Forney, P. D., & Ripley, W. K. (1991). Alcohol use among Black adolescents: Parental and peer influences. *Journal of Alcohol and Drug Education, 36*, 36–46.

Forslund, M. A., & Gustafson, T. J. (1970). Influence of peers and parents and sex differences in drinking by high-school students. *Quarterly Journal of Studies on Alcohol, 31*, 868–875.

Fort, J. (1981). *The addicted society.* New York: Grove Press.

Freud, S. (1969). Adolescence as a developmental disturbance. In G. Caplan & S. Lebovovici (Eds.), *Adolescence* (pp. 39–47). New York: Basic Books.

Friedman, A. S. (1987). Psychopathology as an antecedent to, and as a consequence of, substance use in adolescence. *Journal of Drug Education, 17*, 233–244.

Fuchs, V. R., & Reklis, D. M. (1992). America's children: Economic perspectives and policy options. *Science, 25*, 41–46.

Gans, H. J. (1992). Second generation decline: Scenarios for the economic and ethnic futures of the post-1965 American immigrants. *Ethnic and Racial Studies, 15*, 173–192.

Garmezy, N. (1983). Stressors of childhood. In N. Garmezy & M. Rutter (Eds.), *Stress, coping and development in children* (pp. 43–84). New York: McGraw-Hill.

Gary, L. E. (1983). The impact of alcohol and drug abuse on homicidal victims. In T. D. Watts & R. Wright (Eds.), *Black alcoholism: Toward a comprehensive understanding.* Springfield, IL: Charles C Thomas.

Gibson, M. A. (1995). Additive acculturation as a strategy for school improvement. In R. G. Rumbaut & W. A. Cornelius (Eds.), *California's immigrant children: Theory, research, and implications for educational policy* (pp. 77–106). San Diego: Center for U.S.–Mexican Studies, University of California, San Diego.

Gibson, M. A., & Ogbu, J. U. (1991). *Minority status and schooling: A comparative study of immigrant and involuntary minorities.* New York: Garland Publishing.

Gil, A. G., & Vega, W. A. (1996). Two different worlds: Acculturation stress and adaptation among Cuban and Nicaraguan families. *Journal of Social and Personal Relationships, 13*(3), 435–456.

Gil, A. G., Vega, W. A., & Biafora, E. (1998). Temporal influences of family structure, and family risk factors on drug use initiation in a multiethnic sample of adolescent boys. *Journal of Youth and Adolescence* (forthcoming, Spring 1998).

Gil, A. G., Vega, W. A., & Dimas, J. (1994). Acculturative stress and personal adjustment among Hispanic adolescent boys. *Journal of Community Psychology, 22*, 43–54.

Gilbert, M. J., & Alcocer, A. M. (1988). Alcohol use and Hispanic youth: An overview. *Journal of Drug Issues, 18*(1), 33–48.

Gilbert, M. J., & Cervantes, R. C. (1986). Patterns and practices of alcohol use among Mexican Americans: A comprehensive review. *Hispanic Journal of Behavioral Sciences, 8*, 1–60.

Gillmore, M. R., Hawkins, J. D., Catalano, R. F., Day, L. E., Moore, M., & Abbott, R. (1991). Structure of problem behaviors in preadolescence. *Journal of Consulting and Clinical Psychology, 59*, 499–506.

Girgus, J. S., Nolen-Hoeksema, S., & Seligman, M. E. P. (1989, August). *Why do sex differences in depression emerge during adolescence?* Paper presented at the 97th Annual Convention of the American Psychological Association, New Orleans, LA.

Glaser, D. (1956). Criminality theories and behavioral images. *American Journal of Sociology, 61*, 433–444.

Glazer, J., & Moynihan, P. (1968). *Beyond the melting pot* (10th ed.). Cambridge MA: MIT Press.

Glueck, S., & Glueck, E. (1962). *Family environments and delinquency.* Boston: Houghton-Mifflin.

Glueck, S., & Glueck, E. (1968). *Delinquents and non-delinquents in perspective.* Cambridge, MA: Harvard University Press.

Goode, E. (1993). *Drugs in American society.* New York: McGraw-Hill.

Goodstadt, M. S. (1974). Myths and methodology in drug education: A critical review of the research evidence. In M. S. Goodstadt (Ed.), *Research on methods and programs of drug education.* Toronto: Addiction Research Foundation.

Gordon, M. (1964). *Assimilation in American life. The role of race, religion, and national origin.* New York: Oxford University Press.

Gore, S., Aseltine, R. H., & Colton, M. E. (1992). Social structure, life stress and depressive symptoms in a high school-aged population. *Journal of Health and Social Behavior, 33*, 97–113.

Gottfredson, M., & Hirschi, T. (1989). A propensity-event theory of crime. In W. S. Lafner & F. Adler (Eds.), *Advances in criminological theory* (Vol. 1, pp. 57–68). New Brunswick, NJ: Transaction Publishers.

Gottfredson, M. R., & Hirschi, T. (1990). *A general theory of crime.* Stanford, CA: Stanford University Press.

Grady, K., Gersick, K. E., Snow, D. L., & Kessen, M. (1986). The emergence of adolescent substance use. *Journal of Drug Education, 16,* 203–220.

Graves, T. D. (1967). Psychological acculturation in a tri-ethnic community. *SouthWestern Journal of Anthropology, 23,* 68–77.

Green, L. W. (1985). *Toward a healthy community: Organizing events for community health promotion.* Washington, DC: US Government Printing Office.

Grenier, G. J., & Stepick, A. (1992). In G. J. Grenier & A. Stepick III (Eds.), *Miami now. Immigration, ethnicity, and social change.* Gainesville: University Press of Florida.

Grube, J. W., & Wallack, L. (1994). Television beer advertising and drinking knowledge, beliefs, and intentions among school children. *American Journal of Public Health, 84,* 254–259.

Guinn, R., & Hurley, R. S. (1976). A comparison of drug use among Houston and Lower Rio Grande secondary students. *Adolescence 11,* 43, 456–459.

Gutman, H. (1976). *The black family in slavery and freedom, 1750–1925.* New York: Pantheon.

Gutman, H. (1983). Persistent myths about the Afro-American family. In Michael Gordon (Ed.), *The American Family in Social Historical Perspective* (pp. 459–481). New York: St. Martin's Press.

Guy, S. M., Smith, G. M., & Bentler, P. M. (1994a). Consequences of adolescent drug use and personality factors on adult drug use. *Journal of Drug Education, 24,* 109–132.3.

Guy, S. M., Smith, G. M., & Bentler, P. M. (1994b). The influence of adolescent substance use and socialization on deviant behavior in young adulthood. *Criminal Justice and Behavior, 21,* 236–255.

Hacker, G. A., Collins, R., & Jacobson, M. (1987). *Marketing booze to blacks.* Washington, DC: Center for Science in the Public Interest.

Hamburg, B. A., Braemer, H. C., & Jahnke, W. A. (1975). Hierarchy of drug use in adolescence: Behavior and attitudinal correlates of substantial drug use. *American Journal of Psychiatry, 132,* 1155–1167.

Handlin, O. (1959). *Immigration as a factor in American history.* Englewood Cliffs, NJ: Prentice Hall.

Hansell, S., & White, H. R. (1991). Adolescent drug use, psychological distress, and physical symptoms. *Journal of Health and Social Behavior, 32,* 288–301.

Harford, T. C. (1986). Drinking patterns among black and nonblack adolescents: Results of a national survey. *Annals of the New York Academy of Sciences, 472,* 130–141.

Harlow, L. L., Newcomb, M. D., & Bentler, P. M. (1986). Depression, self-derogation, substance use, and suicide ideation: Lack of purpose in life as a mediational factor. *Journal of Clinical Psychology, 42,* 5–21.

Harris, A. R. (1977). Sex and theories of deviance: Toward a functional theory of deviant typescripts. *American Sociological Review, 42,* 3–16.

Hawkins, D. J., Catalano, R. F., & Miller, J. Y. (1992). Risk and protective factors for alcohol and other drug problems in adolescence and early adulthood: Implications for substance abuse prevention. *Psychological Bulletin, 112,* 64–105.

Hays, R. D. (1991). User's Guide for the Longitudinal Scalogram Analysis Program. Santa Monica, CA: RAND.

Hays, R. D., & Ellickson, P. L. (1991). Guttman scale analysis of longitudinal data: Methodology and drug use applications. *International Journal of Addictions, 25*(11A), 1341–1352.

Herd, D. (1985). *The socio-cultural correlates of drinking patterns in black and white Americans.* Ph.D. dissertation, University of California, San Francisco, Alcohol Research Group.

Herd, D. (1987). Rethinking black drinking. *British Journal of Addiction, 82,* 219–223.

Herd, D. (1990). Subgroup differences in drinking patterns among black and white men: Results from a national survey. *Journal of Studies on Alcohol, 51,* 221–232.

Herskovits, M. J. (1938). *Acculturation: The study of culture contact*. New York: Augustin.

Hirschi, T. (1969). *Causes of delinquency*. Berkeley, CA: University of California Press.

Hirschi, T., & Gottfredson, M. (1983). Age and the explanation of crime. *American Journal of Sociology, 89*, 552–584.

Hoffman, T., Dana, R. H., & Bolton, B. (1985). Measured acculturation and MMPI-168 performance of Native American adults. *Journal of Cross Cultural Psychology, 16*, 243–256.

Homans, G. C. (1967). *The nature of social science*. New York: Harcourt Brace Jovanovich.

Hops, H., Weissman, W., Biglan, A., Thompson, R., Faller, C., & Severson, H. H. (1986). A taped situation test of cigarette refusal skills among adolescents. *Behavioral Assessment, 8*, 145–154.

Hops, H., Sherman, L., & Biglan, A. (1989). Maternal depression, marital discord, and children's behavior: A developmental perspective. In G. Patterson (Ed.), *Depression and aggression in family interactions* (pp. 185–208). Hillsdale, NJ: Erlbaum.

Horwitz, A. V., & White, H. R. (1987). Gender role orientations and styles of pathology among adolescents. *Journal of Health and Social Behavior, 28*, 158–170.

Huba, G. J., & Bentler, P. M. (1980). The role of peer and adult models for drug taking at different stages in adolescence. *Journal of Youth and Adolescence, 9*, 449–465.

Huba, G. J., & Bentler, P. M. (1982). A developmental theory of drug use: Derivations and assessment of a causal modeling approach. In P. B. Baltes & O. G. Brim (Eds.), *Theories on drug abuse: Selected contemporary perspectives* (Research Monograph 30, pp. 95–101). Rockville, MD: National Institute on Drug Abuse.

Huba, G. J., & Bentler, P. M. (1984). Causal models of personality, peer culture characteristics, drug use and criminal behaviors over a five year span. In D. W. Goodwin, K. T. Van Dusen, & S. A. Mednick (Eds.), *Longitudinal research in alcoholism* (pp. 73–94). Boston: Kluwer-Nijhoff.

Huba, G. J., Newcomb, M. D., & Bentler, P. M. (1986). Adverse drug experiences and drug use behaviors: A one-year longitudinal study of adolescents. *Journal of Pediatric Psychology, 11*, 203–219.

Huizinga, D., Loeber, R., & Thornberry, T. P. (1993). Longitudinal study of delinquency, drug use, sexual activity, and pregnancy among children and youth in three cities. *Public Health Reports, 108*, 90–96.

Hundleby, J. D. (1987). Adolescent drug use in a behavioral matrix: A confirmation and comparison of the sexes. *Addictive Behaviors, 12*, 103–112.

Hunt, D. G. (1974). Parental permissiveness as perceived by the offspring and the degree of marijuana usage among offspring. *Human Relations, 27*, 267–285.

Hurricane recovery slow. (1993, April 18). *Miami Herald*, p. B1.2

Inciardi, J. A. (1981). *The drugs-crime connection*. Beverly Hills, CA: Sage.

Jackson, N., Greenaway, C., & Zalesnick, M. (1981). Age of initial drug experimentation among white and non-white ethnics. *The International Journal of Addictions, 16*, 1373–1386.

Jaynes, G. D., & Williams, R. M. (1989). *A common destiny: Blacks and American society*. Washington, DC: National Academy of Sciences.

Jessor, R. (1982). Critical issues in research on adolescent health promotion. In T. Coates, A. Peteresen, & C. Perry (Eds.), *Promoting adolescent health: A dialogue on research and practice* (pp. 447–465). New York: Academic Press.

Jessor, R., & Jessor, S. L. (1977). *Problem behavior and psychosocial development: A longitudinal study of youth*. New York: Academic Press.

Jessor, R., & Jessor, S. L. (1978). Theory testing in longitudinal research on marijuana. In D. B. Kandel (Ed.), *Longitudinal research on drug use: Empirical findings and methodological issues*. Washington, DC: Hemisphere.

Jessor, R., Graves, T. D., Hanson, R. C., & Jessor, S. L. (1968). *Society, personality and deviant behavior: A study of a tri-ethnic community*. New York: Holt, Rinehart & Winston.

Jessor, R., Van Den Bos, J., Vanderryn, J., Costa, F. M., & Turbin, M. S. (1995). Protective factors in adolescent problem behavior: Moderator effects and developmental change. *Developmental Psychology, 31*, 923–933.

Johnson, R. E., & Marcos, A. C. (1988). Correlates of adolescent drug use by gender and geographic location. *American Journal of Drug and Alcohol Abuse, 14*, 51–63.

Johnston, L. D., & O'Malley, P. M. (1985). Issues of validity and population coverage in student surveys of drug use. In *Self-report methods of estimating drug use*, (NIDA Research Monograph No. 57, pp. 31–54). Washington, DC: U.S. Government Printing Office.

Johnston, L. D., Bachman, J. G., & O'Malley, P. M. (1984). *Monitoring the future: Questionnaire responses from the nation's high school seniors, 1983.* Ann Arbor, MI: Institute for Social Research, University of Michigan.

Johnston, L. D., O'Malley, P. M., & Bachman, J. G. (1988). *Illicit drug use, smoking, and drinking by America's high school students, college students, and young adults* (DHHS Pub. No. ADM 89-1602). Washington, DC: U.S. Government Printing Office.

Johnston, L. D., O'Malley, P. M., & Bachman, J. G. (1991). Drug use among American high school seniors, college students and young adults, 1975–1990: Vol. 1. High school seniors. Rockville, MD: National Institute on Drug Abuse.

Johnston, L. D., O'Malley, P. M., & Bachman, J. G. (1994). *Monitoring the Future Study.* Rockville, MD: National Institute on Drug Abuse.

Johnston, L. D., O'Malley, P. M., & Bachman, J. G. (1995). *Monitoring the future study, Preliminary report.* Ann Arbor, MI: Institute for Social Research, University of Michigan.

Johnston, L. D., O'Malley, P. M., & Bachman, J. G. (1996). *National results on drug use from the monitoring the future study, 1975–1995*, 2 Vols. (NIH Publication No. 96-4139). Washington, DC: U.S. Government Printing Office.

Kaestner, E., Frank, B., Marel, R., & Schmeider, J. (1986). Substance use among females in New York State: Catching up with the males. *Advances in Alcohol and Substance Abuse, 5*, 29–49.

Kaftarian, S. J., & Hansen, W. B. (1994). Improving methodologies for the evaluation of community-based substance abuse prevention programs [CSAP Special Issue, Community Partnership Program], *Journal of Community Psychology*, pp. 3–5.

Kandel, D. B. (1975). Stages in adolescent involvement in drug use. *Science, 190*, 912–914.

Kandel, D. B. (1978). Convergences in prospective longitudinal surveys of drug use in normal populations. In D. B. Kandel (Ed.), *Longitudinal research on drug use: Empirical findings and methodological issues* (pp. 3–38). Washington DC: Hemisphere (Halsted-Wiley).

Kandel, D. (1982). Epidemiological and psychological perspectives on adolescent drug use. *Journal of the American Academy of Child Psychiatry, 21*, 328–347.

Kandel, D. B. (1985a). On processes of peer influences in adolescent drug use: A developmental perspective. *Advances in Alcohol and Substance Abuse, 4*, 139–163.

Kandel, D. B. (1985b). Stages in adolescent involvement in drug use. *Science, 190*, 912–914.

Kandel, D. B. (1988). Issues of sequencing of adolescent drug use and other problem behaviors. *Drugs and Society, 3*, 55–76.

Kandel, D. (1995). Ethnic differences in drug use. In G. J. Botvin, S. Schinke, & M. A. Orlandi (Eds.), *Drug abuse prevention with multiethnic youth* (pp. 81–105). Thousand Oaks, CA: Sage.

Kandel, D. B., & Davies, M. (1982). Epidemiology of depressive mood in adolescence. *Archives of General Psychiatry, 39*, 1205–1212.

Kandel, D. B., & Faust, R. (1975). Sequence and stages in patterns of adolescent drug use. *Archives of General Psychiatry, 32*, 923–932.

Kandel, D. B., & Logan, J. A. (1984). Patterns of drug use from adolescence to young adulthood. Periods of risk for initiation, stabilization and decline in use. *American Journal of Public Health, 74*, 660–672.

Kandel, D., & Yamaguchi, K. (1993). From beer to crack: Developmental patterns of drug involvement. *American Journal of Public Health, 83*, 851–855.

Kandel, D., & Davies, M., & Davis, M. (1990). *New York state youth survey.* Albany: New York State Office of Mental Health.

Kandel, D. B., Davies, M., Karus, D., & Yamaguchi, K. (1986). The consequences in young adulthood of adolescent drug involvement. *Archives of General Psychiatry, 43*, 746–754.

Kandel, D. B., Simcha-Fagan, O., & Davies, M. (1986). Risk factors for delinquency and illicit drug use from adolescence to young adulthood. *Journal of Drug Issues, 16*, 67–90.

Kandel, D. B., Kessler, R., & Margulies, R. (1978). Antecedents of adolescent initiation into stages of drug use: A developmental analysis. In D. B. Kandel (Ed.), *Longitudinal research on drug use: Empirical findings and methodological issues* (pp. 73–99). Washington, DC: Hemisphere.

Kandel, D., Yamaguchi, K., & Chen, K. (1992). Stages of progression in drug involvement from adolescence to adulthood: Further evidence for the gateway theory. *Journal of Studies on Alcohol, 53*, 447–457.

Kaplan, H. B. (1975). Increase in self-rejection as an antecedent of deviant responses. *Journal of Youth and Adolescence, 4*, 438–458.

Kaplan, H. B. (1980). *Deviant behavior in defense of self.* New York: Academic Press.

Kaplan, H. B. (1984a). *Patterns of juvenile delinquency.* Beverly Hills: Sage.

Kaplan, H. B. (1984b). Pathways to adolescent drug use: Self-derogation, peer influence, weakening of social controls and early substance use. *Journal of Health and Social Behavior, 25*, 270–289.

Kaplan, H. B. (1995). Drugs, crime and other deviant adaptations. In H. B. Kaplan (Ed.), *Drugs, crime and other deviant adaptations: Longitudinal studies* (pp. 1–46). New York: Plenum.

Kaplan, H. B., & Fukurai, H. (1992). Negative social sanctions, self-rejection, and drug use. *Youth and Society, 23*, 275–298.

Kaplan, H. B., & Johnson, R. J. (1991). Negative social sanctions and juvenile delinquency: Effects of labeling in a model of deviant behavior. *Social Science Quarterly, 72*, 98–122.

Kaplan, H. B., Martin, S., & Robbins, C. (1984). Pathways to adolescent drug use: Self-derogation, peer influence, weakening of social controls, and early substance use. *Journal of Health and Social Behavior, 25*, 270–289.

Kaplan, H. B., Martin, S., & Robbins, C. (1985). Toward an explanation of increased involvement in illicit drug use: Application of a general theory of deviant behavior. In J. R. Greenley (Ed.), *Research in community and mental health* (Vol. 5, pp. 205–252). Greenwich, CT: JAI Press.

Kaplan, H. B., Johnson, R. J., & Bailey, C. A. (1986). Self-rejection and the explanation of deviance: Refinement and elaboration of a latent structure. *Social Psychological Quarterly, 49*, 110–128.

Kaplan, H. B., Martin, S. S., & Johnson, R. J. (1986). Self-rejection and the explanation of deviance: Specification of the structure among latent constructs. *American Journal of Sociology, 92*, 384–411.

Kaplan, H. B., Johnson, R. J., & Bailey, C. A. (1987). Deviant peers and deviant behavior: Further elaboration of a model. *Social Psychology Quarterly, 50*, 277–284.

Kaplan, H. B., Johnson, R. J., & Bailey, C. A. (1988a). Applications of a general theory of deviant behavior: Self-derogation and adolescent drug use. *Journal of Health and Social Behavior, 23*, 274–294.

Kaplan, H. B., Johnson, R. J., & Bailey, C. A. (1988b). Explaining adolescent drug use: An elaboration strategy for structural equations modeling. *Psychiatry, 51*, 142–161.

Keefe, S. E. (1984). Real and ideal extended families among Mexican Americans and Anglo Americans: On the meaning of close family ties. *Human Organization, 43*, 65–70.

Keefe, S. E., & Padilla, A. M. (1987). *Chicano ethnicity.* Albuquerque: University of New Mexico Press.

Kelly, J. G. (1968). Toward an ecological conception of preventive intervention. In J. W. Carter (Ed.), *Research contributions from psychology to community mental health* (pp. 76–101). New York: Behavioral Publications.

Khoury, E. L., Warheit, G. J., Zimmerman, R. S., Vega, W. A., & Gil, A. G. (1996). Gender and ethnic differences in the prevalence of alcohol, cigarette, and illicit drug use in a cohort of young Hispanic adolescents in South Florida. *Women and Health, 24*, 21–40.

Khoury, E. L., Warheit, G. J., Hargrove, M. C., Zimmerman, R. S., Vega, W. A., & Gil, A. G. (1997). The impact of Hurricane Andrew on deviant behavior among a multi-racial/ethnic sample of adolescents in Dade County, Florida: A longitudinal analysis. *Journal of Traumatic Stress, 10*(1), 71–91.

Kilbourne, J. (1991). Deadly persuasion: 7 myths alcohol advertisers may want you to believe. *Media and Values, 54/55*, pp. 10–12.

Kinder, B., Pape, N., & Walfish, S. (1980). Drug and alcohol education programs: A review of outcome studies. *International Journal of the Addictions, 15*, 1035–1054.

Kleinman, P. H., Wish, E. D., Deren, S., & Rainone, G. (1988). Daily marijuana use and problem behaviors among adolescents. *International Journal of the Addictions, 23*, 87–107.

Kluckhohn, C., & Leighton, D. (1946). *The Navajo.* Cambridge, MA: Harvard University Press.

Kluckhohn, F., & Strodbeck, F. (1961). *Variations in value orientations.* Evanston, IL: Row Peterson.

Krohn, M. D., Skinner, W. F., Massey, J. L., & Lauer, R. M. (1983). Social bonding theory and adolescent cigarette smoking: A longitudinal analysis. *Journal of Health and Social Behavior, 24*, 337–349.

Krohn, M. D., Skinner, W. F., Massey, J. L., & Akers, R. L. (1985). Social learning theory and adolescent cigarette smoking: A longitudinal study. *Social Problems, 32*, 455–473.

Kuo, W. H. (1976). Theories of migration and mental health: An empirical testing on Chinese-Americans. *Social Science Medicine, 10*, 297–306.

Labouvie, E. W., Pandina, R. J., White, H. R., & Johnson, V. (1990). Risk factors of adolescent drug use: An affect-based interpretation. *Journal of Substance Use, 2*, 265–285.

Lamke, L. K. (1982). The impact of sex-role orientation on self-esteem in early adolescence. *Child Development, 53*, 1530–1535.

Landrine, H., & Klonoff, E. A. (1996). *African American acculturation.* Thousand Oaks, CA: Sage.

Landrine, H., Richardson, J. L., Klonoff, E. A., & Flay, B. (1994). Cultural diversity in the predictors of adolescent cigarette smoking. *Journal of Behavioral Medicine, 17*, 331–346.

Laub, J. H., & Sampson, R. J. (1988). Unraveling families and delinquency: A reanalysis of the Gluecks' data. *Criminology, 26*, 355–380.

Lavik, N. J., & Onstad, S. (1986). Drug use and psychiatric symptoms in adolescence. *Acta Psychiatrica Scandanavia, 73*, 437–440.

Lazarus, R. S., & Launier, R. (1978). Stress related transactions between person and environment. In L. A. Pervin & M. Lewis (Eds.), *Perspectives in interactional psychology* (pp. 287–327). New York: Plenum.

Lemert, E. M. (1951). *Social pathology: A system approach to the theory of sociopathic behavior.* New York: McGraw-Hill.

Lerner, R. M. (1986). *Concepts and theories of human development* (2nd ed.). New York: Random House.

Lerner, R. M., Petersen, A. C., & Brooks-Gunn, J. (1991). *Encyclopedia of adolescence.* New York: Garland.

Lewis, M. A., Leake, B., Giovannoni, J., Rogers, K., & Monahan, G. (1995). Drugs, poverty, pregnancy, and foster care in Los Angeles, California, 1989 to 1991. *Western Journal of Medicine, 163*, 435–440.

Lewis, O. (1969). Culture of poverty. In D. P. Moynihan (Ed.), *On understanding poverty: Perspectives from the social sciences* (pp. 23–24). New York: Basic Books.

Linton, R. (1940). *Acculturation in seven American Indian tribes.* New York: Appleton-Century-Crofts.

Loeber, R., & Stouthamer-Loeber, M. (1986). Family factors as correlates and predictors of juvenile conduct problems and delinquency. In M. Tonry & N. Morris (Eds.), *Crime and justice* (Vol. 7, pp. 29–149). Chicago: University of Chicago Press.

Luther, S. S., & Zigler, E. (1991). Vulnerability and competence: A review of research on resilience in childhood. *American Journal of Orthopsychiatry, 61,* 6–22.

Lynskey, M. T., & Ferguson, D. M. (1995). Childhood conduct problems, attention deficit behaviors, and adolescent alcohol, tobacco, and illicit drug use. *Journal of Abnormal Child Psychology, 23,* 281–302.

Maccoby, E. E., & Martin, J. A. (1983). Socialization in the context of the family: Parent–child interaction. In E. M. Hetherington (Ed.), *Handbook of child psychology,* Vol. 4, *Socialization, personality, and social development* (pp. 1–101). New York: John Wiley.

Maddahian, E., Newcomb, M. D., & Bentler, P. M. (1985). Single and multiple patterns of adolescent substance use: Longitudinal comparisons of four ethnic groups. *Journal of Drug Education, 15,* 311–326.

Maddahian, E., Newcomb, M. D., & Bentler, P. (1986). Adolescents' substance use: Impact of ethnicity, income, and availability. *Advances in Alcohol and Substance Abuse, 5,* 63–78.

Maddox, G. L., & McCall, B. C. (1964). *Drinking among teenagers; A sociological interpretation of alcohol use by high-school students* (Rutgers Center of Alcohol Studies, Research Monograph No. 4). New Brunswick, NJ: Rutgers Center on Alcohol Studies.

Magnusson, D. (1987). *Paths through life, vol. 1.* Hillsdale, NJ: Erlbaum.

Magnusson, D., & Bergman, L. R. (1988). Individual and variable-based approaches to longitudinal research on early risk factors. In M. Rutter (Ed.), *Studies of psychosocial risk: The power of longitudinal data* (pp. 46–61). New York: Cambridge University Press.

Making Prevention Work (1997). Rockville, MD: Center for Substance Abuse Prevention (CSAP).

Malvin, J., Moskowitz, J., Schaps, E., & Schaeffer, G. (1985). Evaluation of two school-based alternatives programs. *Journal of Alcohol Drug Education, 30,* 98–108.

Marin, G., Sabogal, F., Marin, B. V., Otero-Sabogal, R., & Perez-Stable, E. J. (1987). Development of a short acculturation scale for Hispanics. *Hispanic Journal of Behavioral Science, 9,* 183–205.

Markstrom-Adams, C. (1989). Androgyny and its relation to adolescent psychosocial well-being: A review of the literature. *Sex Roles, 21,* 325–340.

Martin, S. S., & Robbins, C. A. (1995). Personality, social control, and drug use in early adolescence. In H. B. Kaplan (Ed.), *Drugs, crime, and other deviant adaptations: Longitudinal studies* (pp. 145–161). New York: Plenum.

Mason, M. L. (1973). Drug education effects. *Dissertation Abstracts, 34*(4-B), 418.

Mata, A. G. (1986). *Alcohol use among South Texas adolescent youth.* Austin, TX: Texas Commission on Alcoholism.

McAdoo, H. (1983). *Extended family support of single black mothers.* Final report for the National Institute of Mental Health, Rockville, MD: NIMH.

McAlister, A. L., Perry, C. L., & Maccoby. N. (1979). Adolescent smoking: Onset and prevention. *Pediatrics, 63,* 650–658.

McAlister, A. L., Perry, C. L., Killen, J., Slinkard, L. A., & Maccoby, N. (1980). Pilot study of smoking, alcohol, and drug abuse prevention. *American Journal of Public Health, 70,* 719–721.

McBride, A. A., Joe, G. W., & Simpson, D. D. (1991). The prediction of long-term alcohol use, drug use and criminality among inhalant users. *Hispanic Journal of Behavioral Sciences, 13,* 315–323.

McCarthy, J. D., & Hoge, D. R. (1984). The dynamics of self-esteem and delinquency. *American Journal of Sociology, 90,* 396–410.

McCord, J. (1991). The cycle of crime and socialization practices. *Journal of Criminal Law and Criminology, 82,* 211–228.

McCutcheon, A. L. (1987). *Latent class analysis.* Newbury Park: Sage.

McKenzie, R. D. (1933). *The metropolitan community.* New York: McGraw-Hill.

McMillan, B., Florin, P., Stevenson, J., Kerman, B., & Mitchell, R. (1995). Empowerment praxis in community coalitions. *American Journal of Community Psychology, 23,* 699–727.

Mead, M. (1949). *Culture change and character structure.* New York: Oxford University Press.

Menard, S. (1995). *Applied logistic regression analysis* (Sage University paper series on Quantitative Applications in the Social Sciences, series no. 07-106). Thousand Oaks, CA: Sage.

Mensch, B. S., & Kandel, D. B. (1988). Under reporting of substance use in a national longitudinal youth cohort. *Public Opinion Quarterly, 52,* 100–124.

Merton, R. K. (1938). Social structure and anomie. *American Sociological Review, 3,* 672–682.

Merton, R. K. (1957). *Social theory and social structure.* Glencoe, NY: Free Press.

Messner, S. F., Krohn, M. D., & Liska, A. E. (1989). *Theoretical integration in the study of deviance and crime: Problems and prospects.* Albany, NY: State University of New York Press.

Metcalf, A. W. (1995). Child, adolescent, and adult development. In H. Goldman (Ed.), *Review of general psychiatry* (pp. 20–43). Norwalk, CT: Appleton and Lange.

Milgram, C. G. (1993). Adolescents, alcohol and aggression. *Journal of Studies in Alcohol, 11*(Suppl. 11), 53–61.

Miller, W. (1958). Lower class culture as a generating milieu of gang delinquency. *Journal of Social Issues, 14,* 5–19.

Mindel, C. H. (1980). Extended familism among urban Mexican Americans, Anglos, and Blacks. *Hispanic Journal of Behavioral Sciences, 2,* 21–34.

Monitoring the Future Survey. (1994). Washington, DC: National Institute on Drug Abuse, Department of Health and Human Services.

Mooney, D. K., Fromme, K., Kivlahan, D. R., & Marlatt, G. A. (1987) Correlates of alcohol consumption: Sex, age, and expectancies relate differentially to quantity and frequency. *Addictive Behavior, 12,* 235–240.

Moore, D., & Saunders, B. (1991). Youth drug use and the prevention of problems. *International Journal on Drug Policy, 2*(5), 3–8.

Mrazek, P. J., & Haggerty, R. J. (1994). *Reducing risks for mental disorders: Frontiers for Preventive intervention research.* Washington, DC: National Academy Press.

Murray, D. M., Perry, C. L., O'Connell, C., & Schmid, L. (1987). Seventh-grade cigarette, alcohol, and marijuana use: Distribution in a North Central U.S. metropolitan population. *International Journal of the Addictions, 22,* 257–276.

Mussen, P., Conger, J., & Kagan, J. (1974). *Child development and personality* (4th ed.). New York: Harper and Row.

Musto, D. F. (1991). Opium, cocaine, and marijuana in American history. *Scientific American, 265,* 47.

National Center on Addiction and Substance Abuse. (1996). *Substance abuse and the American woman.* New York: National Center on Addiction and Substance Abuse, Columbia University.

National Center for Health Statistics. (1985). Hispanic health and nutrition examination survey. *Vital and Health Statistics,* Series I, No. 19. Hyattsville MD: U.S. Public Health Service.

National drug control strategy: Strengthening communities' response to drug and crime (1995). Office of National Drug Control Office. Washington, DC: US Government Printing Office.

National Institute on Drug Abuse. (1987). *Drug abuse among Hispanics: Mexican Americans, Puerto Ricans, and Cubans.* Rockville, MD: National Institute on Drug Abuse.

National Institute on Drug Abuse. (1988). *Drug abuse warning network.* Rockville, MD: NIDA Press Office.

National Institute on Drug Abuse. (1995). *National household survey on drug abuse.* Office of Applied Studies, SAMHSA. Rockville MD.

National Institute of Justice. (1992). *Drug use forecasting 1991 annual report.* Washington, DC: National Institute of Justice, Office of Justice Programs.

National structured evaluation of alcohol and other drug abuse prevention, executive summary. (1994). Rockville, MD: Substance Abuse and Mental Health Services Administration.

New crime wave. (1996, January 22). *Miami Herald,* p. A1, A6.

New housing overloading Dade's schools. (1995, January 15). *Miami Herald,* p. B1, B2.

Newcomb, M. D. (1995). Drug use etiology among ethnic minority adolescents: Risk and preventive factors. In G. J. Botvin, S. Schinke, & M. A. Orlandi (Eds.), *Drug abuse prevention with multiethnic youth* (pp. 105–129). Thousand Oaks, CA: Sage.

Newcomb, M. D., & Bentler, P. M. (1986a). Substance abuse and ethnicity: Differential impact of peer and adult models. *Journal of Psychology, 120,* 83–95.

Newcomb, M. D., & Bentler, P. M. (1986b). Frequency and sequence of drug use: A longitudinal study from early adolescence to young adulthood. *Journal of Drug Education, 16,* 101–120.

Newcomb, M. D., & Bentler, P. M. (1988). *Consequences of adolescent drug use: Impact on the lives of young adults.* Newbury Park, CA: Sage.

Newcomb, M. D., & Bentler, P. M. (1989). Substance use and abuse among children and teenagers. *American Psychologist, 44,* 242–248.

Newcomb, M. D., & McGee, L. (1989). Adolescent alcohol use and other delinquent behaviors: A one-year longitudinal analysis controlling for sensation seeking. *Criminal Justice and Behavior, 16,* 345–369.

Newcomb, M. D., Huba, G. J., & Bentler, P. M. (1986). Desirability of various life change events among adolescents: Effects of exposure, sex, age, and ethnicity. *Journal of Research in Personality, 20,* 207–227.

Newcomb, M. D., Maddahian, E., & Bentler, P. M. (1986). Risk factors for drug use among adolescents: Concurrent and longitudinal analyses. *American Journal of Public Health, 76,* 525–531.

Newcomb, M. D., Maddahian, E., & Bentler, P. M. (1987). Substance use and psychosocial risk factors among teenagers: Associations with sex, age, ethnicity, and type of school. *American Journal of Drug and Alcohol Abuse, 13,* 413–433.

Newcomb, M. D., Chou, C., Bentler, P. M., & Huba, G. J. (1988). Cognitive motivations for drug use among adolescents: Longitudinal tests of gender differences and predictors of change in drug use. *Journal of Counseling Psychology, 35,* 426–438.

Nisbet, R. A. (1966). *The sociological tradition.* London: Heinemann.

Nolen-Hoeksema, S., & Girgus, J. S. (1994). The emergence of gender differences in depression during adolescence. *Psychological Bulletin, 115,* 424–443.

Nolen-Hoeksema, S., Girgus, J. S., & Seligman, M. E. P. (1991). Sex differences in depression and explanatory style in children. *Journal of Youth and Adolescence, 20,* 233–245.

Novacek, J., Raskin, R., & Hogan, R. (1991). Why do adolescents use drugs? Age, sex, and user differences. *Journal of Youth and Adolescence, 20,* 475–492.

O'Donnell, J., Hawkins, J. D., & Abbott, R. D. (1995). Predicting serious delinquency and substance use among aggressive boys. *Journal of Consulting and Clinical Psychology, 63,* 529–537.

Oetting, E. R. (1993). Orthogonal cultural identification: Theoretical links between cultural identification and substance use. In M. R. De La Rosa & J. L. Recio Adrados (Eds.), *Drug abuse among minority youth: Methodological issues and recent research advances* (NIH Publication No. 93-3479), (pp. 32–56). Washington DC: National Institute on Drug Abuse.

Oetting, E. R., & Beauvais, F. (1987). Peer cluster theory, socialization characteristics, and adolescent drug use: A path analysis. *Journal of Counseling Psychology, 34,* 205–213.

Oetting, E. R., & Beauvais, F. (1991). Adolescent drug use: Findings of national and local surveys. *Journal of Consulting and Clinical Psychology, 58,* 385–394.

Offer, D., & Schonert-Reichi, K. (1992). Debunking the myths of adolescence: Recent findings from adolescent research. *Journal of American Academy, Child Adolescent Psychiatry, 31,* 1003.

Ogbu, J. U. (1978). *Minority Education and Caste: The American System in Cross-cultural Perspective.* New York: Academic Press.

Olson, D. H. (1986). Circumplex Model VII: Validation studies and FACES III. *Family Process, 25,* 337–351.

Olson, D. H. (1989). *Circumplex Model of Family Systems VIII: Family assessment and intervention.* In D. H. Olson, C. S. Russell, & D. H. Sprenkle (Eds.), Circumplex Model: Systematic Assessment and Treatment of Families. New York: Haworth Press.

Osgood, D. W., Johnston, L. D., O'Malley, P. M., & Bachman, J. G. (1988). The generality of deviance in late adolescence and early adulthood. *American Sociological Review, 53,* 81–93.

Overtown Neighborhood Partnerships. (1995). *The cost of poverty in Overtown and in Dade County in 1990: Summary report.* Miami, FL: Overtown Chamber of Commerce.

Padilla, A. M. (1980). *Acculturation theory, models and some new findings.* Boulder, CO: Westview.

Page, J., McCoy, C., Sweeney, J., & Rio, L. (1985). Alcohol and adaptation to exile in Miami's Cuban population. In L. Bennett & G. Ames (Eds.), *The American experience with alcohol* (pp. 41–61). New York: Plenum.

Pandina, R. J., & Schuele, J. A. (1983). Psychosocial correlates of alcohol and drug use of adolescent students and adolescents in treatment. *Journal of Studies on Alcohol, 44,* 950–973.

Park, R. E. (1928). Human migration and the marginal man. *American Journal of Sociology, 33,* 881–893.

Park, R. E. (1936). Succession: An ecological concept. *American Sociological Review, 1,* 171–179.

Park, R. E. (1950). *Race and culture.* London: Glencoe/Collier-Macmillan.

Park, R. E. (1952). *Human communities.* New York: Free Press.

Park, R. E., Burgess, E. W., & McKenzie, R. D. (1925). *The city.* Chicago: University of Chicago Press.

Partnership for a Drug-Free America. (1992). *1987–1991 survey findings.* New York: Author.

Paton, S., & Kandel, D. B. (1978). Psychological factors and adolescent illicit drug use: Ethnicity and sex differences. *Adolescence, 13,* 187–200.

Paton, S., Kessler, R., & Kandel, D. (1977). Depressive mood and adolescent illicit drug use: A longitudinal analysis. *Journal of Genetic Psychology, 131,* 267–289.

Peak of power: Penelas. (1996, October 2). *Miami Herald,* p. A1, A18.

Pearlin, L. I., & Schooler, C. (1978). The structure of coping. *Journal of Health and Social Behavior, 19,* 2–21.

Pearlin, L. I., Lieberman, M. A., Menaghan, E. G., & Mullen, J. T. (1981). The stress process. *Journal of Health and Social Behavior, 22,* 337–356.

Pellegrini, D. S. (1990). Psychosocial risk and protective factors in childhood. *Journal of Developmental and Behavioral Pediatrics, 11,* 201–209.

Penning, M., & Barnes, G. E. (1982). Adolescent marijuana use: A review. *International Journal of Addictions, 17,* 749–791.

Pentz, M. A. (1983). Prevention of adolescent substance abuse through social skills development. In T. J. Glynn, C. G. Leukefeld, & J. P. Ludford (Eds.), *Preventing adolescent drug abuse: Intervention strategies.* (pp. 195–232). Washington, DC: National Institute on Drug Abuse.

Pentz, M. A., Cormack, C., Flay, B., Hansen, W., & Johnson, C. A. (1986). Balancing program and research integrity in community drug abuse prevention: Project STAR approach. *Journal of School Health, 56,* 389–393.

Perry, C. L., Killen, J., Slinkard, L. A., & McAlister, A. L. (1980). Peer teaching and smoking prevention among junior high students. *Adolescence, 9,* 277–281.

Perry, C. L., Telch, M. J., Killen, J., Dass, R., & Maccoby, N. (1983). High school smoking prevention: The relative efficacy of varied treatments and instructors. *Adolescence, 18,* 562–566.

Petersen, A. C. (1993). Female pubertal development. In M. Sugar (Ed.), *Female adolescent development* (pp. 3–27). New York: Brunner/Mazel.

Petersen, A. C., & Taylor, B. (1980). The biological approach to adolescence: Biological change and psychological adaptation. In J. Adelson (Ed.), *Handbook of adolescent psychology* (pp. 000–000). New York: Wiley.

Petersen, A. C., Sarigiani, A. C., & Kennedy, R. E. (1991). Adolescent depression: Why more girls? *Journal of Youth and Adolescent, 20,* 247–271.

Petraitis, J., Flay, B. R., & Miller, T. Q. (1995). Reviewing theories of adolescent substance use: Organizing pieces in the puzzle. *Psychological Bulletin, 117,* 67–84.

Phil, R. O., & Spiers, P. (1978). The etiology of drug abuse. In B. Maher (Ed.), *Progress in experimental personality research* (pp. 22–45). New York: Academic Press.

Phinney, J. S. (1989). Stages of ethnic identity development in minority group adolescents. *Journal of Early Adolescence, 9,* 34–49.

Phinney, J. S. (1992). The multigroup ethnic identity measure. *Journal of Adolescent Research, 7,* 156–176.

Phinney, J. S. (1996). When we talk about American ethnic groups, what do we mean? *American Psychologist, 51,* 918–927.

Piaget, J. (1932). *The moral judgement of the child.* London: Routledge & Kegan Paul.

Piaget, J. (1971). *Biology and knowledge.* Chicago: University of Chicago Press.

Pierce, J. P., Gilpin, E., Burns, D. M., Whalen, E., Rosbrook, B., Shopland, D., & Johnson, M. (1991). Does tobacco advertising target young people to start smoking? *Journal of the American Medical Association, 266,* 3154–3158.

Pirie, P. L., Murray, D. M., & Luepker, R. V. (1988). Smoking prevalence in a cohort of adolescents, including absentees, dropouts, and transfers. *American Journal of Public Health, 78*(2), 176–178.

Portes, A. (1995). Segmented assimilation among new immigrant youth: A conceptual framework. In R. G. Rumbaut & W. A. Cornelius (Eds.) *California's immigrant children: Theory, research, and implications for educational policy* (pp. 71–76). San Diego: University of California, San Diego, Center for U.S.-Mexican Studies.

Portes, A., & Bach, R. L. (1985). *Latin journey: Cuban and Mexican immigrants in the United States.* Berkeley, CA: University of California Press.

Portes, A., & Rumbaut, R. G. (1990). *Immigrant America: A portrait.* Berkeley, CA: University of California Press.

Portes, A., & Stepick, A. (1993). *City on the edge.* Berkeley, CA: University of California Press.

Portes, A., & Zhou, M. (1993). The new second generation: Segmented assimilation and its variants. *The Annals of the American Academy of Political and Social Science, 530,* 74–96.

Postman, N. (1994). *The disappearance of childhood.* New York: Vintage Books.

Prather, J. E., & Fidel, L. S. (1978). Drug use and abuse among women: An overview. *International Journal of the Addictions, 13,* 863–885.

Pulkkinen, L. (1988). Delinquent development: Theoretical and empirical considerations. In M. Rutter (Ed.), *Studies of psychosocial risk: The power of longitudinal data* (pp. 184–199). New York: Cambridge University Press.

Quinney, R. (1977). *Class, state, and crime.* New York: David McKay.

Rachal, J., Williams, J. R., Behan, M. L., Cavanaugh, B., Moore, R. P., & Eckerman, W. C. (1975). *A national study of adolescent drinking behaviors, attitudes and correlates* (Final Report to the National Institute on Alcohol Abuse and Alcoholism, contract No. HSM-42-73-80. NTIS No. PB-246-002; NIAAA/NCALI-75-27). Rockville, MD: NIAAA.

Rachal, J. V., Guess, L. L., Hubbard, R. L., Maisto, S. A., Cavanaugh, E. R., Waddell, R., & Benrud, C. H. (1982). Facts for planning No. 4: Alcohol misuse by adolescents. *Alcohol Health and Research World, 12,* 61–68.

Radloff, L. S. (1977). The CES-D scale: A self-report depression scale for research in the general population. *Applied Psychological Measurement, 3,* 385–401.

Rappaport, J. (1987). Terms of empowerment/Exemplars of prevention: Toward a theory of community psychology. *American Journal of Community Psychology, 15,* 121–147.

Reckless, W. C. (1967). *The crime problem* (4th ed.). New York: Appleton-Century-Crofts.

Reckless, W. C., Dinitz, S., & Murray, E. (1956). Self-concept as an insulator against delinquency. *American Sociological Review, 21,* 744–746.

Redfield, R., Linton, R., & Herskovits, M. J. (1936). Memorandum on the study of acculturation. *American Anthropologist, 38,* 149–152.

Reebye, P. M., Moretti, M. M., & Lessard, J. C. (1995). Conduct disorder and substance use disorder: Comorbidity in a clinical sample of preadolescent and adolescents. *Canadian Journal of Psychiatry, 40,* 313–319.

Reis, E. C., Duggan, A. K., Adger, H., & DeAngelis, C. (1992). The impact of anti-drug advertising on youth substance use. *American Journal of Diseases of Children, 146,* 519–521.

Rierdan, J., Koff, E., & Stubbs, M. L. (1989). A longitudinal analysis of body image as a predictor of the onset and persistence of adolescent girls' depression. *Journal of Early Adolescence, 9,* 454–466.

Ringwalt, C. L., & Palmer, J. H. (1990). Differences between white and black youth who drink heavily. *Addictive Behaviors, 15,* 455–460.

Robbins, C. A. (1989). Sex differences in psychosocial consequences of alcohol and drug abuse. *Journal of Health and Social Behavior, 30,* 117–130.

Robbins, C. A., & Martin, S. (1993). Gender, styles of deviance, and drinking problems. *Journal of Health and Social Behavior, 34,* 302–321.

Robins, L. N. (1980). The natural history of drug abuse. *Acta Psychiatrica Scandinavica, 62*(Suppl. 284), 7–20.

Robins, L. N. (1984). The natural history of adolescent drug abuse. *American Journal of Public Health, 74,* 656–657.

Robins, L. N., West, P. A., & Herjanic, B. L. (1975). Arrests and delinquency in two generations: A study of black urban families and their children. *Journal of Child Psychology and Psychiatry, 16,* 125–140.

Rogler, L., Cortes, D., & Malgady, R. (1991). Acculturation and mental health status among Hispanics. *American Psychologist, 6,* 585–597.

Romelsjo, A. (1987). Decline in alcohol-related problems in Sweden greatest among young people. *British Journal of Addiction, 82,* 1111–1124.

Ronan, L. (1986, Winter). Alcohol-related health risks among black Americans. *Alcohol Health & Research World,* pp. 36–39.

Rosaldo, R. (1993). *Culture and truth. The remaking of social analysis.* Boston: Beacon Press.

Rosenbaum, E., & Kandel, D. B. (1990). Early onset of adolescent sexual behavior and drug involvement. *Journal of Marriage and the Family, 52,* 783–798.

Rosenbaum, M. (1996). *Kids, drugs, and drug education: A harm reduction approach.* San Francisco, CA: The National Council on Crime and Delinquency.

Rosenberg, F., & Simmons, R. (1975). Sex, sex-roles, & self-image. *Journal of Youth and Adolescence, 4,* 229–258.

Rosenberg, M. (1989). Self-esteem and adolescent problems: Modeling reciprocal effects. *American Sociological Review, 54,* 1004–1018.

Rosenblitt, D. L., & Nagey, D. A. (1973). The use of medical manpower in a seventh grade drug education program. *Journal of Drug Education, 3,* 39–56.

Rothman, J., Erlich, J. L., & Teresa, J. G. (1981). *Changing organizations and community programs.* Beverly Hills, CA: Sage.

Rumbaut, R. G. (1994a). The crucible within: Ethnic identity, self-esteem, and segmented assimilation among children of immigrants. *International Migration Review, 28*(4), 748–794.

Rumbaut, R. G. (1994b). Origins and destinations: Immigration to the United States since World War II. *Sociological Forum, 9,* 583–621.

Rumbaut, R. G. (1995). The new Californians: Comparative research findings on the educational progress of immigrant children. In R. G. Rumbaut & W. A. Cornelius (Eds.), *California's immigrant children: Theory, research, and implications for educational policy* (pp. 17–70). San Diego: University of California, San Diego, Center for U.S.-Mexican Studies.

Rutter, M. (1986). The developmental psychopathology of depression: Issues and perspectives. In M. Rutter, C. Izard, & P. Read (Eds.), *Depression in young people: Developmental and clinical perspectives* (pp. 3–30). New York: Guilford.

Rutter, M. (1987). Psychosocial resilience and protective mechanisms. *American Journal of Orthopsychiatry, 57,* 316–331.

Schaps, E., Bartolo, R. D., Moskowitz, J., Palley, C. S., & Churgin, S. (1981). A review of 127 drug abuse prevention program evaluations. *Journal of Drug Issues, 12,* 17–43.

Scheier, L. M., Newcomb, M. D., & Skager, R. (1994). Risk, protection, and vulnerability to adolescent drug use: Latent-variable models of three age groups. *Journal of Drug Education, 24,* 49–82.

Schinke, S. P., & Gilchrist, L. D. (1983). Primary prevention of tobacco smoking. *Journal of Primary Prevention, 5,* 48–56.

Schinke, S., Botvin, G., & Orlandi, M. (1991). *Substance abuse in children and adolescents: Evaluation and intervention.* Newbury Park, CA: Sage.

Schlegel, A., & Barry, H., III (1991). *Adolescence: An anthropological inquiry.* New York: Praeger.

School crimes, year by year. (1996, December 2). *Miami Herald,* p. A1, A6.

Segal, B. (1991). Adolescent initiation into drug-taking behavior: Comparisons over a five-year period. *International Journal of the Addictions, 26,* 267–279.

Shaw, C. R. (1929). *Delinquency areas.* Chicago: University of Chicago Press.

Shaw, C. R., & McKay, H. D. (1942). *Juvenile delinquency in urban areas.* Chicago: University of Chicago Press.

Shedler, J., & Block, J. (1990). Adolescent drug use and psychological health: A longitudinal inquiry. *American Psychologist, 45,* 612–630.

Shoemaker, D. J. (1990). *Theories of delinquency: An examination of explanations of delinquent behavior* (2nd ed.). New York: Oxford University Press.

Simmons, R. G., & Blyth, D. A. (1987). *Moving into adolescence: The impact of pubertal change and school context.* New York: Aldine de Gruyter.

Simmons, R. G., Rosenberg, F., & Rosenberg, M. (1973). Disturbance in the self-image at adolescence. *American Sociological Review, 38,* 553–568.

Skolbekken, J. A. (1995). The risk epidemic in medical journals. *Social Science in Medicine, 40,* 291–305.

Smart, R. G., & Fejer, D. (1972). Drug use among adolescents and their parents: Closing the generation gap in mood modification. *Journal of Abnormal Psychology, 79,* 153–160.

Smith, G. M., & Fogg, C. P. (1978). Psychological predictors of early use, late use, and nonuse of marijuana among teenage students. In D. B. Kandel (Ed.), *Longitudinal research on drug use: Empirical findings and methodological issues* (pp. 101–114). New York: Hemisphere.

Special Populations Report, No. 4 (1996). *Hispanic Population Estimates By Age and Sex for Florida and Its Counties, 1996.* Gainesville, FL: University of Florida, Bureau of Business and Economic Research.

Stacy, A. W., & Newcomb, M. D. (1995). Social-psychological influences on deviancy. In H. B. Kaplan (Ed.), *Drugs, crime and other deviant adaptations: Longitudinal studies* (pp. 99–127). New York: Plenum.

Stacy, A. W., & Newcomb, M. D., & Bentler, P. M. (1992). Interactive and higher-order effects of social influences on drug use. *Journal of Health and Social Behavior, 33,* 226–241.

Steffensmeier, D. J., & Steffensmeier, R. H. (1980). Trends in female delinquency: An examination of arrest, juvenile court, self-report, and field data. *Criminology, 18,* 62–85.

Stein, J. A., Newcomb, M. D., & Bentler, P. M. (1992). The effect of agency and communality on self-esteem: Gender differences in longitudinal data. *Sex Roles, 26,* 465–483.

Stonequist, E. V. (1937). *The marginal man: A study in personality and culture conflict.* New York: Charles Scribner's Sons.

Strasburger, V. C. (1989). Why just say no won't work. *Journal of Pediatrics, 114,* 676–681.

Strasburger, V. C. (1995). *Adolescents and the media: Medical and psychological impact.* Thousand Oaks, CA: Sage.

Straus, R., & Bacon, S. D. (1953). *Drinking in college.* New Haven: Yale University Press.

Sue, S., & Moore, T. (1984). *The pluralist society.* New York: Human Sciences Press.

Susman, E. J., Nottelmann, E. D., Inoff-Germain, G. E., Dorn, L. D., & Chrousas, G. P. (1987).

Hormonal influences on aspects of psychological development during adolescence. *Journal of Adolescent Health Care, 8,* 492–504.

Sussman, S., Stacy, A. W., Dent, C. W., Simaon, T. R., Galoif, E. R., Moss, M. A., Craig, S., & Johnson, C. A. (1995). Continuation high schools: Youth at risk for drug use. *Journal of Drug Education, 25,* 191–209.

Sutherland, E. H. (1934). *Principles of criminology.* Chicago: Lippincott.

Sutherland, E. H. (1939). *Principles of criminology* (2nd ed.). New York: Lippincott.

Sutherland, E. H. (1947). Principles of criminology (3rd ed.). New York: Lippincott.

Sutherland, E. H., & Cressey, D. R. (1930). *Criminology.* 3rd ed. Philadelphia: J. B. Lippincott.

Sutherland, E. H., & Cressey, D. R. (1960). *Principles of criminology* (6th ed.). Philadelphia: Lippincott.

Sutker, P. B., Archer, R. P., & Allain, A. N. (1978). Drug abuse patterns, personality characteristics, and relationships with sex, race, and sensation seeking. *Journal of Consulting and Clinical Psychology, 46,* 1374–1378.

Swadi, H. (1988). Drug and substance use among 3,333 London adolescents. *British Journal of Addiction, 83,* 935–942.

Swaim, R. C., Oetting, E. R., Edwards, R. W., & Beauvais, F. (1989). Links from emotional distress to adolescent drug use: A path model. *Journal of Consulting and Clinical Psychology, 57,* 227–231.

Swaim, R. C., Beauvais, F., Chavez, E. L., & Oetting, E. R. (1997). The effect of school dropout rates on estimates of adolescent substance use among three racial/ethnic groups. *American Journal of Public Health, 87,* 51–55.

Szapocznik, J., & Hernandez, R. (1988). The Cuban American family. In C. H. Mindel, R. W. Habenstein, & R. Wright (Eds.), *Ethnic families in America* (pp. 82–104). New York: Elsevier.

Szapocznik, J., & Kurtines, W. (1980). Acculturation, biculturalism and adjustment among Cuban Americans. In A. Padilla (Ed.), *Psychological dimensions on the acculturation process: Theory, models, and some new findings* (pp. 56–78). Boulder, CO: Westview Press.

Szapocznik, J., Daruna, P., Scopetta, M., & Arnalde, M. (1977). The characteristics of Cuban immigrant inhalant abusers. *American Journal of Drug and Alcohol Abuse, 4,* 377–389.

Szapocznik, J., Scopetta, M., Kurtines, W., & Arnalde, M. (1978). Theory and measurement of acculturation. *International Journal of Psychology, 12,* 113–130.

Szapocznik, J., Ladner, R., & Scopetta, M. (1979). Drug abuse and subjective distress in a Hispanic population. In C. Beshner & R. Friedson (Eds.), *Youth drug abuse* (pp. 61–95). Lexington MA: Heath.

Szapocznik, J., Scopetta, M., & Tillman, W. (1979). What changes, what stays the same and what affects acculturative change in Cuban immigrant families. In J. Szapocznik & M. Herrera (Eds.), *Cuban Americans: Acculturation, adjustment, and the family* (pp. 1–23). Miami, FL: Universal Press.

Taylor, D., Biafora, F., Warheit, G., & Gil, A. (1994). Racial mistrust and attitudes towards the law among African-American, Haitian, and other Caribbean Island boys. *Law and Human Behavior, 18,* 291–303.

Terrell, F. (1980). *The development of an inventory to measure certain aspects of cultural mistrust among blacks.* Paper presented at the Fifth Conference on Empirical Research in Black Psychology, Howard University, Washington, DC.

Terrell, F., Terrell, S., & Taylor, J. (1981). Effects of race of examiner and cultural mistrust on the WAIS performance of black students. *Journal of Consulting Clinical Psychology, 49,* 750–751.

Thoits, P. (1985). Social support and psychological well-being: Theoretical possibilities. In G. Sarason & B. R. Sarason (Eds.), *Social support: Theory, research, and applications* (pp. 51–72). The Hague, Netherlands: Martinus Nijhoff.

Thomas, W. I., & Znaniecki, F. (1918–20). *The Polish peasant in Europe and America* (5 Vols.). Chicago: University of Chicago Press.

Thomas, W. I., & Znaniecki, F. (1927). *The polish peasant in Europe and the United States* (Vol. 2). New York: Knopf.

Thrasher, F. (1927). *The gang*. Chicago: University of Chicago Press.

Tobler, N. S. (1986). Meta-analysis of 143 adolescent drug prevention programs: Quantitative outcome results of program participants compared to a control or comparison group. *Journal of Drug Issues, 16*(4), 537–567.

Trauma after the storm: Children are still suffering Hurricane Andrew's wrath. (1993, April 5). *Newsweek*, p. 65.

Triandis, H. C. (1994). *Culture and social behavior*. New York: McGraw-Hill.

Trickett, E. J. (1984). Toward a distinctive community psychology: An ecological metaphor for the conduct of community research and the nature of training. *American Journal of Community Psychology, 12*, 261–280.

Trickett, E. J., & Birman, D. (1989). Taking ecology seriously: A community development approach to individually based preventive interventions. In L. A. Bond & B. E. Compas (Eds.), *Primary prevention and promotion in the schools* (pp. 361–390). Newbury Park, CA: Sage.

Trickett, E. J., Watts, R., & Birman, D. (1993). Human diversity and community psychology: Still hazy after all these years. *Journal of Community Psychology, 21*, 264–279.

Tschann, J. M., Adler, N. E., Irwin, C. E., Millstein, S. G., Turner, R. A., & Kegeles, S. M. (1994). Initiation of substance use in early adolescence: The roles of pubertal timing and emotional distress. *Health Psychology, 13*, 326–333.

Turner, J. R., Wheaton, B., & Lloyd, D. (1995). The epidemiology of social stress. *American Sociological Review, 60*, 104–125.

U.S. Bureau of the Census. (1990). *Census of population and housing: Summary of social, economic, and housing characteristics, CHP-2-11*. Washington, DC: U.S. Department of Commerce.

U.S. Bureau of the Census. (1990). *Census of population and housing: Summary of social, economic, and housing characteristics: Florida, CHP-5-11*. Washington, DC: U.S. Department of Commerce.

U.S. Bureau of the Census. (1992). *Census of population and housing (CPH-1)*. Washington, DC: U.S. Department of Commerce.

U.S. Department of Health and Human Services (USDHHS). (1985). Report of the secretary's task force on black and minority health volume VII, chemical dependency and diabetes. Washington, DC: US Government Printing Office.

U.S. Department of Health and Human Services (USDHHS). (1993). The second national conference on preventing and treating alcohol and other drug abuse, HIV infection, and AIDS in black communities: From advocacy to action. *CSAP Monograph* No. 13.

U.S. Department of Health and Human Services. (1995). *Preliminary estimates from the 1994 national household survey on drug abuse*. Advance report no. 10, September 1995.

Unrecovered: Many lives still shattered in south Dade. (1994, March 7). *Miami Herald*, p. B1.

Urban, J., Carlson, E., Egeland, B., & Stroufe, L. A. (1991). Patterns of individual adaptation across childhood. *Development and Psychopathology, 3*, 345–450.

Vega, W. A. (1990). Hispanic families in the 1980s: A decade of research. *Journal of Marriage and the Family, 52*, 1015–1024.

Vega, W. A. (1992). Theoretical and pragmatic implications of cultural diversity for community research. *American Journal of Community Psychology, 20*, 375–391.

Vega, W. A., Zimmerman, R. S., Warheit, G. J., Apospori, E., & Gil, A. G. (1993). Risk factors for early adolescent drug use in four racial/ethnic groups. *American Journal of Public Health, 83*, 185–189.

Vega, W. A., Gil, A. G., & Zimmerman, R. S. (1993). Patterns of drug use among Cuban Americans, African Americans, and White non-Hispanic boys. *American Journal of Public Health, 83*, 257–259.

Vega, W. A., Gil, A. G., Warheit, G. J., Zimmerman, R. S., & Apospori, E. (1993). Acculturation and delinquent behavior among Cuban American adolescents: Toward an empirical model. *American Journal of Community Psychology, 21*, 113–125.

Vega, W. A., Kolody, B., Hwang, J., & Nobel, A. (1993). Prevalence and magnitude of perinatal substance exposures in California. *New England Journal of Medicine, 32,* 850–854.

Vega, W. A., Khoury, E., Zimmerman, R. S., Gil, A. G., & Warheit, G. J. (1995). Cultural conflicts and problem behaviors of Latino adolescents in home and school environments. *Journal of Community Psychology, 23,* 167–179.

Vega, W. A., Apospori, E., Gil, A. G., Zimmerman, R. S., & Warheit, G. J. (1996). A replication and elaboration of the esteem-enhancement model. *Psychiatry, 59,* 128–144.

Vega, W. A., Zimmerman, R. S., Warheit, G. J., & Gil, A. G. (1998). Acculturation stress and Latino adolescent drug use. In A. Maney (Ed.), *Stress, psychological disorder, and prevention strategies.* Rockville, MD: National Institute of Mental Health, in press.

Vega, W. A., Kolody, B., Porter, P., & Noble, A. (1997). Effects of age on perinatal substance abuse among Whites and African Americans. *American Journal of Drug and Alcohol Abuse, 23*(3), 431–451.

Vickers, A. (1992). Why cigarette advertising should be banned. *British Medical Journal, 304,* 1195–1196.

Violence follows hurricane. (1992, September 3). *Miami Herald,* p. A1.

Wallace, J. M., & Bachman, J. G. (1991). Explaining racial/ethnic differences in adolescent drug use: The impact of background and lifestyle. *Social Problems, 38,* 333–357.

Wallack, L., & Corbett, K. (1990). Illicit drug, tobacco, and alcohol use among youth: Trends and promising approaches in prevention. In H. Resnik, S. E. Gardner, R. P. Lorian, & C. E. Marcus (Eds.), *Youth and drugs: Society's mixed messages* (pp. 5–29) (OSAP Prevention Monograph-6). Rockville, MD: U.S. Department of Health and Human Services.

Warheit, G. J. (1979). Life events, coping, stress and depressive symptomatology. *American Journal of Psychiatry, 136,* 502–507.

Warheit, G. J., & Auth, J. B. (1985). The mental health and social correlates of alcohol use among differing life cycle groups. In G. Maddox, L. Robins, and N. Rosenberg (Eds.), *Nature and Extent of Alcohol Problems Among the Elderly* (USDHHS Publication (ADM) 84-1321: 29–82). Rockville, MD: National Institute on Alcohol Abuse and Alcoholism.

Warheit, G. J., Biafora, F. A., Vega, W. A., & Zimmerman, R. S. (1995). Self-rejection, derogation and peer factors and substance use among a sample of Hispanic, Black, and non-Hispanic white adolescents. *Journal of Addictions, 30,* 97–116.

Warheit, G. J., Zimmerman, R. S., Khoury, E. L., Vega, W. A., & Gil, A. G. (1996). Disaster related stresses, depressive signs and symptoms and suicidal ideation among a multi-racial/ethnic sample of adolescents: A longitudinal study. *Journal of Child Psychology and Psychiatry, 37*(4), 435–444.

Warheit, G. J., Vega, W. A., Khoury, E. L., Gil, A. G., & Elfenbein, P. R. (1996). A comparative analysis of cigarette, alcohol, and illicit drug use among an ethnically diverse sample of young adolescents. *Journal of Drug Issues, 26,* 901–922.

Watters, J. K., Reinarman, C., & Fagan, J. (1985). Causality, context and contingency: Relationships between drug abuse and delinquency. *Contemporary Drug Problems, 12,* 351–373.

Watts, W. D., & Wright, L. S. (1990). The relationship of alcohol, tobacco, marijuana, and other illegal drug use to delinquency among Mexican-American, black, and white adolescent males. *Adolescence, 97,* 171–181.

Watzlawick, F., Weakland, J. H., & Fisch, R. (1974). *Change: Principles of problem formation and problem resolution.* New York: Norton.

Webb, J. A., Baer, P. E., McLaughlin, R. J., McKelvey, R. S., & Caid, C. D. (1991). Risk factors and their relation to initiation of alcohol use among early adolescents. *Journal of the American Academy of Child and Adolescent Psychiatry, 30,* 563–568.

Weil, A. (1972). *The natural mind.* Boston, MA: Houghton-Mifflin Company.

Wells, K. (1980). Gender-role identity and psychological adjustment in adolescence. *Journal of Youth and Adolescence, 9,* 59–73.

Wells, L. E., & Rankin, J. H. (1983). Self-concept as a mediating factor in delinquency. *Social Psychological Quarterly, 46*, 11–22.

Welte, J. W., & Barnes, G. M. (1987). Alcohol use among adolescent minority groups. *Journal of Studies on Alcohol, 48*, 329–336.

Werch, C. E., Anzalone, D. M., Brokiewicz, L. M., Felker, J., Carlson, J. M., & Castellon-Vogel, E. A. (1996). An intervention for preventing alcohol use among inner-city middle school students. *Archives of Family Medicine, 5*, 146–152.

Weschler, H., & McFadden, M. (1976). Sex differences in adolescent alcohol and drug use: A disappearing phenomenon. *Journal of Studies on Alcohol, 37*, 1291–1301.

Weschler, H., Davenport, A., Dowdall, G., Moeykens, B., & Castillo, S. (1994). Health and behavioral consequences of binge drinking in college: A national survey of students at 140 college campuses. *Journal of the American Medical Association, 272*(2), 1672–1677.

White, H. R., Johnson, V., & Garrison, C. G. (1985). The drug-crime nexus among adolescents and their peers. *Deviant Behavior, 6*, 183–204.

Wicker, A. (1986). Behavior settings reconsidered: Temporal stages, resources, internal dynamics, context. In D. Stokols & I. Altman (Eds.), *Handbook of environmental psychology* (pp. 613–633). New York: Wiley & Sons.

Wilsnack, R. W., & Wilsnack, S. C. (1978). Sex roles and drinking among adolescent girls. *Journal of Studies in Alcohol, 39*, 1855–1874.

Wilsnack, S. C., Klassen, A. D., & Wright, S. I. (1985). Gender-role orientations and drinking among women in a U.S. national survey. In S. C. Wilsnack (Ed.), *Women and alcohol: Health-related issues* (pp. 15–28). Rockville, MD: National Institute on Alcohol Abuse and Alcoholism, Division of Extramural Research.

Wilson, W. J. (1993). The underclass: Issues, perspectives, and public policy. In W. J. Wilson (Ed.), *The ghetto underclass* (pp. 1–24). Thousand Oaks, CA: Sage.

Windle, M. (1991). Alcohol use and abuse: Some findings from the national adolescent student health survey. Special focus: Alcohol and youth. *Alcohol-Health-and Research-World, 15*, 5–10.

Windle, M. (1993). A retrospective measure of childhood behavior problems and its use in predicting adolescent problem behaviors. *Journal of Studies in Alcohol, 54*, 422–431.

Wirth, L. (1928). *The ghetto.* Chicago: University of Chicago Press.

Wirth, L. (1931). Culture conflict and delinquency. *Social Forces, 8*, 484–490.

Wittke, C. (1952). *Refugees of revolution: The German forty-eighters in America.* Philadelphia: University of Pennsylvania Press.

Wu, P., & Kandel, D. B. (1995). The roles of mothers and fathers in intergenerational behavior and transmission. In H. B. Kaplan (Ed.), *Drugs, crime, and other deviant adaptations: Longitudinal studies* (pp. 49–81), New York: Plenum.

Zimmerman, R. S., & Langer, L. M. (1995). Improving prevalence estimates of sensitive behaviors: The randomized lists technique and self-reported honesty. *Journal of Sex Research, 32*, 107–117.

Zimmerman, R. S., Vega, W. A., Gil, A. G., Warheit, G. J., Apospori, E., & Biafora, F. (1994). Who is Hispanic? Definitions and their consequences. *American Journal of Public Health, 84*(12), 1985–1987.

Zinberg, N. (1984). *Drug, set, and setting.* New Haven: Yale University Press.

Index

Teachers, adolescents' need for approval by, 143
Television programs, commercial content of, 185
Tobacco, as gateway drug, 88, 91; *see also* Cigarettes; Smoking
Tobacco use, *see also* Cigarettes; Smoking
legal prohibitions against, 40
by school dropouts, 178
Tranquilizer use, 157

United Kingdom, harm reduction education in, 186
University of Chicago, urban sociology development at: *see* Chicago School of Urban Sociology
Urban areas
adolescent behavior in, 1–3
adolescent development in, 5–6
residential transitions in, 7
social characteristics of, effect on crime rates, 9
Urbanization, societal effects of, 6

Values
deviant, adolescents' acceptance of, 9
flux of, 8
materialistic, 9
Violence, adolescent, 2

War on Drugs, 178
White males, alcohol use, 162–163
White non-Hispanic adolescents
alcohol use, 67
deviant behavior and, 59–60, 61, 62, 63–64, 169
gender differences in risk factors for, 108, 109, 112, 115, 122
lifetime prevalence, 52–53, 65, 157
magnitude of, 57, 58
past-month prevalence, 157
past-year prevalence, 164
regular/past month prevalence, 55, 56, 66

White non-Hispanic adolescents (*cont.*)
cocaine use, 162
drug use
deviant behavior and, 59–60, 61, 62, 63, 64, 65, 169
past-year prevalence, 164
progression of, 89, 89–90
hallucinogen use, 88
inhalant use, 66, 157
lifetime prevalence, 53, 54, 65, 158
past-year prevalence, 164, 165
regular/past month prevalence, 55, 56
marijuana use, 67
gender differences in risk factors for, 108, 109, 111, 112, 115, 116, 117
lifetime prevalence, 52–53, 65
magnitude of, 58, 59
past-year prevalence, 164–165
protective factors against, 83–87
regular/past month prevalence, 55, 56
risk domain analysis of, 78–82
methamphetamine use, 88
as risk factor studies reference group, 73–74
smoking
gender differences in risk factors for, 109, 110, 112, 115
lifetime prevalence, 51, 52, 65, 157
magnitude of, 57, 58, 59
past-year prevalence, 164
regular/past month prevalence, 54, 55, 65, 66, 156–157
substance abuse rates among, 66–67, 156
White non-Hispanic population, of Dade County, Florida, 17–18
Women
alcohol use by, African American/White American comparison of, 150
social role of, 96

Youth-serving organizations, drug use prevention interventions with, 192